Nepal

STEVE RAZZETTI

Climbing Consultant: VICTOR SAUNDERS

Interlink Books

An imprint of Interlink Publishing Group, Inc.
Northampton, Massachusetts

First American edition published in 2009 by
INTERLINK TRAVEL
An imprint of Interlink Publishing Group, Inc.
46 Crosby Street, Northampton, Massachusetts 01060
www.interlinkbooks.com

ISBN 978-1-56656-728-2

Commissioning Editor: Ross Hilton
Series editor: Pete Duncan, Kate Michell
Design: Alan Marshall
Cartography: William Smuts
Production: Marion Storz

Front cover: Macchapuchhare, Annapurna Range. Back cover:
author with friends at Taplejung. Cover spine: Climbing to French
Pass (trek 8). Title page: Paldor summit ridge (trek 14).
Opposite contents page: Kanchendzonga from Drohmo Ri (trek
25). Contents page top: trekker and dog in Tibet (trek 4); middle
top: monks at Tengboche Gompah (trek 18); middle bottom:
trekkers in Ghunsa valley (trek 25); bottom: yak at Ramtang
(trek 25).

Reproduction by Modern Age Repro Co. Ltd, Hong Kong
Printed and bound in Malaysia by Times Offset (M) Sdn Bhd

To request our free 40-page full-color catalog, please write to us
at Interlink Publishing, 46 Crosby Street, Northampton, MA
01060, visit our website at www.interlinkbooks.com or e-mail us
at info@interlinkbooks.com

Dhaulagiri Himal from approach to Ghorepani (trek 6).

CONTENTS

ABOUT THIS BOOK

Covering Nepal from west to east, this book is divided into five regional chapters: western Nepal, the Annapurna region, the Langtang region, the Everest region and eastern Nepal. Each regional chapter gives in-depth coverage of a number of recommended trekking routes plus selected climbing peaks that can be accessed during the course of the treks.

Like the trekking routes themselves, the peaks featured range in difficulty (from an easy scramble to a moderately technical climb) but mostly fall well within the horizon of any properly equipped and experienced party. They are presented as a natural highpoint of trekking in a high-altitude region.

Three introductory sections precede the regional chapters. An opening chapter provides a brief snapshot of Nepal, its geography, people and culture. The second chapter provides all the practical advice you should need on arrival in the country and for travel by motorised transport as far as the trailhead; while the third covers all the practicalities thereafter – the logistics of setting off on trek and the possible extra requirements that may be involved in climbing peaks en route.

Regional directories at the end of each regional chapter consolidate the general advice given in the introductory sections with specific listings information.

Appendices on the mountain environment, minimal impact trekking, mountain photography, and health and safety for trekkers complete the book.

LEGEND

══════	Highway	✈	International airport
═══════	Provincial road	✗	Airport/airstrip
───────	Secondary road	▲	Temple
┅┅┅┅┅	Track	Kang La ✗	Mountain pass
▬▬▬▬	Trek route	Kang ▲ 6556m (21510ft)	Peak in metres (feet)
▰▰ ▰ ▰▰	International boundary	Duwo Glacier	Glacier
••••••••••	Railway	dam river	Water features
▣ KATHMANDU	City		Altitude contour (4000m/13125ft on trek maps)
◉ BIRATNAGAR	Major town		Ridge
◎ Taplejung	Town	ANNAPURNA HIMAL	Mountain range
○ Ghunsa	Village	❶➤	Trek number

Trek Essentials boxes summarize each trek, including approximate number of days required, means of access to the start and finish, highest elevations reached, trekking style involved and official restrictions, if any. Also mentioned are notable variations on the route.

Top-class **mapping** pinpoints the route of each trek, with ridge lines, selected altitude contours, glaciers, passes and nearest roads included. Also illustrated in fainter dotted lines are alternative trails.

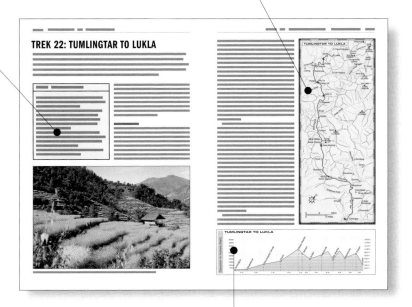

Strip maps illustrate the elevation profile of each trek, including key passes and village spot heights, as well as walking times.
(NB Strip maps are illustrative and not designed for cross-reference between treks.)

Specially sourced **topo photographs** show the general approach route to each climbing peak, with the route clearly marked in red.

Climb Essentials boxes summarize the characteristics of each climbing route, including summit height, principal camps and grade of climb.

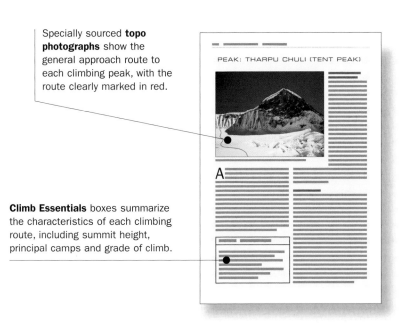

1

INTRODUCTION TO
NEPAL

Nepal has captivated the imagination of mountaineers, explorers and all manner of foreign visitors since it first opened its doors in the 1950s.

This extraordinary country contains some of the most breathtakingly beautiful mountain scenery in the world, ranging from lush, terraced farmland and rice paddies, sub-tropical forest and sweltering valleys, to arid, windswept high-altitude plains, remote mountain passes and the summits of the highest peaks on earth.

Home to cultures and religions that have shaped the philosophical outlook of the civilized world for thousands of years, Nepal is a Mecca for adventurous travellers and a visit is both a scenic revelation and an education in itself.

Sunset over Annapurna Himal from Bara Pokhari.

Hindus ritually bathing in the Bagmati River at Pashupatinath, Kathmandu.

THE LAND

Nepal is a landlocked country, approximately 800km (500 miles) long and between 90 (56 miles) and 230km (144 miles) wide, with an area of approximately 140,000km² (54,686 sq miles). Its borders are with India to the south and west, Sikkim to the east and Tibet to the north. It is characterized by several east–west chains of hills of increasing height. From the fertile plains of the Terai in the south, the country rises through the Siwalik and Mahabharat hills, also known as the middle hills, to the Greater Himalaya and the Tibetan plateau in the north. This represents the biggest altitude variation in the world, from less than 100m (328ft) above sea level to the summit of Everest at 8848m (29028ft), the highest point on earth.

Climate

The main factor governing weather patterns in Nepal, and indeed the entire Himalaya, is the monsoon from the Bay of Bengal. Carrying rain clouds that are the lifeblood of the entire Indian subcontinent, the air-currents of the monsoon sweep across the land from the southeast and are prevalent through most of the **summer** season, from late May until early September. During this time it rains almost daily, with the southeast receiving the heaviest precipitation, and the northwest the lightest. The air is hot and humid, and trails in the hills turn into leech-infested quagmires of mud. As the monsoon recedes in September the skies miraculously clear and **autumn** is the most popular season for trekking. Visibility is then superb, and the weather mostly settled and fine. The onset of **winter** in December brings bitterly cold nights and biting winds at altitude, but the country is sufficiently far south to ensure mild winters at lower elevations. It rarely snows below 2000m (6560ft). In **spring** the rhododendrons bloom, bringing a riot of colour to the hills. However, after the long, dry winter there is dust in the air and this, combined with the increasing humidity and cloud build-up as the monsoon approaches, conspires to reduce visibility even at higher altitudes.

As may be expected, temperatures vary dramatically with altitude. As a rough guide, during March–April and October–December in Kathmandu and the lower valleys, daytime temperatures can easily hit 30°C (86°F), dipping at night to a minimum of 20°C (68°F). At elevations of 4000m (13124ft) the maximum daytime temperature is 15°C (59°F), dropping to –5°C (23°F) at night; while above 5500m (18045ft) daytime temperatures barely attain 3°C (37°F) and may plunge to –25°C (–13°F) at night.

HISTORY

The first recorded rulers of the Kathmandu valley were the Kirats, hailing from the east of Nepal. They are mentioned in the Hindu epic *Mahabharata*. Between the 4th and 7th centuries the Malla dynasty was ascendant, and their culturally rich epoch lasted almost a millennium, producing a fantastic heritage of temples, statues and works of art.

By the 18th century there were small principalities and fiefdoms dotted all over Nepal – 24 in the far west alone. One of these, Gorkha, was ruled by the Shah dynasty, and in 1768 Prithvi Narayan Shah defeated the Malla kings and succeeded in unifying Nepal for the first time.

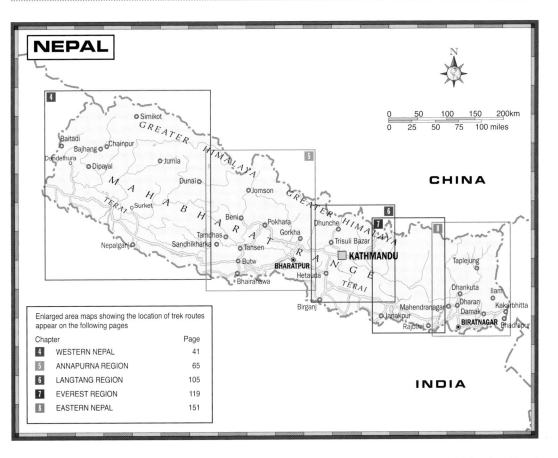

NEPAL

CHINA

INDIA

The present monarch, King Gyanendra, is a direct descendant of his.

Another force instrumental in shaping the political and economic landscape of Nepal today emerged in 1846, when the Prime Minister, Jung Bahadur Rana, conspired with the queen regent to take over the country. In what became known as the Kot Massacre, Jung Bahadur ambushed and killed the senior political and military leaders of the day. Stamping his authority thereafter, he decreed that the post of Prime Minister would become hereditary amongst his descendants. The Ranas ruled for over a century, during which little economic progress was made and the country was increasingly isolated from the outside world. The last queen, Aishowrya, was a Rana.

Short-lived Democratic Reform

Increasing public discontent under Rana rule came to a head in 1951, when, with assistance from India and backed by the Nepal Congress Party, King Tribhuvan instigated an armed rebellion to reinstate the rule of the Shah dynasty. He instituted a series of democratic political reforms, and it was during the 1950s that Nepal was first opened to visiting foreigners. By the end of the decade a road into the Kathmandu valley from Raxaul on the Indian border had been completed, the rumble of diesel trucks and buses forever banishing tranquillity to the more distant uplands.

However, King Tribhuvan's reforms floundered in a mire of petty squabbling and corruption, and after his death his son Mahendra set about tackling the problem. In 1962 Mahendra banned all political parties and introduced the *panchayat* ('five councils') system, wherein the council of ministers was drawn from the highest democratic assembly, the Rastrya Panchayat, but the King still appointed key legislators, effectively retaining control. This status quo was maintained when Mahendra died in 1972 and was succeeded by his son Birendra.

In 1989 Nepal's Trade and Transit agreement with India expired. Angered by Nepal's increasing trade links with China, India declined to renegotiate, and instead imposed harsh economic sanctions, closing border crossings and precipitating an acute oil shortage. During the winter of 1989-90 the population of the Kathmandu valley suffered badly as the scarcity of kerosene, the most widely used cooking fuel, caused prices to spiral upwards. Allegations of profiteering and corruption were laid against government officials, and public unrest as the administration spectacularly failed to resolve the issue soon reached crisis levels. The banned political parties temporarily overcame their mutual distrust and united under Ganesh Man Singh, to launch a fierce critique of the *panchayat* government, accusing it of human rights violations, incompetence and corruption.

Return to Democracy
On 6 April 1990 there was an unprecedented public protest on the streets of the capital, which would have passed off peacefully had nervous policemen not turned on the crowds with batons and guns. Several people were killed and hundreds wounded. The following day, despite a curfew on the city, a number of police officers were killed in revenge attacks. On the evening of 8 April, the king finally relented and rescinded the old ban on political parties. The modern democratic era had begun.

A general election was held in 1991, which the Nepal Congress Party won comfortably. Sadly, inexperience and corruption soon paralyzed the administration. The government violently suppressed communist opposition, and the situation deteriorated until 1994, when parliament was dissolved and fresh elections were announced. No government has lasted more than a year since.

Civil War and the New Millennium
In the face of ineffectual and corrupt minority governments and the complete neglect of rural areas by successive administrations, the Nepal Communist Party (Maoist) began a violent campaign in 1996 to destabilize the government and abolish the monarchy. From Dolpo and Mugu in the far north-west, this soon spread throughout the country as the demands of the Maoists under their enigmatic leader Prachandna struck a resonant note with the impoverished rural population. In what became known as "The Peoples' War", over 12,000 Nepalis lost their lives and the tourism industry was severely affected. Nepal's image as a safe destination was also tainted abroad. Visitor numbers plummeted as stories of curfews, hijackings and general mayhem circulated in the world's media.

As if this wasn't enough, on June 1st, 2001, Crown Prince Dipendra went on a drunken rampage at the Royal Palace in Kathmandu and shot dead both his father King Birendra and his mother Queen Aiswarya. Thirteen other members of the royal family were also shot, eight of them fatally. Dipendra then shot himself, and in a strange twist of fate ascended to the throne for three days whilst in a coma, before dying and being succeeded by his uncle Gyanendra.

Gyanendra's authoritarian streak did not go down well in a climate of increasing popular suffering and unrest. Twice – in 2002 and 2005 – he dismissed parliament and assumed the powers of government for himself, becoming a virtual dictator. The citizens of Nepal, particularly those of the Kathmandu valley, had by now had quite enough of this overbearing monarch, Strikes, protest marches and increasingly violent clashes between citizenry and police eventually persuaded him that the game was up, and in a historic televised address to the nation on 24th April 2006 he reinstated parliament. Within two months that same parliament had passed legislation stripping him of all effectual power. The days of "The Kingdom of Nepal" were over.

Realising that the population were thoroughly weary of the escalating violence of their campaign, the Maoists announced a unilateral ceasefire on April 27th 2006, and this was reciprocated by the government on May 3rd. Much behind-the-scenes manoevring had been going on, and finally, on November 21st peace negotiations yielded a deal between Pachandna and Prime Minister Girija Prasad Koirala bringing the Maoists into the government and placing their weapons under United Nations guard. At the time of writing, elections are scheduled for November 2007.

Nepal Today
Today the population of Nepal is over 29 million, an alarming figure when compared with just five million in 1949 and ten million in 1960. This growth rate shows no sign of slowing. Tourism has long surpassed remittances from Gurkha soldiers as the main source of foreign exchange dollars for the treasury, though during the Civil War huge numbers of Nepalis took up lucrative employment in the Gulf States. An international airport and numerous land routes now bring over 400,000 foreign visitors to the country annually.

THE PEOPLE
Essentially, two distinct cultures meet in Nepal and dominate the life of the country. From the north have come groups of Sino-Mongoloid peoples, with their Buddhist faith, while from the

south have come Hindu Indo-Caucasians. Their intermingling has blurred the edges of these cultural and ethnic backgrounds and produced a wonderful, unique society in which the festivals of each religion are celebrated by the entire population. This is particularly true of the Kathmandu valley, of which it has often been said that there are almost as many different temples and shrines as there are people.

The fabric of Nepali society is complex, with both caste and tribal origin complicating the basic dichotomy mentioned above. Although Nepali is the *lingua franca* of the country, most people – especially in remote areas – speak it only as a second language. In total there are approximately fifty languages spoken in Nepal.

Throughout the country you will encounter high-caste Hindu **Brahmin**, various clans of Hindu **Chhetris** such as the **Ranas** and **Thakuris**, and **Newars**, who may be either Buddhist or Hindu. The Newars were the original inhabitants of the Kathmandu valley, and their skill as artisans is manifested throughout the kingdom in their temples and characteristic houses. Newari women wear distinctive black sarees with crimson trim, and their cuisine is reputed to be the finest in the land.

Middle Hills
Travelling through the middle hills almost anywhere in Nepal you will meet Buddhist **Tamangs**, while in the east of the country you will also encounter the **Kiranti** – either the **Rai** clan in the Dudh Khosi and Arun areas or the **Limbu** clan east of the Arun and in the Kangchendzonga region. In the Annapurna region the middle hills are populated by **Gurungs**, and it is from this group that British Gurkha regiments traditionally recruit. Other inhabitants of the middle hills include **Magars**, **Thakalis** and **Sunwars**.

Upland Areas
The north of the country is populated almost exclusively by people of Tibetan origin, the general term for whom is **Bhotias**. In the high Himalaya you may find Buddhist **Sherpas** living anywhere from Helambu to the border with Sikkim in the east – beyond in fact, as many live in both Sikkim and Darjeeling. Their traditional homeland is the Khumbu, though, and their association with the exploits of mountaineering expeditions in Nepal has become the stuff of legend. From the arid country north of Annapurna come another distinct people of Tibetan origin, the **Manangis**. These are some of the richest, most powerful businessmen

---

FESTIVALS

The Hindu pantheon has as many gods as there are days in the year, and the Nepali calendar is liberally sprinkled with Hindu festivals. **Dasain**, also called Durga Puja, usually occurs in October and is the biggest festival in Nepal. The core of this ten-day celebration is the victory of the goddess Durga over evil, and it is traditional for city office workers to return to their villages during Dasain. **Tihar** is the Nepali name for the Indian festival of Diwali – the festival of lights. The highlight of this week-long celebration is Laxmi Puja, during which people paint their houses, clean their temples and light candles or butter lamps to appease Laxmi, the goddess of wealth. Children take delight in tossing firecrackers at the feet of passing pedestrians, and gambling, otherwise illegal in Nepal, is temporarily tolerated. **Holi** is the water-throwing festival, during which children and youths pelt each other with coloured water and powder paints. A popular sport in Kathmandu at this time is dropping balloons or condoms full of paint from the roofs of buildings onto the heads of unsuspecting tourists below.

---

in the country, with lucrative contacts throughout southeast Asia thanks to privileges granted to them by the king in 1784 and enjoyed to this day. Other separate groups are the **Dolpo-pa** who live west of Dhaulagiri, and the **Lo-pa** of Mustang.

Children at Tashigaon in the upland area of eastern Nepal.

2
ARRIVING IN NEPAL

After the initial excitement of arriving in Nepal, it doesn't take long to discover that travel to the trekking regions beyond the Kathmandu valley can be fraught with excitement or setbacks. The country's road network is poorly developed, and access to distant regions is usually by air, often involving landings at nerve-jangling airstrips.

Radar and modern navigation aids have yet to arrive in Nepal, and air services are frequently disrupted by bad weather. As an old sign at Kathmandu airport's domestic terminal used to read, 'Passengers Please Note: In Nepal we do not fly through clouds, as here they often have rocks in them!'

However, with suitable preparation and some patience you will find the initial stages of your journey in Nepal both rewarding and entertaining. This chapter is your primer.

Afternoon crowds in Kathmandu's Durbar Square, cultural heart of the old city and a living museum of Nepal's rich and diverse architectural heritage.

TRAVELLING TO NEPAL

Most foreign visitors arrive in Nepal by plane at Kathmandu's new Tribhuvan International Airport (TIA). There are now 18 airlines providing scheduled international connections to Kathmandu. These are Gulf Air (Bahrain & Dammam), Xpressair (Kuala Lumpur & Bangkok), Royal Nepalese Airlines (Delhi & Dubai), Indian Airlines (Kolkata & Delhi), Qatar Airways (Doha), Thai Airways (Bangkok), Biman Bangladesh (Dhaka), Jet Airways (Delhi), Druk Air (Paro & Delhi), Ethihad Airways (Abu Dhabi), Air Sahara (Delhi), Air Arabia (Sharjah), GMG Airlines (Dhaka), Silk Air (Singapore), China Southern Airlines (Guangzou), Pakistan International (Karachi), Korean Air (Seoul) and Air China (Lhasa). Some travel companies also operate charter flights.

There are eight road entry points to Nepal from India, but those most likely to be considered by overland travellers are Mahendranagar or Nepalganj in the far west, Sanauli for Pokhara, Birganj for Kathmandu and Rani Sikijahi or Kakarbhitta in the far east. From Tibet there is only one road crossing into Nepal, via the Friendship Highway at Kodari. The border crossing from Purang (on the route from Mount Kailas) into Humla in northwest Nepal is open, but only on foot – it's a five-day hike from the roadhead at Sher to the airstrip at Simikot.

Visas

All foreign nationals except Indians require visas to enter Nepal, available either at Nepal embassies and consulates overseas or at the airport/frontier on arrival. Allow plenty of time to get your Nepal visa if you are applying by post – applications usually take two to three weeks to process. Often a better option is to hand in your passport at a Nepal embassy or consulate in person. It will then be processed overnight for you to collect next day. Theoretically you will need a passport photograph if applying for a visa on arrival, but this is usually waived if you don't have one.

Visas obtained on arrival must be paid for in US$ cash. A standard tourist visa for 60 days costs US$30. Note that your visa does not allow unrestricted access throughout the country. Travel in certain regions requires a trekking permit (see page 26).

Visa extensions may be obtained from the Department of Immigration, Bhrikuti Mandap, Kathmandu tel (01) 4223590/4222453/ 4223681 , fax (01) 4223127, www.immi.gov.np deptimi@ntc.net.np, 0900 – 1700 Mon-Fri or from the Pokhara Immigration Office, Dam Side, Pokhara tel (061) 521167. Be sure to have your passport, the correct fee, passport photographs and completed application fee ready before joining the queue. Visa extensions currently cost US$30 per month ($50 per month with multiple entries).

NEPALESE EMBASSIES/CONSULATES OVERSEAS

Australia
Embassy: Suite 2.02, 24, Marcus Clarke Street (PO Box 2889), Canberra City, ACT 2601 tel: (02) 6162 1554 / 6162 1556 fax (02) 6162 1557 embassyofnepal@grapevine.com.au, nepalembassy@bigpond.com
Consulate General: Level 5, 203-233 New South Head Road, Edgecliff, Sydney NSW 2027 tel (612) 9328 7062 fax (612) 9328 0323 info@nepalconsulate.org.au

France
45, bis Rue des Acacias, 75017, Paris, tel 01 46 22 48 67, fax 01 42 27 08 65

Germany
Im Hag 15, D-5300, Bonn, tel 0228 343097, fax 0228 856747

India
1, Barakhamba Road, New Delhi 110001, tel 011 332 9969, 011 332 7361, fax 011 332 6857, ramjanaki@del.2.vsnl.net.in
19, Woodlands, Sterndale Road, Alipore, Calcutta 700027, tel 033

479 1224, 033 479 1085, fax 033 479 1410

Italy
Piazzale Medaglie d'Oro 20, 00136 Roma, tel 348175, 341055

Japan
14-9 Tokoroki 7-chome, Setagaya-ku, Tokyo T158, tel 03 3705 5558, fax 03 3705 8264, nepembjp@big.org.jp

Holland/The Netherlands
Keizersgracht 463, 1017 DK Amsterdam, tel 020 624 1530, fax 020 624 6173 consulate@nepal.nl www.nepal.nl

United Kingdom
12a, Kensington Palace Gardens, London W8 4QU, tel 020 7229 1594, 020 7229 6231, fax 020 7792 8861 http://www.nepembassy.org.uk

USA
Embassy: 2131 Leroy Place NW, Washington DC 20008, tel (202) 667 4550 fax (202) 667 5534 www.nepalembassyusa.org
Consulate General: Suite 202, 820, Second Avenue, New York, NY 10017 tel (212) 370 3988 / 9 fax (212) 953 2038

Customs/Immigration

There is a 'green channel' on arrival at Tribhuvan International Airport, but all hand and check-in luggage will be x-rayed. Photographic film may be removed and inspected visually. You may be asked if you are carrying video cameras, radio equipment or computers. Note that any such items declared will be registered in your passport – failure to produce them when you leave will almost certainly result in you missing your flight or parting with a large sum of money.

Long-distance coaches from India are rigorously inspected for contraband at the border (a process which can take up to eight hours) and frequently stopped and searched again en route to Kathmandu, especially at Thankot on the rim of the Kathmandu valley.

There are limits on the amount of duty-free goods you may import into Nepal, but cigarettes and alcohol are inexpensive.

Time differences

Nepal is 5hrs 45min ahead of GMT/UTC.

MONEY

The unit of currency in Nepal is the rupee, usually abbreviated to NRs. Exchange rates at the time of writing were US$1 = NRs66, £1 = NRs135.

The currency black market has virtually disappeared in Nepal, and though almost any carpet shop or hotel will change cash dollars and pounds at a rate marginally above that offered by the banks, only banks and authorized money-changers will change travellers' cheques. Keep your exchange receipts if you want to change back any excess rupees (up to a maximum of 15 per cent) at the airport on departure (but remember to keep sufficient rupees aside to pay your airport tax).

Travellers' cheques from the major companies (Visa, Amex, Thomas Cook) are acceptable almost anywhere in Kathmandu or Pokhara, and US$ travellers' cheques may be used to purchase internal air tickets. However, you will only be given change in rupees. Elsewhere, cash is easier. ATM's are now proliferating in Kathmandu and Pokhara. If you're setting off for the hills, try to break your Nepalese money into smaller denominations, though it's not necessary to carry a rucksack full of one and two rupee notes!

INTERNATIONAL AIRLINES

The following international airlines have offices in Kathmandu.

BIMAN Bangladesh Airlines, Nagpokhari, Naxal, tel (01) 434982, 434740, 434869, fax (01) 434869 bimanktm@wlink.com.np

China South West Airlines, Kamaladi, tel (01) 411302, 419770, 434936, fax (01) 416541 www.cswa.com

Druk Air, PO Box 4794, Durbar Marg, tel (01) 4225166, 4225794, fax (01) 4227229, travels@shambhala.wlink.com.np

Gulf Air, Hattisar, PO Box 1307, tel (01) 4435322, 4493323, fax (01) 4435301, gfktm@mos.com.np

Indian Airlines, PO Box 300, Hattisar, tel (01), 4414596, 4429468, fax (01) 4419649

Pakistan International Airlines (PIA), Hattisar, tel (01) 4439324, 4439563, fax (01) 4439564, pia@mail.com.np

Qatar Airways, PO Box 4163, Kantipath, tel (01) 256579, 257712, fax (01) 266599, zenith@ktmpc.mos.com.np

Nepal Airlines, NAC Building, PO Box 401, Kantipath, tel (01) 4220757, 4244055, fax (01) 4225348 info@nac.com.np www.royalnepal-airlines.com

Silk Air, Durbar Marg, tel (01) 4220759, fax (01) 4226795 www.silkair.net

Thai Airways, PO Box 12766, Durbar Marg, tel (01) 4223656, 4221247, 4224387, fax (01) 4221130 thai@ntc.net.np, www.thaiairways.com

Jet Airways , Durbar Marg tel (01) 4222121 fax (01)

Korean Air Kamaladi, tel (01) 4252048, 4252049, fax (01) 4220267 universal1@mail.co.np

Air China North Gate of Royal Palace, tel (01) 4440651, fax (01) 4440641 ktmddca@wlink.com.np

Tipping

Tipping has become the accepted norm throughout the Indian subcontinent, and Nepal is no

A welcome tea-stop en route to Kathmandu by long-distance coach.

DOMESTIC AIRLINES

The domestic airlines currently operating in Nepal are:

Buddha Air, GPO Box 2167 Hattisar, tel (01) 5521015, 5522694, fax (01) 5537726, buddhaair@buddhaair.com, www.buddhaair.com Serves Pokhara, Bhairawa, Nepalganj and Britnagar using Beech 1900D aircraft

Cosmic Air, Lal Durbar, tel (01) 4215771, 4215563, reservation@cosmicair.com, www.cosmicair.com Serves Bhadrapur, Bharatpur, Jomsom and Pokhara using Fokker 100 aircraft

Gorkha Airlines, Hattisar, tel (01) 4435121, 4445510, fax (01) 4435430, e-mail: gorkha@mos.com.np, www.gorkhaairlines.com Serves Pokhara, Tumlingtar, Bharatpur using 18-seat Dornier 228 aircraft

Nepal Airlines, NAC Building, PO Box 401, Kantipath, tel (01) 4220757, 4244055, fax (01) 4225348 info@nac.com.np www.royalnepal-airlines.com Serves all destinations using 18-seat Twin Otter and 44-seat Avro aircraft

Yeti Airways, Lazimpat, tel (01) 4417455, 4423577, fax (01) 4421294, lazimpat@yetiairlines.com Thamel office tel (01) 4213002, 4213011, fax (01) 4213005 thamel@yetiairlines.com www.yetiairlines.com Serves Tumlingtar, Lukla, Pokhara, Simara, Jomsom, Dolpa, Simikot, Biratnagar, Nepalganj using 19-seat Twin Otter & 30 seat Jetstream 41 aircraft

Sita Air, Hattisar, tel (01) 4445012, 2004144, fax 4490546, www.sitaair.com.np Serves Lukla, Tumlingtar, Biratnagar, Nepalganj, Simikot, Jumla & Pokhara, using 18-seat Dornier 228-202 aircraft

exception. Ten rupees will keep luggage porters and the likes at your hotel happy (unless it's five-star, where they might expect a dollar!), and as a rule of thumb for restaurant waiters and trek staff the figure should be roughly 10 per cent of the bill or their wages for the trip. This can be rounded up or down, depending on your satisfaction with the service provided. Generally speaking there should be a very good reason for not giving a tip at all in such situations, as this will be taken as a serious put-down.

TRANSPORT
Kathmandu Valley

There are plenty of motorized rickshaws and taxis available for longer journeys in the Kathmandu valley area, but if your driver refuses to use the meter be sure to negotiate a fare before you set off. Gullible tourists have led to an unwarranted hike in taxi fares charged to foreigners in Kathmandu. No self-respecting Nepali would dream of travelling in a taxi or rickshaw without using the meter, but in ignorance of this many tourists happily pay as much as three times the correct fare – Bargain hard.

Traffic volumes have increased to nightmare proportions in the city over recent years. There were less than 7500 vehicles in the country in 1978, and over 355,000 in 2002. This has resulted in drastic increases in air pollution, rising noise levels and chronic congestion. Many residents and tourists now use face-masks when on the street. The smog that hangs over the city on most days has been alleviated somewhat by the government's recent ban on the poorly maintained two-stroke engined auto-rickshaws imported from India. Attempts to introduce electric versions of these noisy abominations have been moderately successful, but the numbers in operation are still tiny. They are easily identifiable, being white and bearing the 'SAFA Tempo – non-polluting vehicle' logo in bold green letters.

By far the best way to explore the maze of narrow streets and alleys that make up the old city is to walk, but if you simply cannot face going on foot, take a cycle rickshaw. Known locally as Nepali helicopters, on account of the umbrellas which their drivers vigorously twirl whilst touting for business, they are great fun to ride in.

Hiring bikes is another alternative. Heavy, gearless machines of Indian or Chinese manufacture are widely available and fine for getting about the city if you are used to riding in traffic. More adventurous folk will find an increasing number of mountain bikes on hire, which are excellent for longer outings in the valley and beyond.

Countrywide
By Air

Internal flights, though often subject to delays on account of bad weather, technical or other problems, are by far the most time-efficient way of reaching the starting point for a trek. Nepal boasts some of the most remote and spectacular STOL (short take-off and landing) airstrips in the world, and flying in to one of these by plane can save as much as two weeks on ground alternatives. The huge Russian Mi-17 helicopters that temporarily revolutionized internal air travel in Nepal have now all been grounded after being refused international classification as passenger carriers. Be aware that the baggage allowance in most cases is only 15kg (33lb) per person on internal flights, and that excess capacity on small planes is very limited.

A Russian Mi-17 helicopter unloading cargo at Simikot airstrip; these powerful craft are no longer licensed for passenger use in Nepal.

dalbat with a bottle of liquor, while rural Nepalis frequently travel in the company of farm animals. Riding on the roof of buses may be preferable, and any preconceptions you may harbour about safety standards should be thoroughly exorcized before embarking on such a journey. The state of some vehicles plying routes in the more backward and rural areas of the country is truly shocking. If none of this puts you off, you will probably find travelling by bus in the company of Nepali country folk entertaining and rewarding. As is true for all modes of travel and accommodation in Asia, the more you pay, the more you insulate yourself from the real country.

The longer routes within Nepal are covered by night-coach services, and your ticket – ideally purchased several days in advance – will guarantee a reclining, almost comfortable seat. Such journeys are less hair-raising than daytime ones, as the roads are then free of wandering cattle,

Booking and reconfirming internal flights yourself is a complicated, stress-inducing procedure. The demand for seats to popular destinations is so great that tour companies often block-book up to two years in advance, and the entire business runs on favours and patronage. RNAC may tell you that there are no seats to your destination for six months, but a well-connected agency can often have you on a flight the very next day. In any case it's always important to reconfirm each flight. Seats on flights out of the hills are only reconfirmed the day before, so trekkers may have to send somebody ahead with their tickets once sure they will reach the airstrip on time.

All foreigners have to pay for internal flights in US dollars, and tourists pay more than double the local rate. Having a 'dollar ticket' often works in your favour trying to get a seat on a flight from a more obscure airstrip, but Lukla is famous for chaotic and sometimes violent scenes as trekkers and mountaineers squabble over seats after cancelled flights. Theoretically, those holding reservations for a specific flight have priority over those waiting after previous cancellations. If the weather has been bad for days you may go from standing hopefully in a departure room with boarding card in hand to the bottom of a 300-person waiting list in ten minutes!

By Bus
Local buses in Nepal are cheap and often dangerously overloaded, while the seats, if you manage to occupy one, are no more than cramped wooden benches. Drivers often wash down their lunchtime

---

CONSULATES IN NEPAL

Various countries have embassies/consulates in Kathmandu:
Australia: Bansbari, GPO Box 879, tel (01) 4371678, 4371466, fax (01) 4371533 www.nepal.embassy.gov.au
France: Lazimpat, GPO Box 452, tel (01) 4412332, 4413839, 4414734, fax (01) 4419968 www.ambafrance-np.org
Germany: Gyaneshwor, GPO Box 226, tel (01) 4412786, fax (01) 4416899, www.deutschebotschaft-kathmandu.org.np
India: 336, Kapurdhara Marg, GPO Box 292, tel (01) 4410900, 4414990, 4411699, fax (01) 4428279, www.south-asia.com/Embassy-India/
Italy: Baluwatar, GPO Box 275, tel (01) 4252801-4, 4412280, fax (01) 4413879
Japan: Pani Pokari, GPO Box 264, tel (01) 4426680, fax (01) 4414101, www.np-emb.go.jp
Netherlands: Bakhundole Height, GPO Box 1966, tel (01) 5522915, 5523444, fax (01) 5523155, www.netherlandsconsulate.org.np
New Zealand: Dillibazar, GPO Box 224, tel (01) 4412436, fax (01)4414750
United Kingdom: Lainchaur, GPO Box 106, tel (01) 4410583, 4414588, fax (01) 4411789, www.britishembassy.gov.uk BEKathmandu@fco.gov.uk
USA: Maharajganj, tel (01 4007200, 4007280, fax (01) 4007272 www.nepal.usembassy.gov usembktm@state.gov

families driving their herds of goats to market, drunkards on bicycles, boys playing cricket and other hazards. There have, however, been reports of hold-ups by bandits. Local and long-distance buses from Kathmandu tend to depart from the New Bus Park at Gongabu, 5km (3 miles) north of the city on the Ring Road. Various companies operate 'tourist buses' to Pokhara and Chitwan from Kathmandu, and in 1997 a new Green Line luxury coach service with a depot on the corner of Kantipath and Tridevi Marg in Thamel began between Kathmandu and Pokhara. Recommended bus operators include:

Greenline Intercity Bus Service, Tridevi Marg, Kathmandu, PO Box 1307, tel (01) 253885, 257544, fax (01) 253885, email: greenline@unlimit.com www.catmando.com/greenline Pokhara office; Lakeside tel 061-31472
Swiss Travel, Tridevi Marg, Kathmandu tel (01) 4412964
Blue Sky Travel, Thamel tel (01) 4441322
Loyal Travel, Thamel tel (01) 4267890

ACCOMMODATION

Comfortable accommodation in the regional cities of Nepal, such as Nepalganj and Biratnagar, is

The 'pilot' of a 'Nepali helicopter', or pedal rickshaw, takes a nap.

limited. However, both Kathmandu and Pokhara (the main town in central Nepal) offer innumerable hostels, guesthouses and hotels offering rooms from the most basic cells to deluxe air-conditioned suites with panoramic mountain views, 24-hr room service and satellite television. You can pay anything from NRs50 to US$200+ a night.

In Kathmandu, budget accommodation for foreigners is concentrated in the Thamel area of town, but this has become a veritable tourist ghetto, far removed in character, atmosphere and price from the rest of the city. Anyone who has been to Nepal can recommend favourite lodgings in Kathmandu or Pokhara, and it is an unfortunate fact that any place recommended in the more popular travellers' guidebooks will be packed during peak season. If the mayhem of Thamel is too much, seek out more peaceful, cheaper accommodation at Bodnath or in Patan or Bhaktapur.

FOOD AND DRINK

The variety of food on offer in the restaurants of Kathmandu and Pokhara is as diverse as the accommodation available in hotels. You can find anything from basic *dalbat* in a roadside hovel for NRs15 to international *haute cuisine* costing US$30 or more.

Restaurants in Kathmandu's Thamel vie with each other to provide the most comprehensive and imaginative menus, though often the food and service are mediocre. European and continental fare almost always disappoints, and by far the best way of finding good service and food is to seek out the places where Nepalis eat. Traditional Newari cuisine and Indian food are good bets. Getting a table at any of the more popular and well established restaurants in town during peak season requires prior booking.

Countrywide, the staple diet is *dalbat* (dal = lentils cooked as a watery soup, *bat* = boiled rice), typically eaten twice a day. Nepalis don't eat breakfast as such, but take their first *dalbat* late in the morning. They then eat again after sunset, when the work of the day is done.

In poor rural houses the *dalbat* may be unaccompanied, but usually it is supplemented with some sort of *takaari* (vegetables), *dahi* (yoghurt or curds) and *achaar* (spicy pickles). In more affluent settings it may become an elaborate spread, with several different vegetable dishes, egg or fish and perhaps even some different types of meat. It is thus similar to the *thalis* served in India, and, in the same way, the price of a *dalbat* in a Nepali restaurant will include as many top-ups as you can eat.

Drink

Nepal may be a Hindu and Buddhist country (beliefs which eschew intoxicating liquor), but the consumption of alcohol is as central to Nepali traditions of socialising and celebration as it is in any heathen western nation. Typically, Nepalis cannot 'take their drink' though, and your smiling, peace-loving companions may quickly become knife-wielding homicidal maniacs given a supply of *raksi*.

The three home-brewed liquors you are most likely to be offered in Nepal are *chang*, *raksi*, and – in the east – *thungba*. *Chang* is best compared with beer, and is typically fermented from rice, barley or corn. Depending on the skill or tastes of those preparing it, the resultant brew can vary from something akin to runny alcoholic porridge to a coarse wine. When sampling it, remember that the water used in its production will certainly not have been purified.

Raksi is distilled from the fermented mush of whatever grain or fruit happens to be in abundance at the time of manufacture. Rice, barley, apples or bananas are favourites. Its high concentration of alcohol makes it less likely to leave you with dysentery, but don't count on being able to see straight or walk for a week!

From the Arun valley eastwards you are less likely to be offered *chang* than the local variant, *thungba*. Millet grains are pounded and fermented in large vats, after which the resultant alcoholic pulp is scooped into a cylindrical wooden vessel, often elaborately decorated with brass bands, and boiling water is poured in. A tight fitting lid is then placed on the top and a dab of butter placed on the rim as a blessing. The warm liquid inside is drunk through a thin bamboo straw called a *pising*. The potency of this comforting drink only becomes apparent when you attempt to stand.

Water

In cities all water other than bottled mineral water should be regarded as contaminated. This includes the water used to make ice-cubes. You should never, especially in Kathmandu, and doubly so in the rainy season, even brush your teeth with tap water.

Once on trek, either boil (just bringing water to the boil, at any altitude, is now

accepted to be sufficient to sterilise it) or treat all drinking water with tincture of iodine (2–4 drops per litre, left for 15-20 minutes, depending on the level of contamination and temperature). If you're using juice powder or any other flavouring, add this after treatment. About 50mg of vitamin C added to each litre of iodine treated water will effectively neutralise the bad taste. Iodine tincture is widely available in Kathmandu. Chlorine-based purification agents are less effective, and filters are heavy and unreliable. Do not use mineral water on trek! It is ridiculously expensive, and discarded plastic water bottles have far surpassed toilet paper as the biggest polluter of popular trekking routes.

HEALTH AND HYGIENE

The most common illness suffered by visitors to

Chang is traditionally drunk from small cups made from turned rosewood.

Many colourful street food markets start at dawn in the city of Kathmandu.

Most forms of diarrhoea are self-limiting, and antibiotics are rarely necessary. Also, don't neglect personal hygiene. Do wash your hands!

COMMUNICATIONS

The modern telecommunications age has arrived in Nepal with a vengeance. There are countless telephone, fax and email bureaus providing almost cost-price access to international communications all over Kathmandu, and to a lesser extent in other major towns. These offer telephone and fax services at a fraction of the costs charged by hotels, and similarly cheap email/internet services. The use of internet has revolutionized the way the international travelling community keeps in touch.

For those who still wish to avail themselves of more conventional postal services, the General Post Office (GPO) in Kathmandu is at Sundhara, open 10:00–17:00 Sun–Fri. There are *poste restante* facilities available. If you are staying in Thamel, it will save you a long trip to the GPO to use one of the many posting services offered by places such as Pilgrims Bookshop and most hotels. For a modest fee they will take your letters and cards there and see them franked. Always use airmail; surface mail – via India – is unreliable.

Nepal is diarrhoea, and this problem, though often temporarily debilitating, is rarely serious. The onset of travellers' diarrhoea can be brought about by one of several factors, or a combination. Intercontinental travel places many demands on your body, as you simultaneously ask it to cope with jet lag and disrupted sleep patterns, the stress and excitement of setting off on an adventure, a complete change of environment (physical and cultural), strange and exotic food and a whole new set of bacteria in the environment. A few precautionary measures religiously adhered to will greatly reduce your chances of getting sick.

In particular, pay attention to your diet. Eat sensibly – refrigeration is almost unheard of in Nepal, so try to eat only freshly cooked food. Avoid salads, cut fruit and anything that has been left out on display. If you do get diarrhoea, rest, eat nothing for 24 hours, drink plenty of (safe!) water and replenish your salts by using one of the widely available oral rehydration preparations.

ELECTRICITY

Nepal's electricity supply, theoretically 220V/50Hz, fluctuates widely. Powercuts are frequent, though most major hotels in cities will have generators. Note that a voltage stabilizer is essential if you're using sensitive equipment like a laptop computer or television.

Batteries

Duracell and other such alkaline and lithium batteries for cameras, etc are widely available in Kathmandu and Pokhara, but most are copies made in the far east and do not perform any better than the cheaper Indian equivalents. It is strongly recommended that you bring sufficient for your needs with you from home. Also note that such cells contain highly toxic chemicals and should not under any circumstances be thrown away in the hills.

LANGUAGE

If there is one thing that will enrich any visit to Nepal it is a knowledge – however rudimentary – of the Nepali language and a willingness to attempt conversation with those you meet during your travels. Carrying a simple phrase book will pay enormous dividends, and if you are fortunate enough to travel with a Nepali who speaks some English you will have much fun learning the basics of spoken Nepali. Its linguistic roots are in Sanskrit, the ancient Indo-European literary language of India, and like Hindi, with which it has much in common, it is normally written in the Devanagiri script.

SECURITY

The vast majority of Nepalis are friendly, helpful and scrupulously honest, but constant exposure to what can only be perceived as giddy levels of affluence and the carefree attitudes of foreigners in the more popular areas has led many into temptation. A level of vigilance and care is required in these places – to keep honest folk honest as much as anything. There have been increasing reports of theft, and even violent crimes, particularly in regional areas such as Annapurna and Helambu. Avoid ostentatious displays of wealth, and keep valuable items with you. Apart from obviously appealing items like cameras and binoculars, boots are very desirable objects in the eyes of poor Nepalis – do not leave them outside the door of your hotel room or tucked under the flap of your tent.

A sense of sartorial modesty is also called for, as figure-revealing women's clothes and behaviour that would be considered innocent enough at home may be perceived as open invitations by some Nepali men. Note that nudity and public displays of physical affection are offensive to Nepalis and should be avoided.

NEPALI WORDS AND PHRASES

Namaste!	(Universal greeting – literally 'I salute the God within you' – often accompanied by holding the palms of the hands together in a gesture akin to that of prayer)	Ramro	Good, fine (as in *tapailay ramro chha?*)
		Amaa	(Term of address for woman old enough to be your mother)
		Didi	(Term of address for older sister)
Namaskaar	(More formal and polite form of the above, used to address elders)	Baahini	(Term of address for younger sister)
		Baabu	(Term of address for man old enough to be your father)
Danyabaad	Thank you (not used often in conversation)		
Kaana	Food	Daai/Daaju	(Term of address for older brother; though if you are familiar with the person, try *chacha* – 'uncle')
Meetho	Tasty/delicious (as in *meetho chha* – 'it is tasty'; this can be turned into the question 'is it tasty?' by raising the tone of *chha*)		
		Baai	(Term of address for younger brother)
Paani	Water	Huunchha	Yes/OK
Chiyaa	Tea (sweet, with milk)	Hoinaa	No
Malaai chang dheri manparchhaa	I like *chang* (a kind of alcohol) very much	Ramro din	Good weather (literally 'good day')
		Din na ramro	Bad weather
Poinchha	Available	Suberaatri	Goodnight
Diinos	Please give me	Kusto boyo suudnu?	Did you sleep well?
Chhainaa	I don't have (use when children ask for sweets)	Bistaare	Slowly
		Cheeto	Quickly
Maagnu hundaaina	You shouldn't beg	Ukaalo	Uphill
Baatho	Path/trail (as in *raatho maatho chipalo baatho* – 'red mud, slippery path!')	Uuraalo	Downhill
		Tapaaiko nam ke ho?	What is your name?
Ke Garne?!	What to do?! (as in *ke garne, aiyotha nabaai arko bir garne!* – 'what can I do? If you don't marry one you'll marry another!')	Mero nam Natalie ho	My name is Natalie
		Malaai pisaab/disaa garnu parchha	I need to urinate/defecate
Kati baijo	What time is it? (literally 'how many bells')	NUMBERS	1 = *ek*, 2 = *dui*, 3 = *teen*, 4 = *chha*, 5 = *paanch*, 6 = *cheh*, 7 = *saat*, 8 = *aat*, 9 = *naau*, 10 = *daas*, 25 = *pachis*, 50 = *pachas*
Tapailay kusto chha?	Are you fine?		
Sanche chha	I'm perfect!		

3

TREKKING AND CLIMBING IN

NEPAL

When Bill Tilman stepped into the luxurious shade of the British Embassy compound on arrival in Kathmandu in May 1949, he can have had little idea that the odyssey upon which he was about to embark would eventually bring fame, fortune and hundreds of thousands of people from every corner of the globe to the tiny kingdom of Nepal.

His exploratory forays to the Kali Gandaki, Helambu and the Khumbu were the first ever foreign treks in Nepal, beginning a tradition that has transformed the country. In 1960 the first trekking permits were issued, and the following year British climber Eric Shipton led the first commercial trek – to the base camp of Everest.

Realising the appeal of trekking and the potential commercial benefits, in 1965 Colonel 'Jimmy' Roberts, who had accompanied Tilman on his jaunts, founded the first trekking agency, Mountain Travel. Today, nearly a quarter of all visitors to Nepal come to trek.

Heading up through Kunjiri village towards Sinchewa Banjang on the second day of the approach to Kangchendzonga (trek 25).

NEPAL'S TREKKING REGIONS

Approximately 100,000 people a year apply for trekking permits in Nepal and head for the hills. Of these, some 60 per cent are bound for the Annapurna region, 17 per cent to the Everest region, 13 per cent to the Langtang region and 10 per cent to the rest of the country.

There can be few pastimes as stimulating and rewarding as a long walk in the Nepal Himalaya. Except in the highest, most remote areas, trekking is seldom a wilderness experience, as the hill country is extensively populated and farmed. Whilst the trails in the Annapurna, Langtang and Everest regions may be thronging with cosmopolitan hordes of trekkers, even in the backwoods you are likely to pass pilgrims, traders and government officials from far and wide. For many Nepalis, long-distance travel on foot is a fact of life.

Trekking Permits

Probably largely as a result of difficulties policing their use during the Maoist insurgency, trekking permits for the more popular destinations – Annapuna, Everest and Langtang – are no longer required. Current information at the time of writing (Nov 2007) is that Maoists in many areas are still collecting fees from trekkers and issuing receipts, but this may change in the near future. In October 2006, after much lobbying by the Trekking Agents Association of Nepal, the government introduced the controversial Trekkers Registration Certificate (TRC). This was mandatory for all trekkers, everywhere in Nepal, only issued through accredited agencies and carried with it the stipulation that at least one member of staff from the issuing agency had to accompany the trekker *en route*. This was effectively the end of independent trekking in Nepal. Due to "administrative" difficulties, the scheme was withdrawn early in 2007, but it may yet surface again. Meanwhile, the only areas requiring permits are the so-called "restricted areas" – briefly, Dolpo, Kangchendzonga, Makalu, Mugu, Darchula, Mustang and Humla. This list is not exhaustive – see individual trek sections for detailed information. These permits are only issued through accredited agencies, and carry with them a set of conditions and regulations – see information box.

TREKKING STYLES

There are various ways of travelling on foot through Nepal. When planning a trek think carefully about the different styles of trekking available. Remember that when hiking in any major range of mountains it makes sense to go with at least one well chosen companion, as a slip and a sprained ankle can occur at any time. It is also prudent to register with your embassy before setting off, and to sign in at any police checkpoints along the way.

Teahouse

This is the way Nepalis usually travel, making their overnight halts at primitive *bhattis*, and carrying minimal luggage. In the three main trekking areas, these *bhattis* have evolved into sophisticated trekkers' lodges which today offer private rooms, sun-terraces, hot showers, varied and exotic menus and supplies of beer portered in from downcountry. In popular regions the availability of such

---

RESTRICTED AREAS

These essentially consist of everywhere outside of the popular routes in the Annapurna, Everest and Langtang regions. Access to 'restricted' areas is permitted only on the following terms and conditions.

· Only groups are allowed.
· Agent must arrange the entire trek.
· Liaison officer is required on certain routes.
· Agent is responsible for security of group; in the event of police assistance being required, the agent must meet their personal expenses.
· Medical care during the trek is the responsibility of the agent.
· No fuel wood may be used.
· Tins, bottles, etc may only be disposed of at designated sites.
· You may only travel on the authorised route.
· No money/gifts/charity may be distributed to local residents or students during the trip.
· Entry to certain religious/cultural sites prohibited to foreigners.
· You may not perpetrate or allow any acts that destroy religion, culture or the environment.
· All Nepali staff must be insured.
· Groups going to Lo Manthang (Mustang) must submit a list of all goods and equipment carried to the Tourist Information Service, Jomsom, and take all rubbish to them for disposal on their return. Clearance will then be given, and this must be submitted to the Ministry of Tourism.
· Liaison officer must be provided with all food, lodging and expenses, and paid per day. Tent, sleeping bag etc. must be provided for the duration of the trek / expedition, medical treatment provided as necessary and the liaison officer must be insured.
·Permits must be obtained within 21 days of Ministry of Tourism recommendation.

accommodation gives you the flexibility to adjust your itinerary on a daily basis and travel light. The only piece of equipment you will need is a sleeping bag. However, to adopt this mode of travel in more remote areas you must be prepared for very crude and often insanitary conditions, monotonous food, smoky interiors and zero privacy. You will also need to speak at least basic Nepali.

Drawbacks of this approach include being totally dependent on facilities in villages and having to stay on the main routes. Depending on your perspective, you may find the constant company of large numbers of other trekkers and the teahouse 'scene' appealing or nauseating.

Backpacking

Although backpacking (carrying everything you need to be self-sufficient on your own back) is widely practised in mountain areas elsewhere in the world, it is seldom appropriate in Nepal. Backpacking is a mode of travel for wilderness areas, and few parts of Nepal actually fall into this category.

Despite the possible sense of satisfaction to be gained from being completely self-sufficient, carrying stoves, fuel and supplies of freeze-dried food for an outing of over four or five days is unnecessary and arduous. With some exceptions, fresh food is widely available throughout Nepal – nutritious, delicious and digestible. By contrast, even the most expensive freeze-dried food is practically inedible and has alarming effects on the digestive system. Given that most Himalayan treks involve at least two weeks on the trail, and longer ones well over a month, backpacking is usually a non-

---

LIAISON OFFICERS

In its attempts to alleviate the acute environmental pressures brought to bear on popular destinations by the ever increasing volume of trekkers, the Nepalese government has been cautiously opening up a number of delectable previously off-limits areas to foreign visitors. Strict conditions (see box opposite) apply to the issue of permits, and the use of liaison officers has been made mandatory, making it impossible to go it alone and teahouse trek as one can elsewhere. The negative impact of insensitive, inexperienced holidaymakers and travellers, for whom a trek in Nepal is the first and only mountain journey they will ever make, and for whom the availability of pizza, cold beer and a hot shower are the key criteria when selecting a place to stay overnight, should thus be averted.

---

starter. The trails are brutally steep and your pack will be very heavy. On the positive side, you will be free to camp wherever you please, but be aware that in certain areas there is a security and safety risk.

With a Porter

If you are fit and prepared to rough it and carry some of your own kit, you and your friends can quite feasibly trek almost anywhere in Nepal with one or two porters each. Finding good porters is not always easy, especially during the peak trekking seasons and in areas where major construction work is going on. If you strike it lucky though, this is a very rewarding way to travel in Nepal. In the company of a local you will see and experience much that would otherwise pass you

Humli porters enjoying a smoke on the trail from Simikot to the Tibetan border (trek 4).

TREKKING AGENCIES

Over 800 trekking agencies are registered with the Ministry of Tourism in Nepal, from small family operations to international companies. Here is a selection of reputable, well-established firms.

Kathmandu
Asian Trekking, GPO Box 3022, Tridevi Marg, tel (01) 4424249, 4426947, 4432867, fax (01) 4411878, www.asian-trekking.com
Explore Himalaya Amrit Marg, Bhagwan Bahal, Thamel, GPO Box 4902, tel (01) 4418100, 4418400, fax (01) 4412888, www.explore-himalaya.com
Highland Sherpa, GPO Box 3597, Bishal Nagar, tel (01) 4442454, email: trek@economail.com.np
Himalaya Expeditions, GPO Box 105, Nuwakot Ghar, Sanepa Chowk, Lalitpur-2, tel (01) 5545900, 5544999, fax (01) 5526575, www.himex-nepal.com
International Trekkers, GPO Box 1273, Dhumbarahi, tel (01) 4371537, 4371397, 4370714, fax (01) 4371561, www.intreka-sia.com
Malla Treks, PO Box 5227 Kathmandu tel (01)4410089, fax (01) 4423143 www.mallatreks.com
Sherpa Trekking Service, GPO Box 500, Kamaladi, tel (01) 4421551, fax (01) 4227243, www.sts.com.np
Thamserku Trekking, GPO Box 3124, Basundhara tel (01) 4354491, 4354764, 4354044, fax (01) 4354323 www.thamserkutrekking.com

Pokhara
Most of the Kathmandu agencies have offices in Pokhara
Sunrise Trekking, GPO Box 125, Damside tel (061) 521147, fax (061) 522810 www.sunrisenepal.com

by, learn more of the Nepali language and make real Nepali friends. Your porters will be much better than you at buying any provisions you may require, negotiating for places to camp or sleep, route-finding and all manner of other intricate tasks. You will also be able to enjoy the walk unencumbered by a monster pack and have the energy left at the end of the day to appreciate your surroundings. This is a great way to go.

With a Sirdar and Crew
For a group of friends agreed on at least the outline of a proposed route, this is a highly recommended way to travel. Depending on your situation and previous contacts made in Nepal, a trekking outfitter in Kathmandu should be able to provide you with 'full service trekking' at a surprisingly economical price. Obviously, if you make contact with an outfitter via a tour operator abroad the price quoted to you will include an extra commission, though if you have no previous experience in Nepal this extra expense does buy you some peace of mind.

There are hundreds of trekking companies working out of Kathmandu and Pokhara, and no official rating system to indicate the efficiency or honesty of each. They can provide services ranging from simply obtaining your permits to furnishing an entire crew. Many people report high levels of satisfaction from the most basic, small operators, whilst some people report problems experienced with crews provided by well known companies. When tendering for quotes, be sure to enquire about the food provided, tents used (mess tent? kitchen tent? latrine?), the number of sherpa and kitchen staff, and, especially if you plan to go above the snowline, the type and quality of equipment supplied to the porters.

If arranging this type of trek from home, allow six months to get things sorted out, and insist on written confirmation. Most agencies have email and fax facilities, so this should not be a problem. If you want to arrange things on the spot in Kathmandu or Pokhara, you may find that all the best sirdars and cooks are already out on trek and that porters are in short supply. Allow a minimum of a week to get this sort of venture off the ground.

Trek cook preparing lunch on a wood fire – try to ensure that kerosene stoves are used.

Given a group of friends with shared objectives and sufficient time, a professional sirdar and a properly equipped kitchen-crew and porters, this is undoubtedly my preferred mode of travel in Nepal. The itinerary can be altered as the trip pans out, days lengthened or shortened to suit terrain, and time in the hills enjoyed completely. Nothing beats being out in the mountains of Nepal, far off the beaten track, with a group of good friends in the company of a professional team of Nepalis. For a sense of adventure, camaraderie and sheer pleasure, this is tops.

With a Commercial Operator

Adventure travel is big business today, and those with sufficient funds but only limited time available away from their jobs will find a seemingly endless array of commercial treks and expeditions on offer. By signing up for such a trip you do commit yourself into the company of strangers for the duration. Most (but not all!) groups hit it off, and many people make lifelong friends during the course of this kind of trekking holiday.

Commercially organized trekking groups, by definition, have a preordained itinerary, thus pre-

---

NEPAL ONLINE

FOREIGN & COMMONWEALTH OFFICE (UK)
http://www.fco.gov.uk/travel List of UK diplomatic missions abroad and information on potential hot spots.

NEPAL GOVERNMENT, MINISTRY OF TOURISM
http://www.tourism.gov.np/ Latest mountaineering regulations, peak permits, fees & and a wealth of ohter information.

NEPAL GOVERNMENT DEPARTMENT OF IMMIGRATION
http://www.viewnepal.com/immigration/ For latest information about visas, trekking permits, restricted areas and lists of accredited trekking agents.

NEPAL TOURIST BOARD
http://www.welcomenepal.com Lots of general information & links

NEPAL HOME PAGE
http://www.info-nepal.com Excellent site with information on travel, news, arts, culture and society, development issues, links.

DESTINATION HIMALAYAS – WHERE EARTH MEETS SKY
http://library.thinkquest.org/10131 Includes interactive exhibits, critical information sources and an atlas of Himalayan maps.

HIMALAYAN EXPLORERS CLUB
http://www.hec.org Now broadened in scope and renamed the International Mountain Explorers Connection, this is a club site promoting responsible and sustainable mountain travel.

KATHMANDU ENVIRONMENTAL EDUCATION PROJECT (KEEP)
http://www.keepnepal.org Ecological information, links to other sites and ideas for eco-action.

CIWEC
http://www.ciwec-clinic.com This is the most trusted medical centre in Kathmandu for expatriates and trekkers alike.

NEPALNEWS
http://www.nepalnews.com Excellent site providing news from Nepal as it happens.

NEPAL MOUNTAINEERING ASSOCIATION (NMA)
http://nma.com.np The organization that controls permits and fees for climbing peaks in Nepal. The site includes a list of all the current official 'trekking peaks' and details of peak fees.

HIMALAYAN RESCUE ASSOCIATION (HRA)
http://www.himalayanrescue.org Information on preparation, trail conditions, weather, dealing with altitude, arranging rescues, and a good list of links.

HIGH ALTITUDE MEDICINE GUIDE
http://www.high-altitude-medicine.com Excellent resource provided by Oregon based Thomas E Dienz, MD. Detailed information on altitude-related matters.

INTERNATIONAL PORTER PROTECTION GROUP
http://www.ippg.net Organisation promoting the welfare of mountain porters.

CAN (COMMUNITY ACTION NEPAL)
www.canepal.org.uk Charity and trekking organization founded by British mountaineer Doug Scott "to help mountain people help themselves" by initiating health and education projects. Web site contains a wealth of practical information.

THE NEPAL TRUST
www.nepaltrust.org
Truly inspirational charitable trust working amongst the most deprived and isolated communities in Nepal.

TREK INFO
http://www.trekinfo.com
Info for the independent trekker, with links and message board.

cluding spontaneous diversions and rest days. Life within such a group can be a bit introverted, and participants often find themselves communicating with each other rather than with locals, though this doesn't have to be the case. Some companies design their itineraries to include a degree of flexibility and this should be apparent from their literature. The group always camps together, but it is by no means necessary to walk together in single file (as many do!). An experienced leader and a professional trek crew should enable those who would otherwise never dream of experiencing the joys of trekking to find out exactly what all the fuss is about.

Take it easy and drink plenty, especially at the start.

Trekking Style Considerations
Women
As a woman, trekking alone is definitely not advisable. If you do not wish to go with a group, it is safest to hire a porter/guide from a reputable company in Kathmandu or Pokhara. There are now agencies that specialize in providing female Nepali staff for women trekkers – for up-to-date information, enquire at the Kathmandu Environmental Education Project (KEEP) office in the new Thamel Bazaar, Jyatha Tole, Kathmandu.

That said, as a woman you will have unique opportunities to get to know local people in Nepal. Sisterhood is strong in Nepali society and, if you show an interest and learn even a little Nepali, you will often be invited into kitchens and gardens to meet aunties, grandmas and daughters.

Children
Trekking with children in the Himalaya obviously requires extra effort and planning, but nearly every family that tries it loves it. Even if your kids are too young to remember daily events a few years hence, the experience of travelling in a mountainous land where there are no roads, machinery or television will leave a lasting, positive impression.

It's not ideal if you have no previous experience

of trekking, but otherwise having children with you is likely to enrich the entire experience for everyone. Plan shorter days, make sure their gear is as good as yours, and hire extra staff to look after them and to carry those under the age of eight if the going gets tough. Many agencies now have experience catering for families on trek, and some foreign commercial operators do provide tailor-made family itineraries.

HIRING PORTERS
If you have any reliable contacts in the trekking business in Kathmandu, use them! Porters hired through an agency are more likely to have a reasonable idea of what they're letting themselves in for, and you will have some sort of come-back in the event of a problem or dispute. If you decide to wait until you reach the trail-head before engaging your porters, be sure that you all know what you are agreeing to before setting off. Obviously a rudimentary knowledge of Nepali is necessary here, as it is highly unlikely that any Nepali offering his or her services as a porter will speak any English. Establish whether or not they have walked your proposed route before, and ask to see any references they may have been given by previous employers. Agree daily rates of pay, the size of the loads, arrangements for the porters' food and accommodation and, if you are going high, make sure they have sufficient clothing and bedding. It is usually prudent (but not always possible) to change lowland porters for Bhotias (Tibetans) as soon as you start to get high, as these men will be more accustomed to the cold and altitude. Depending on the area you are walking in and the time of year, expect to pay between NRs250 and NRs400 per porter per day. It's probably simplest and best to have them agree on a rate and feed themselves.

Legally, you are required to insure the life of each porter for NRs100,000, and NRs200,000 if they are carrying loads above a mountain base camp. This is almost never done, but you must at least adopt a responsible, caring attitude. There

Striking camp near Yalbang in the Humla Karnali valley north of Simikot. In remote areas such as this, self-sufficiency is the rule.

have been shocking instances in the past of trekkers abandoning porters to fend for themselves after storms or accidents in high country. In the aftermath of terrible storms in November 1995, many trekkers showed an alarming and callous disregard for their Nepali staff. As helicopters flew in to groups stranded in isolated locations and demanded US$400 per person for evacuation, westerners scrambled aboard leaving their porters to dig their way out. A young Rai boy froze to death on the Zatrwa La above Lukla, dressed only in thin cotton trousers and a shirt, whilst in the load he was carrying was the trekker's down clothing that would have saved his life. An entire group of snow-blind porters was abandoned near French Pass as their employers made a dash for safety. Such conduct is unacceptable.

Remember that once you engage porters you are as responsible for their welfare and safety. Without the dedicated hard work and companionship shown to foreigners by porters, kitchen staff, cooks and sirdars, no expedition or trek would even reach the mountains. To repay this effort and good humour by betraying them the minute conditions get difficult is inhuman.

BASIC TREKKING EQUIPMENT
The choice of equipment always provokes heated debate. Use your own experience to guide your choices – recommendations here are made without deferring to the cost of particular items.

BOOTS. Fabric boots may be light and comfortable, but they are never totally waterproof, provide less ankle support and are less durable than leather boots.

TREK STAFF

There is a definite order of rank amongst staff running the typical commercial trekking expedition in Nepal. In charge is the sirdar, responsible for running the whole show – hiring and paying porters, adjusting loads, organising campsites and stages en route and liaising with the trekking group. Assisting him (or her) will be a number of sherpas, depending on the size of the group. The term 'sherpa' as a job description has come about as a result of the fact that originally this role was exclusively performed by Sherpas, though today a sherpa may well be from any upland hill tribe. Their job is to help around camp and to look after the group on the trail, and many trekkers strike up lasting friendships with them.

Of equal rank to the sirdar on the catering side is the cook, who oversees the kitchen operation. He will usually be assisted by as many as six kitchen staff, who do most of the hard work washing up and maintaining the stoves. A typical career in trekking for a Nepali usually starts with a stint as a porter. This may then lead to secondment either into the kitchen or sherpa crews and thence, after years of experience, to the position of sirdar or cook.

Looking towards the Mera La from Tagnag (trek 21) after an autumn snow storm.

GAITERS. These are an essential item if you're going on snow.

SANDALS. For use in camp and wading rivers, a pair of Teva-type sports sandals are unbeatable. Carry them with you always, and change into them whenever you stop. Airing your boots and socks every lunchtime will keep your feet happy.

WALKING POLES. These are not cheap, but don't dismiss them until you've tried them. Modern, lightweight, adjustable walking poles will save your knees a lot of punishment on descents, especially if you're carrying a heavy pack. Many models are now available.

SLEEPING BAG. Though it may be hot in the valleys, night-time temperatures can plummet below freezing at any time of year above 4500m (14765ft). If you're camping, a warm sleeping bag will make the difference between misery and bliss. Down is still, weight for weight, 100 per cent more efficient than the best synthetics. Keep it dry and air it daily.

Generally, but especially if you will be going above the snow line, a well broken-in pair of leather walking boots is a wise choice. The less stitching on the uppers the better. Keep them waxed.

SOCKS. Modern loopstitch construction is recommended, with as high a percentage of wool as possible. Synthetics stink, cheap ones rub.

SLEEPING SHEET LINER. Choose either cotton (adequate) or silk (luxury). It keeps your grime off the sleeping bag and is great at lower altitudes when you would fry in a down bag. A liner is far easier to wash than a sleeping bag.

SLEEPING MAT. There are some people still using closed-cell foam mats – but only those who have not tried Thermarests. Carry a repair kit.

RUCKSACK. Err on the generous side in terms of size. A capacity of 40 litres should be sufficient for lowland trekking, 60 litres if you're planning a longer tour or going high. A large rucksack half full will carry better than a small one stuffed to the brim. Choose one with a padded hip-belt, contoured shoulder harness and effective closures. Make sure it fits you correctly – many manufacturers offer different back-lengths.

STOVE. The only fuel widely available in Nepal is kerosene, and the quality is usually poor. High-tech stoves hate it. If you're going to rely on a stove, take one you can easily strip down and clean – by far the best is the MSR XGK.

HELICOPTER RESCUE

If you find yourself in a situation where a helicopter rescue is essential, do the following:

1. Select a person to carry the message – preferably another trekker or an English-speaking Nepali.
2. Write the request with waterproof ink in legible capital letters, stating:
   Degree of urgency – 'Most Immediate' for cases where death is likely in 24hrs, 'ASAP' otherwise.
   Exact location and altitude (the maximum height for helicopter rescue is ±5000m/16400ft).
   Name, age, sex, nationality and passport number of casualty.
   Trekking agency/insurance policy details/emergency contact numbers.
   Concise medical information – is a stretcher or oxygen needed? Is a doctor present/required?
   Name, nationality, organisation of person sending message.
3. Wait. A rescue may take several days, depending on availability of aircraft and prevailing weather conditions. If you mark your location with brightly coloured clothing or a sleeping bag, remove it as soon as the pilot has spotted you. The blast from a helicopter's rotors will destroy tents.

Clothing

Generally you should be prepared for extremes of temperature during a trek. In the lowlands it is likely to be swelteringly hot and humid, whilst above 5000m (16405ft) it can be dry, intensely cold and very windy. Never underestimate the burning power of the sun, especially at altitude or on snow.

For trekking in the lowlands, generously cut shorts or light cotton/synthetic trekking pants are ideal. Women may find skirts more comfortable and convenient. I often wear the baggy *shalwar* trousers favoured by men in Pakistan – the Nepali equivalents are called *suruwal*. These have a drawstring waist, can be tailor-made for you in a few hours in Kathmandu for a small fee and are supremely comfortable. Cotton t-shirts are ideal in the heat, though chilly when soaked in sweat at altitude.

Modern mountaineering clothing for higher altitudes is not cheap, but the technology involved in fabric manufacture today has revolutionised the levels of comfort provided. Basically you should choose your high-altitude wear according to the layering principle. Next to the skin, wear a set of thermal underwear made of some sort of wicking material that takes sweat away from the surface of the skin before it can perform its natural cooling function. Patagonia's Capilene is a good example.

Over that, use a combination of different weights of fleece fabric, depending on conditions. The latest types are durable, light and quick-drying. Their function is to trap a layer of still air which acts as thermal insulation. Wind-proof versions are also available, but many are far from soft and snug – Patagonia's R4 fabric is a notable exception.

Finally, bring an outer shell layer. This should be windproof, waterproof, and (if the whole system is to function during aerobic activity) breathable. Many such fabrics are now available, but the original is still the best – Goretex.

Apart from the superb way that this system works when used together, its other major advantage is that each element may be used individually, giving the flexibility required to meet a variety of climatic conditions. Use the same basic principles to keep your extremities warm – gloves, hats and socks.

If you're planning on spending much time over 4500m (14765ft), or going between late November and March, a down jacket is probably worthwhile. These are not cheap. Chinese versions can occasionally be purchased in Kathmandu, or you may be able to rent one.

Equipment Hire in Kathmandu.

Many of the more expensive items of kit mentioned above can be hired at very reasonable rates in Kathmandu or Pokhara, though finding the correct size or a particular type of jacket or

SUNDRY ITEMS

SUNGLASSES. At altitude, particularly on snow, the glare from the sun during the daytime is sufficiently strong to cause permanent retinal damage, even with mediocre eye-protection. Snow-blindness, though temporary, is excruciating. Your eyes are precious, so buy the best glasses you can afford – preferably with lenses that filter out 100 per cent UV and IR radiation, and over 75 per cent of all light. Vuarnet glasses are a good example. Choose a design that fits your face closely or has removable leather side-flaps. Plastic lenses are light in weight but scratch easily.

SUN HAT. Avoid sunstroke by keeping the sun off your head. A headscarf is versatile and will suffice.

SUNSCREEN. Intense UV is carcinogenic. Use plenty of high-factor sunscreen – you'll get a serious tan anyway. Lip balm will keep you kissing-fit.

SEWING KIT. Either buy an expensive one or carry any that may have been left for you in your hotel in Kathmandu.

REPAIR KIT. This is especially useful on longer trips. Include super-glue, all-purpose adhesive, patching materials, adhesive tape etc.

STUFF-SACS. Choose waterproof ones, with drawstring tops, for keeping your stuff separate and dry in your kit bag/rucksack. Plastic bags will do at a pinch.

HEAD TORCH. How does anyone manage without one? Petzl headtorches are excellent – take spare batteries and bulbs, and always keep it in your rucksack with you in case you get caught out after dark.

WATER BOTTLE. Find one that doesn't leak! It should hold at least 1.5 litres (2½ pints) and be able to stand boiling water.

PENKNIFE. The 'Swiss Army' type is perfect – scissors, can-opener and tweezers are especially useful.

ALTIMETER. This is more useful for measuring your daily rate of ascent and descent than ascertaining precise elevations. It is also invaluable as an aneroid for keeping an eye on the weather. The Casio/Avocet watch–altimeters are popular with mountaineers and trekkers alike.

sleeping bag may be difficult. There is also a great deal of second-hand equipment for sale, but prices are high. Recently Kathmandu has been flooded with counterfeit clothing and equipment bearing authentic-looking labels of top US and European manufacturers. North Face, Lowe and Patagonia are particularly common, and some of the gear really does look OK. However, a new North Face 'Goretex' jacket for NRs1500 most certainly is not Goretex, and probably isn't remotely waterproof. There are hundreds of trekking equipment shops in Thamel, but a good place to begin your search is at Shona's Alpine Rentals in Jyatha, opposite Kilroy's Restaurant.

PERSONAL FIRST-AID KIT

Commercial trekking groups will usually carry a full expedition medical kit. If you are travelling independently you may want to base your own kit on the following list (refer to the bibliography for more advice). NB While many of the pharmaceuticals listed require a prescription in Europe and America, all are available over the counter at pharmacies in Asia at far less cost. Note that some of them are strong medications, the administration of which in inappropriate circumstances could have serious consequences. Familiarize yourself with current medical practice before carrying them in the hills. Enquire about allergies before administering them to others.

Insect repellent (Repel 100 or Jungle Formula)
Antiseptic cream (Bruladine)
Sun cream and lip salve
Throat lozenges
Deep Heat or Tiger Balm
Anti diarrhoearal (Diacalm or Immodium)
Anti protozoan (Flagyl or Tineba – for treating giardia)
Antibiotics (choose broad-spectrum antibiotics for treating a variety of infections – carry a course of each)
Mild analgesics (Aspirin/Paracetamol for headaches, etc – NOT Codein-based painkillers, as these suppress the breathing function and are not advisable at altitude)
Strong analgesics (Co-proxamol/Ponstan/Temgesic – use with care)
Anti-inflammatories (Nurofen or diclofenac sodium – stomach irritant)
Eye drops (Optrex or Murine)
Plasters and moleskin/blister kit (Compede is recommended)
Bandages and safety pins
Re-hydrant salts (ORS – available cheaply in Nepal; carry several sachets)

Dextrose/glucose tablets
Multi-vitamin tablets
Iodine-based water purification tablets or a small bottle of tincture of iodine with a dropper (chlorine-based water purifiers are not suitable)
Povidone iodine (for cleaning wounds)
Zinc oxide tape
Crepe bandages and safety pins
Butterfly (paper) sutures or Steri-Strips
Cotton wool/swabs
Melolin dressings
Clinical thermometer
Scissors
Crepe bandages and safety pins
Butterfly (paper) sutures or Steri-Strips
Cotton wool / swabs
Melolin dressings
Clinical thermometer
Scissors

INSURANCE

Your normal holiday travel insurance will almost certainly *not* cover you for rescue, evacuation and subsequent medical expenses in the event of an accident, illness or storm in the mountains. Taking out a specialist policy to cover these contingencies is strongly recommended. If you are trekking alone or independently, register with your embassy before departing. If you are arranging your trek through a Kathmandu agency, make sure that you leave details of your insurance cover with them in case they need to organize a rescue for you. Always carry a photocopy of the certificate or a note of important details – policy number, emergency contact numbers – with you in the mountains. Most adventure travel operators insist on this type of cover, and unless you can demonstrate that you are in fact insured, or have sufficient cash (US$) on your person, you will find securing a ride in a helicopter very difficult. The cost of chartering a helicopter is roughly US$1000 per hour of flying time, and in most cases a rescue will cost between US$1500 and US$3000. You will be responsible for any such cost. Many foreign companies now carry satellite phones but resist this expensive intrusion! Before going into a remote area, find out the locations of the nearest telephones and radio-transmitters.

HEALTH CONSIDERATIONS ON TREK
Dehydration

Trekking, especially at the altitudes on many of the routes described in this book, is a physically demanding activity. Whilst not requiring the fitness of an athlete, the fitter you are in before setting off, the more easily you will cope. In order to give your body the best possible chance of adjusting to increased levels of activity and high altitude, maintaining your fluid and salt levels is imperative. As an infallible rule of thumb, you should drink sufficient liquid to maintain a clear and copious urine. If your piss is yellow, you are not drinking enough – it's that simple. Allowing yourself to become dehydrated can bring on symptoms that are almost indistinguishable from altitude sickness – dizziness, headaches, nausea, sweats, chills, muscle cramps, insomnia and lack of appetite. Especially at lower elevations (below 3500m/11480ft), anyone suffering from these symptoms who suspects an altitude-related cause should first eliminate dehydration as a potential factor.

Altitude

A complex and as yet not fully understood set of physical and biochemical changes occurs as the human body is exposed to the decreased levels of oxygen available in the air breathed at high altitude. The general term used to describe these changes is acclimatisation.

Ascending too fast for adequate acclimatisation to take place can result in a person experiencing symptoms of Acute Mountain Sickness (AMS). It is essential that anyone contemplating a trek in the Himalaya has a basic knowledge of the symptoms of AMS, what can be done to prevent them, and what must be done should they occur. Failure to recognise and address these simple criteria can have disastrous, even fatal, consequences. See Health and Safety on page 169 for a discussion of AMS. Recommended further reading on health, first aid and altitude-related topics can also be found in the bibliography.

You must also be psychologically prepared. There is no way of knowing beforehand who will be susceptible to AMS, or when a particular individual will experience it. Age, sex, physical fitness, will-power and pressing itineraries have absolutely no bearing on AMS, and you must be ready at all times to respond appropriately, should a problem develop. It is an interesting fact that 80 per cent of all fatalities due to AMS occur with people on organized treks, while such people only account for 40 per cent of those trekking in Nepal. This imbalance points to several things. Groups have itineraries to stick to, and members may suppress or ignore symptoms for fear of disrupting the schedule. Inexperienced leaders may be reluctant to either hold up an entire group or take on the logistical problems of splitting a party. Such scenarios must be avoided, and the best way of doing this is to ensure that you communicate with and look after each other right from the start.

CLIMBING IN NEPAL

Several attempts to climb the world's highest mountain, Everest, were made in the 1920s and 30s from the Tibetan side of the Himalaya. When Nepal was subsequently opened up to foreigners, a vast array

Descending from Damphus Pass towards Marpha at the end of the Dhaulagiri circuit (trek 8).

of new challenges presented themselves to adventurous climbers. Over the following 30 years, however, what began as near free access to the mountains, including Everest and the sacred Machhapuchhare (Fish Tail), gradually became restricted to a few named expedition peaks. These mountains required a hefty peak fee and liaison officer in addition to unusually onerous bureaucracy and months of pre-planning.

In 1978, under the control of the newly formed Nepal Mountaineering Association (NMA), 18

CLIMBING EQUIPMENT

A number of the treks in this book can be combined with ascents of minor climbing peaks. To climb these peaks you will need some or all of the following equipment in addition to that required for normal trekking:

Expedition-grade plastic climbing boots	Map and compass
Fleece mitts	Harness
Over-mitts	Descender
Thin gloves	Prussik cord
Ski goggles	Short slings
Ski hat	Wires (stoppers)
Balaclava	Pegs (pitons)
Weatherproof overtrousers	Ice screws
Down jacket	Extenders
Fleece trousers (pants)	Karabiners
Cook set	Climbing rope
Hill food	Ice axe
Lighters	Crampons
Light tent	Ice hammer

mountains between 5587m (18331ft) and 6654m (21832ft) were opened to foreigners without the restrictions of the expedition peaks. The bureaucracy was streamlined, a permit could be obtained from the NMA with the minimum of fuss after arriving in Nepal and a liaison officer was not required. These sub-7000m mountains became – misleadingly – known as the "trekking peaks".

Seeking to dispel notions that one may simply "trek" up these often technically challenging peaks, the NMA has recently expanded the list and re-categorized the peaks. There are now 15 "Climbing Peaks" and 16 "ExpeditionPeaks" on the NMA's lists–fulldetails are at http://www.nepal-mountaineering.org/nma_peaks.php. Peaks above 7000m are subject to a whole separate permit structure, administered by the Ministry of Culture, Tourism & Civil Aviation. Full details are at http://www.tourism.gov.np/mountaineering.php

GRADING

Himalayan climbs do not easily fit into normal grading systems because the major difficulties are often not so much technical as those associated with acclimatisation: high altitude and/or large vertical intervals (the difference in height between base camp and the summit). That said, it has become most common to use the French Alpine Grading system.

F	Easy scree or gentle snow or short slopes up to 30°
PD	Scrambling ground, slopes maybe 40°
AD	Some pitched climbing on rock, snow/ice 45–50°
D	Sustained pitched climbing on rock, ice up to 50-60°
TD	Serious technical climbing, vertical ice
ED1	Expect sustained vertical or overhanging sections
ED2...	The ED series is open ended, and gets harder with each generation

Climbing Permits

The NMA peaks attract a fee, which has to be paid in addition to any fee for the trek approaching the mountain. The fees and the lists of peaks have been under review in recent years and the situation is fluid. If you intend to climb any NMA peaks, check the current lists and fees before departing.

The fees for the "Climbing Peaks" on the NMA's list at the time of writing were US$350 for up to four persons, then $40 per extra person up to 8 and then $25 per extra person up to a maximim of 12. For the "Expedition Peaks" the fees are $500 for up to seven members, then $100 for each extra person up to a maximim of 12. A $250

Heading for a high camp on the Yalung La above the lakes at Ramdung base camp, with the Trakarding Glacier beyond (trek 16).

garbage deposit is also payable, and this is refunded as per NMA regulations. Permits are granted by the NMA, PO Box 1435, Nagpokhari, Naxal, Kathmandu, tel (01) 4434525 fax (01) 4434578, e-mail: office@nepal-mountaineering.org www.nepal-mountaineering.org Applications can be made directly though it is easier to use the services of a government-recognised trekking agency. Parties must be accompanied by an NMA-recognised sherpa guide.

Information on royalties, and newly opened peaks is available from the NMA website (URL above).

Climbers on Mera Peak summit (see trek 21), with Everest, Lhotse and Makalu beyond.

Climbing Styles

Although there are straightforward routes on many of these peaks, they certainly should not be underestimated. Several have no easy way up them. The routes selected for this volume are generally the easier ones, mostly around Alpine grade PD, with two ADs and a couple of Fs. All require the use of rope, axe and crampons; ice screws, snow stakes (pickets) and often a small selection of nuts and pegs (pitons) may be useful. Many of the climbs cross seriously crevassed ground and should not be attempted without a firm grounding in the fundamentals of glacier rope-work and crevasse rescue.

Most of the additional climbing equipment needed for trekking peaks can be hired or purchased in Kathmandu, and often sold back again if necessary.

MAPPING

For years, the Schneider maps of the Annapurna, Rolwaling, Langtang and Khumbu regions were the only reliable maps available for trekkers in Nepal. Fortunately, this situation has recently improved dramatically in the 1990's with the publication of an extensive new series of 1:100 000 maps by the Nepal Map House. These cover almost the entire country. For information, contact: Himalayan Map House, GPO Box 3924, Kathmadu, tel (01) 4228965, fax (01) 4228340, email: maphouse@wlink.com.np More recently, the Finnish Government and HMG Survey of Nepal have produced a magnificent series of 1:50,000 maps covering most of the country. They are available from the SS Centre Map House, Thapathali tel (01) 422 1820, 4244056, but will be hard to find outside of Nepal, as production is limited. Details are at www.finnmap.com/nepal2.html and can be ordered from www.cordee.co.uk or www.mapsworldwide.com

THE NMA PEAKS

Previously known as 'trekking peaks' – these are serious mountains and their *official* heights are listed below. Peaks in italic are featured in this book.

CLIMBING PEAKS (NMA LIST)

Manang Himal: Chulu West 6419m (21061ft), *Chulu East* 6584m (21602ft), *Pisang* 6091m (19985ft)
Annapurna Himal: Hiunchuli 6441m (21133ft), Singi Chuli (Fluted Peak) 6501m (21330ft), Mardi Himal 5587m, Tharpu Chuli (Tent Peak) 5663m, Pisang 6091m
Rolwaling Himal: *Ramdung* 5925m (19440ft), *Parchamo* 6187m (20300ft)
Khumbu Himal: Kusum Kangru 6367m (20890ft), Kwangde 6011m (19722ft), *Lobuche East* 6119m (20076ft), *Imja Tse (Island Peak)* 6160m (20211ft), Pokhalde 5806m, Khongma Tse (Mehar Peak) 5849m
Langtang Himal: Naya Kanga 5844m
Ganesh Himal: Paldor 5896m

EXPEDITION PEAKS (NMA LIST)

Langtang Himal: Yala 5732m
Khumbu Himal: Mera Peak 6654m, Cholatse 6440m, Machhermo 6237m, Kyazo Ri 6186m, Nirekha 6186m, Phari Lapcha 6017, Ombigaichen 6340m, Lobuje West 6145m, Abi 6097m, Chhukung Ri 5550m
Jugal Himal: Langsisa-Ri 6427m
Rolwaling Himal: Chekijo 6257m
Kanchendzonga Himal: Bokta 6143m

4
WESTERN NEPAL

From the Kali Ganga and the frontier with India in the west to the Dhaulagiri Himal in the east, the tract of hill-country drained by the Karnali and its tributaries is the wildest, most remote and least trekked part of Nepal.

It is a fantastically beautiful place. Here are peaks every bit as stunning as their famous eight-thousand metre neighbours. Obscure and wondrous beauties like Api, Nampa, Saipal, Kagmara and Kanjiroba. Names that friends back home will never have heard of, but that surely have a special place in the hearts of all who have stood in their shadows.

High and wild in the far west of Nepal – the Sankha Lagna in Humla on a clear December day (see trek 4), with the east face of Saipal beyond.

The medieval village of Rimi, north of the Chankel Lekh en route to Humla from Rara (trek 3).

Tsangpo-Brahmaputra. From one arid corner of south-western Tibet, waters divide and flow the entire length of the Himalaya, finally reaching the ocean as far apart as the Bay of Bengal and the Arabian Sea.

Humla, Mugu and Dolpo are the mountainous districts in northwestern Nepal. Lying in the rain-shadow of the Dhaulagiri and Annapurna Himalaya, this area receives far less of the monsoon's precipitation, and is comparatively arid, less intensively farmed and sparsely populated.

Culturally as well as geographically isolated from the rest of the country, the region's broad, rolling *lekhs* are forested with ancient blue pines, spruces and enormous cedars, and the villages nestling amongst them are populated by Chhetris, Brahmin, Thakuris and Bhotias. Here, over centuries of seclusion from centres of thought and scholarship in India and Tibet, the distinctive features of Hindu and Buddhist beliefs have become blurred. Trans-Himalayan trading patterns that began thousands of years ago still continue to this day, and there is a degree of cultural and economic interaction between Hindu and Buddhist unparalleled elsewhere in the Himalaya.

Added to this are the remnants of the ancient Tibetan Bon religion and animist beliefs which predate even Hinduism. This is the land of *dhamis* and dharma, of pilgrims and traders. It was here that the Malla dynasty had its stronghold, and it is here that the fairytale magic and antiquity of Nepal is still palpable. Along age-old byways traders and pilgrims still walk today, spinning wool, clicking prayer beads, muttering mantras or in silent reverie.

To the north in Tibet, across difficult passes and wind-ravaged plains, lies Mount Kailas. The physical embodiment of Mount Meru, site of legendary duels of magic and home of Lord Shiva, Mount Kailas is the holiest mountain in Asia. Until the Chinese came and sealed all the crossings, the far-flung communities living in these borderlands sustained themselves by

Like the Arun in the East, the mighty Karnali predates the Himalaya, and rises north of the main range in Tibet. The Karnali is one of four great rivers having their sources in the Mount Kailas region – the other three being the Indus, Sutlej and

FREEDOM OF THE HILLS

In 1991 and 1992 I spent several months in Humla and on both occasions my friends and I were the only trekkers within a hundred kilometres of Simikot. The police at the check post there had no idea about restricted areas, liaison officers or trekking permits, and happily gave us their blessings to wander at will in the fascinating hill country north and west of Simikot.

With the opening of the border came officials from the Department of Immigration and newly enlightened police officers. In 1993 over 300 trekkers passed through Humla in organised groups on their way to Mount Kailas (trek 4), and by the time I arrived again in 1994 the Limi valley had been declared a restricted zone, requiring a prohibitive US$700 permit for a visit. On that occasion, and again in 1996, my friends and I crossed the magnificent Sankha Lagna into the Kuwari Khola west of the Humla Karnali. By 1997 the red ink of the bureaucrats had marked that route as restricted too. The freedom of the hills today carries a high price.

trading with their cousins as far abroad as Lhasa and Delhi. The entire region is now in desperate economic decline. Traditional *melas*, or trade fairs, no longer take place, Tibetan traders no longer wander the villages selling turquoise, salt and medicine and bringing news. Today, chartered aircraft bring consignments of rice to feed the impoverished children of Humla and Dolpo.

Trekking in western Nepal is not easy to organise. You need to plan meticulously and be completely self-sufficient, as there are absolutely no facilities. Some particularly alluring areas like Limi in Humla and Shey in Dolpo require exorbitantly expensive permits. Re-supplying with food is impossible, and fuel is so scarce that I have on occasion failed to purchase a single litre of kerosene in Humla's capital, Simikot. Willing porters are hard to find amongst the high-caste Hindu clans of the middle-hills, and tracking down

NEPALGANJ

Access to the far west of Nepal is usually gained via Nepalganj, a sleepy town in the Terai very close to the Indian border and the Royal Bhardia National Park. Accommodation in the town is limited; other than one or two reasonable hotels, there are various squalid establishments around Birendra Chowk in the centre of town. Nepalganj has a sizeable Moslem population, and due to its proximity to the Indian border has occasionally been the scene of major disturbances in the past as Hindu fundamentalists stir up trouble.

the more reliable and competent Bhotias may take time. In short, you will have to make a great effort before you set off on the steep and distant trails of the west. Needless to say, the rewards are great.

TREK 1: APPROACH TO NAMPA AND API

To the uninitiated, a trek to Annapurna or Everest in Nepal may sound like the ultimate adventure. Amongst those familiar with the more popular areas of this divine mountain kingdom, however, there is an increasingly prevalent notion that the country is over-trekked and that opportunities for true exploration are long gone. Surely, in these days of satellite imaging the Himalaya can no longer hold any secrets?

TREK ESSENTIALS

LENGTH (4-5 weeks ex Kathmandu.) Walking from Bajhang: 6 days to Dahachaur, 5 days return trip to Urai Lagna, 4-5 days to Chhelli, 6 days to Api base camp, 9 days to Baitadi.

ACCESS *To start* Flight Nepalganj-Bajhang. *On finish* Flight Baitadi-Nepalganj. Or bus Baitadi-Nepalganj.

HIGHEST POINT Urai Lagna, 5207m (17084ft).

TREK STYLE Tents and kitchen required.

RESTRICTIONS Permits US$90 for the first 7 days, then US$15 per extra day; liaison officer required; park/conservation fees NRs2000.

FURTHER OPTIONS Leave trek at Seti Khola and cross (south of Saipal) via either Jugar Danda or Chauki Lekh ridge to Karnali watershed and Mugu and Humla districts (see trek 3).

The Saipal Himal at sunset from the Bankya Lekh.

Happily this is not true and, while some may berate me for daring to mention it, there is a vast and complex tract of hills northwest of and even more remote than Humla and the Saipal Himal. Separated from India's Garhwal Himalaya by the deep gorge of the Kali Ganga is the Byas Rikhi Himal. A veil of mystery still shrouds this region. What maps there are often prove wildly inaccurate, and route-finding may prove tortuously slow on occasion. As yet no regular itineraries have been worked out, so travel here with an open mind, plenty of time, and be prepared to improvise.

The earliest forays into the area were by two British men, Henry Savage Landor and Tom Longstaff, in 1899 and 1905 respectively. They were followed in 1936 by Swiss geologists Arnold Heim and August Gansser and sporadic subsequent climbing expeditions. Japanese teams climbed the principal summits of the Byas Rikhi Himal, Api (7132m/23400ft) and Nampa (6754m/22160ft), in 1960 and 1972 respectively, but otherwise there have been few exploratory journeys undertaken. Most of the deep approach valleys and rolling ridges here have yet to bear the imprint of a foreign boot.

Mountaineering expeditions to the Byas Rikhi Himal have tended to approach their objective up the most convenient valley, attempt their peak and then retreat down the same valley. Very little is known about routes traversing the country. From ridges sweeping away south from the high peaks in this disregarded corner of Nepal one may gain rare glimpses of the

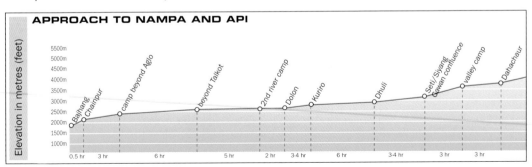

APPROACH TO NAMPA AND API

Elevation in metres (feet)

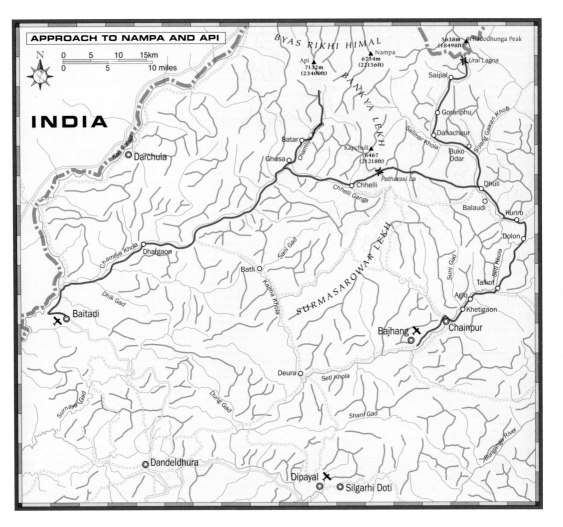

forbidden peaks of the northern Garhwal in India – of Kamet, Trisul and Nanda Devi.

Bajhang to Urai Lagna

The Seti Khola, rising between Nampa and Saipal and flowing south to join the Karnali, drains the southern flanks of the Byas Rikhi. The route suggested here begins at Bajhang in the valley of the Seti and takes in the upper Salimar Khola and the headwaters of the Seti below the Urai Lagna.

Undertaking an outing such as this is a serious matter. A liaison officer will be assigned to you in Chainpur, and you will need the assistance of an experienced sirdar. Men in the lowlands here have almost no experience of portering, and

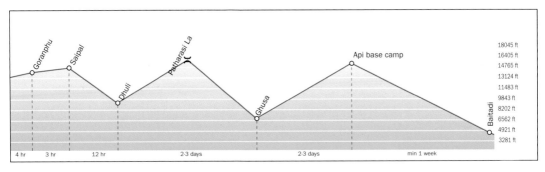

Trekkers heading into Dahachaur village in the Seti Khola.

you may have difficulty recruiting sufficient numbers to carry your kit as far as Dhuli, where more reliable Bhotias may be taken on. Trail conditions vary dramatically from season to season, and being able to elicit information from local shepherds and hunters who frequent the high country may well prove to be crucial in the success or otherwise of any venture.

Like the trail into Humla, the route up the Seti valley from Chainpur to Saipal, via Dolon, Dhuli and Dahachaur, takes you through a land untouched by the hand of time, past ancient orange and lemon groves, flagstoned mediaeval villages and extensive farmland. Under dense forest canopies tribes of langur monkeys cavort and swing, and in obscure quiet grottoes ancient temples are home to monkey, wild cat and luxuriant moss.

Urai Lagna to Api Base Camp via Dhuli

West of the Salimar Khola, the high ridge of the Bankya Lekh descends from the southern flanks of Nampa and its magnificent subsidiary peaks of Bobaye (6808m/ 22337ft) and Jetibohurani (6849m/ 22472ft). By retracing your steps from Urai Lagna as far as Dhuli, it is possible to cross the Bankya Lekh eastwards via the Patharasi La (±4900m/16075ft). The available mapping of this stretch of route is notably poor, but beyond the Patharasi La the route descends into the north of the Chhelli Khola. Continue east as far as Ghusa, where another trail heads north up the valley of the Chamliya Khola, the other major river draining the Byas Rikhi, to eventually reach Api base camp.

Api Base Camp to Baitadi

For the walk-out from Api base camp, follow the Chamliya Khola to where it joins the Kali Ganga and the town of Baitadi on its eastern bank. Allow at least a week to reach Baitadi. On the final approach to Baitadi, note that access to the western banks of the Kali, along which there is a major pilgrim trail heading for Kailas via the Lipu Lekh, is prohibited to foreigners.

SAVAGE LANDOR

The first European to set foot in this area was Henry Savage Landor, euphemistically described in the Alpine Journal as the 'most extravagant and picturesque of travellers'. In 1899 he arrived in the Nampa Khola from India, where he overpowered the Nepalese frontier guards before continuing to Tibet. At the first brush with a Tibetan official, his actions were equally swift:

'Throwing myself upon him, I grabbed him by his pigtail and landed his face a number of blows straight from the shoulder. When I let him go, he threw himself down crying and imploring my pardon. To disillusion the Tibetan on one or two points, I made him lick my shoes clean with his tongue... he tried to scamper away but I caught him once more by his pigtail...'

Savage Landor was eventually captured in Tibet, manacled, imprisoned and soundly thrashed for almost a month before being unceremoniously repatriated to India.

TREK 2: JUMLA TO RARA LAKE

Rara Lake nestles like a sparkling jewel amongst verdant forested hills at the heart of Nepal's least visited National Park. At just over 5km (3 miles) in length, it is the largest body of water in the country and lies at an altitude of 2935m (9630ft) in the district of Mugu. The populations of several villages were relocated to the Terai when the park was inaugurated in 1975, and today the only people living within its boundaries are wardens, police and army officers. Though comparatively short, the hike in from Jumla is strenuous, passing through tranquil valleys and mysterious, magical coniferous forests reminiscent of British Columbia.

To reach Jumla, either fly from Nepalganj or walk from Surkhet. At an altitude of 2370m (7776ft), this dusty town is the starting point for routes heading east into Dolpo, north into Humla and west into Bajura. A few stores line the 200-m (180-yd) flagstoned main street, but despite the presence of the new Karnali Technical School on the outskirts of town, Jumla retains an atmosphere of almost total inertia. Bustling it isn't. The cultural centre of town is the flag-swathed Chandan Nath temple, from within which can be heard bell-ringing and horn-blowing *pujas* every afternoon. The inhabitants of Jumla are mainly high-caste Thakuri and Chhetri Hindus who do not like working as porters.

There are two routes to Rara from Jumla – via Bumri to the east or Sinja to the west. The eastern route is the shorter and lower of the two, though also the more strenuous.

Jumla to Rara via Bumri

The Bumri route has two alternative starts of its own. If there is snow on the hills immediately above Jumla you would be wise to begin along the lower trail into the valley of the Lah Gad via Padmara and the Khali Lagna. Given good weather, however, a more direct and steeper trail crosses the Danphya Lagna (3600m/11812ft), visible due north of Jumla town.

Due to the elevation reached at this first pass, the best way to cross it without a headache is to spend an entire day in Jumla on arrival, and then set out after lunch the next day for Charya Chaur (±3000m/9840ft). It's a peach of a spot in a meadow amongst beautiful pines, with stunning views south across the Tila Khola. The final ascent is steep and best tackled early the next morning.

Recommended overnight camps for the rest of the walk are Bumri, Jhari Khola and Rara. The trail is faint, weaving its way through a wilderness of dense forest and periodically emerging into idyllic

TREK ESSENTIALS

LENGTH (2 weeks ex Kathmandu.) Walking from Jumla: 4 days in to Rara via Bumri, 2 days rest at Rara, 5 days out via Sinja.
ACCESS Flight Nepalganj–Jumla. Or local bus Nepalganj–Surkhet (or night coach Kathmandu–Surkhet) then walk to Jumla via Dai Lekh, Chilkaya and Tila Khola.
HIGHEST POINT Highest trekking point: Chuchemara Danda, ±3800m (12470ft). Highest camp: Rara, 2935m (9630ft).
TREK STYLE Tents and kitchen required.
RESTRICTIONS Permits US$90 for the first 7 days, then US$15 per extra day; park entry NRs1000.
FURTHER OPTIONS Extend trek at Rara to continue to Humla (see trek 3).

clearings and hanging valleys. Camp below Bumri village by the Lah Gad stream on your second night out, and cross the Gurchi Lekh (3400m/11155ft) to the Jhari Khola on the third day. If you are going slowly, there's a perfect camping place at Bulbhule in the Chautha valley as you head north onto this ridge, with a bubbling spring and shady pines.

Spectacular autumn colours in the forests along Rara's northern shoreline.

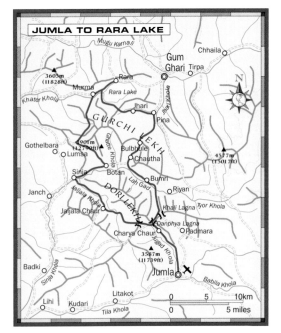

JUMLA TO RARA LAKE

Once at Rara you'll be reluctant to leave. It has a rare peace and tranquillity and a captivating beauty. With no grazing animals in the park the woods have reverted to their natural state with dense undergrowth alive with monkeys and chattering birds. You may be lucky and spot some of the other animals that the park sustains – red pandas, musk deer, Himalayan tahr and noisy wild boar. There are otters too, and the lake is an important stopover for migrating waterfowl.

Spend one of your days here walking round the lake on the path built for King Mahendra to mark his visit in 1964. Look out for ancient Malla stelae and the overgrown temples of Rara and Chapra villages on the north side of the lake.

Walk-out via Sinja

To return to Jumla via the western Sinja route, leave Rara at the bridge where the Khater Khola flows out of the lake in its northwestern corner. Follow the north bank of the river for a couple of kilometres and then turn south up a steep 1000m (3280ft) ascent onto the Chuchemara Danda (the extension west of the Gurchi Lekh). The views north into Humla from this ridge are superb and the airy trail a joy to walk. Recommended overnight camps are at Gorosingha, Sinja and Jaljala, but an extra day would be well spent along the way, as it's fascinating country steeped in history and tradition. There are two paths between Gorosingha and Sinja. The shorter, steeper one via Okarpata has more open mountain vistas but misses out the stunning Gatte Khola valley and Botan.

Sinja used to be the winter capital of the Malla kingdom, but its old ruined town (Kotgaon) lies on the other side of Sinja Khola and is now overgrown. After a long walk from Sinja up the forested Jaljala Khola, the final campsite at Jaljala is in a vast open meadow where spirited wild horses graze on the lush grass. The trail then crosses an unnamed pass at 3500m (11484ft), before skirting around the valley of the Jugad Khola to rejoin the easterly route at Charya Chaur.

From Jhari Khola the main trail descends north to Pina village and the Mugu Karnali – look out for a small wooden sign in English pointing out the 'Way To Rara' and the tiny *maati baato* (upper path) heading off west to Jhari village and Rara. This is truly trekking in wonderland. The path is often barely discernible, climbing through pristine forested hill country, past Jhari's cluster of flat-roofed dwellings and up onto a delightful open ridge that eventually drops away to the southern shore of Rara. On the hillside above Jhari are some of the most magnificent Himalayan cedar trees I've ever seen.

Don't dally long if you want to pitch your tents in daylight at Rara. The park headquarters and campsite look close across the lake to the north, but it takes a good two hours to walk around to them. Camping is not permitted anywhere else on Rara's shores, and the ban on firewood use and fishing is strictly enforced. Be sure to bring sufficient kerosene, as your porters will have to cook with it.

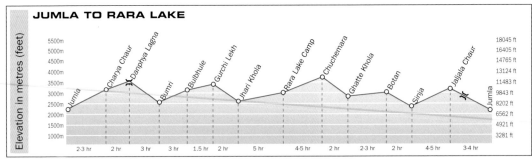

TREK 3: NORTH INTO HUMLA

'Humla. The name resonates like a hymn. Vast and humbling, Humla echoes in whispers'. These are the opening words of Thomas Kelly and Carol Dunham's beautiful paean to this magical corner of far northwestern Nepal, *The Hidden Himalaya*. This marvellous book, sadly no longer in print, inspired my first trek there, and after six visits Humla remains a firm but esoteric favourite. I have walked the route described below three times and never passed a single other trekker.

Having hiked in to Rara Lake (trek 2) and spent a day or two relaxing there, you will be well and truly under the sublime spell cast upon visitors by these western regions, and ready for the trails north into Humla. You will also be sufficiently acclimatised to enjoy the rigours of the days ahead, for these are not gentle ways. The grain of the land here does not lie even or straight, and any trail across it constantly rises to cross ridges only to plunge away down again to the next river. *Ukaalo baato*, *uraalo baato* ('path going up, path going down') will be your mantra in Humla. Allow at least a week to reach Simikot from Rara.

Rara to Rimi

Leaving Rara eastwards from the northern shore of the lake, the way to Humla soon climbs to reach the crest of a broad *lekh* before plunging away northwards into the valley of the Mugu Karnali. Gum Ghari, the administrative centre of the Mugu district, with solar electricity, government offices and a dusty string of poorly stocked

TREK ESSENTIALS

LENGTH (3 weeks ex Kathmandu, including trek 2 to Rara). Walking from Rara: 7-8 days to Simikot.
ACCESS *To start* Trek 2 to Rara. *On finish* Flight Simikot-Nepalganj.
HIGHEST POINT Highest trekking point: crossing the Chankel Lekh, 3640m (11942ft). Highest camp: on the Chankel Lekh, ±3450m (11320ft).
TREK STYLE Tents and kitchen required.
RESTRICTIONS Permits US$90 for the first 7 days, then US$15 per extra day; park entry NRs1000.
FURTHER OPTIONS Continue to Mt Kailas (trek 4); this involves entry to Limi area – US$700 for 10 days, then US$10 per day.

shops, is reached after a couple of hours. It may be possible to re-provision with basic food-stuffs here.

The Mugu Karnali drains a vast, difficult and thoroughly enticing stretch of mountain country

Crossing the new suspension bridge over the Mugu Karnali below Gum Ghari on the trail to Humla.

AROUND SIMIKOT

Simikot is situated on an airy spur at 3000m (9843ft), high above the main Humla Karnali river. The surrounding country consists of steep, pine-forested hills that soon rise towards jagged, snow-covered peaks. Make time if you can to explore the vicinity, for this is a unique and special part of Nepal. Dominating the skyline to the northeast of town are the Changla and Gorakh Himalaya, and into these run the restricted Dozom and Lurupya Khola valleys. For a glimpse into this hidden world, take a day hike up to Torpa and Limithang – Nyimba villages perched high above the Dozom Khola as it cuts deep into the Changla Himal. At remote settlements in this Tolkeinesque valley live communities of Khampa refugees from Tibet who fled there across the 5200m (17061ft) Chang La. Between Torpa and Limithang is the first of the Nepal Trust's health posts, built in 1995 in a cooperative effort between local villagers and western volunteers, and three hours further on, at ±4000m (13120ft), lies Ralling Gompah in a rocky cwm below the sacred peak of *Shel Mo Gang* (Crystal Mountain).

north of Dolpo and the Kagmara Himal. The Bhotias of this valley once conducted their own trade with Tibet via the Nanza La; today they are obliged to make a long and arduous detour to the only open border crossing via the Humla Karnali. High above the turquoise waters of the river, sleepy Gum Ghari makes even Jumla feel sophisticated.

The complexity of the ridge systems in this area makes for many alternative possibilities, and if you are trekking with porters unfamiliar with the trails beware of losing your way. The valleys are deep, the trails steep and navigational errors can be exhausting and time-consuming to rectify. From Gum Ghari the best way to reach Humla is via the Chankel Lekh, but before the climb onto this major watershed dividing the Mugu and Humla districts can be commenced, the Mugu Karnali must be crossed. The new suspension bridge to the west below Gum Ghari is at only 1700m (5578ft), a descent of over 1200m (3937ft) from Rara.

Camp high on the Chankel Lekh to give yourself the best chance of clear views north across Humla from the pass first thing in the morning. This is the highest point (3640m/11942ft) on the walk-in to Simikot, and as the trail emerges from dense conifer and rhododendron forest on the south side of the *lekh* onto the grassy knoll at the crest, the landscape is instantly transformed. Ahead the skyline is a distant wall of magnificent snowy peaks, dominated by the broad bulk of the Saipal Himal (7025m/23049ft) in Humla and Gurla Mandata across the border in Tibet. Beneath these seldom seen peaks Humla is finally revealed, with ridge after blue ridge blending into an increasingly arid distance. Turquoise rivers snake their way through deep valleys and ravines thousands of metres below in deceptive silence. Vivid golden grass appears iridescent against a sky of intense azure while sun-bleached prayer flags flutter in the breeze and eagles soar overhead. This utterly enchanting country is as close to mountain wilderness as you will find in Nepal.

Rimi to Simikot

The huge valley before you now is that of the Tankh Khola, which flows down from the east and another old trading route to Tibet, the Kang La (5358m/17580ft), before joining the Humla Karnali 10km (6 miles) to the west. The trail descends into this valley via the tributary Rowali Khola, passing the Chhetri villages of Rimi and Darma. Primitive and poor, these isolated settlements and the way of life of their inhabitants have changed little over the last few centuries. In the fields women sing heartily as they go about their laborious work. Men constantly spin wool as they herd their livestock, and almost everyone smokes a pungent mix of tobacco and molasses called *tamak* in elaborate clay and copper pipes called *sulpas*. Their houses, constructed of enormous timbers and arranged in labyrinthine mediaeval

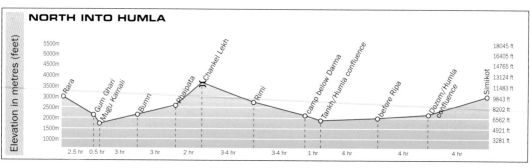

Porters near Ripa village on the trail towards Simikot in the valley of the Humla Karnali.

clusters, cling to impossibly steep hillsides. In summer all of life's chores are performed on the flat roofs of these solid buildings, which are linked by networks of polished single-log stairways. Living conditions for these folk are harsh.

From the Chankel Lekh to Simikot will take a minimum of four days. Do not be deceived by the comparatively short distances indicated on the maps; these are precipitous valleys, and the trails through them are pedestrian roller coasters. The scenery is wild, magnificent and ever changing, the only constant factor being the thundering green torrent of the Humla Karnali river. Set off at dawn each day, and walk through misty bamboo groves as gentle sunlight filters through the canopy overhead and turns the scene into a living Chinese watercolour.

By the time you toil up the final thousand-metre climb to Simikot at the end of this walk, Humla will have worked its magic on you. Its tranquillity and ancient charm are powerful antidotes to the stresses of modern life elsewhere, and a welcome reprieve from the teahouse trails of Nepal's more popular areas. Go properly prepared. Be meticulously sensitive in all aspects of your conduct and enjoy this precious, fragile corner of the Nepal Himalaya. Even if you're not planning to go on to Tibet and Mount Kailas, be sure to give yourself time for further travels north of Simikot.

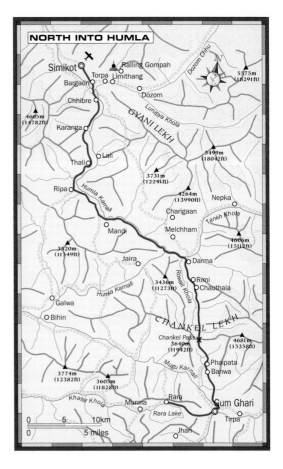

JETH PURNI FESTIVAL

One of the main highlights of the Tibetan year is the festival of Saga Dawa, celebrating the birth anniversary of the Buddha Sakyamuni. In the Humla region this is celebrated as Jeth Purni by Buddhist and Hindu together at the tiny Ralling Gompah. This monastery is situated in a peaceful corrie high on the side of Shelmogang mountain above the village of Limithang (see trek 4), in the valley of the Dozom Chhu. It's a marvellously relaxed yet intensely spiritual celebration, as well as a welcome break from lives of otherwise ceaseless toil. Saga Dawa is an auspicious time to make pilgrimages. It takes place on the full-moon day of the fourth month of the Tibetan calendar – Jeth – usually May or June. However, like all things in Nepal its celebration in Humla is subject to variation due to seasonal and local imperatives. In 1997, for example, the festival at Ralling was postponed for a month on account of late snowfall, and then again due to the death of an elder in Limithang, finally taking place in late June.

Chhetri woman at a Jeth Purni festival

The Day Dawns

The main day of *puja* during Jeth Purni dawns with the thick, sweet-scented smoke of juniper billowing from the chimneys of stupa-shaped rooftop hearths. It's manna for the gods. The houses of the Nyinbas – the Tibetans living in this area – are like miniature mediaeval fortresses, solidly built of huge timbers and dressed stone. Most rise to three storeys, and have grain stores, shrines and guestrooms on their flat roofs. As the juniper crackles and spits into flame the residents joyfully chant 'Om mani padme hum', the Buddhist mantra which is perpetually on their lips.

From before first light the dimly lit interiors of the houses will have been a buzz of activity as folk busy themselves with preparations. Babies howl with disbelief as they endure the novel sensation of being immersed in bowls of warm water and scrubbed. Daughters pour pitchers of water through the hair of their mothers and sisters, and sit patiently working mustard seed oil into their locks before braiding them in the Nyinba fashion. Carpets and blankets are brought out and beaten, saddles dusted down, picnic hampers made ready.

The Hanging Valley

Up at the *gompah*, monks will have been chanting in the tiny temple all night. Pilgrims from local villages start out very early to make their way into the Dozom valley and climb the steep 900m (2950ft) mountainside to Ralling, arriving from far and wide by late morning.

The trail is a festival on foot and horseback. Groups of young and exquisitely bejewelled Nyinba girls in their finest silks skip along, arm in arm, singing gaily. Roguish men on finely caparisoned ponies race on up, their maroon *chuba* coats billowing open at the waist, wide-brimmed Tibetan felt hats worn at rakish angles. All are sweating as they emerge from the precipitous slopes into the secluded hanging valley where the *gompah* lies, surrounded by jagged snow-covered peaks.

The day passes in an exuberant whirl of *puja*, picnic and dance. To the sound of drums and chanting, the *dhamis* – human oracles and village shamans – make their way up in a dignified procession of white turbans and tie-dyed *chubas*. Although Ralling is a Buddhist *gompah*, the people of Humla practise beautifully tolerant forms of their Hindu and Buddhist religions, and both communities join together in celebrating Jeth Purni. The old ways have not been abandoned, and elements of Masta animism and the ancient shamanist Bon religion of Tibet still colour contemporary

Nyinba elders performing ritual dances – *Shon* - during the long afternoon procession down the mountain from Ralling *Gompah*.

religious practice. The *dhamis* play a central role in village life, being consulted on everything from sickness to marriage and business matters. Their participation in these festivities is a central feature, and they ritually circle the tiny *gompah* three times before the feasting and drinking can begin.

Party All Night

As the events of the day draw to a close, a seemingly endless line of Nyinbas in their finest gowns and jewels files through a low cave temple, pressing foreheads to the sacred rocks before moving on into the *gompah* to receive blessings from *lamas*. Eventually, with the sun dropping towards the horizon, the exodus back down the hill begins. There is now a lightness in the air – an unfettered joy and rejoicing. At a place called

Togra halfway back to Limithang a camp is set up, and the chanting, singing, feasting and socialising continues unabated until the afternoon of the following day.

Witnessing and participating in an event such as the Jeth Purni festival at Ralling is like being reborn into a lost but reassuringly familiar realm. Whilst tour companies may offer itineraries to outlandish places, all it really takes is to step out alone into parts of rural Nepal like Humla to discover that time travel is indeed possible.

Anyone contemplating a visit to Humla or Limi should seek out *Kailash Mandala*, a guidebook by Tsewang Lama. As a source of information on the culture and geography of this region it is a unique and book (pub. 2000 by HCDA, Simikot ISBN 9-99337-600-0).

TREK 4: HUMLA TO MOUNT KAILAS

The opening of the border between Humla in northwest Nepal and Ngari in southwest Tibet in May 1993 marked a turning point in the history of this sleepy backwater. Pilgrims and traders had long been permitted to cross into Tibet from Nepal in carefully monitored groups, but the coming of western tourist traffic was something quite new and a real eye-opener for Humlis living along the trail to Tibet. For the visitor, walking the trails of Humla is like passing a parade of the most exotic cultures surviving in Nepal today.

TREK ESSENTIALS

LENGTH (3-4 weeks ex Kathmandu.)
Walking from Simikot: 5 days to Yari, 8-10 days in Tibet, 4 days return to Simikot.
ACCESS Flight Nepalganj–Simikot.
HIGHEST POINT Highest trek point: Dolma La, 5660m (18570ft). Highest camp: above Diraphuk Gompah, ±5210m (17090ft).
TREK STYLE Tents and kitchen required
RESTRICTIONS Permits US$90 for the first 7 days, then US$15 per extra day. Liaison officer required. Costs in Tibet circa US$1000.
FURTHER OPTIONS Treat as continuation of route from Jumla to Humla (trek 3).

Flights to Simikot now make Humla readily accessible, though getting yourselves and all your food and equipment there on a given day requires some logistical acumen and luck. You will be competing with experienced Humlis bent on getting crates of fresh fruit and other bulky treats for their families onto the flight at Nepalganj. Charter flights regularly carry freight on this sector, and having an agent arrange this in advance of your arrival is a good idea. You also have to register with the police at the check post south of the airstrip on arrival, and if you need to organise any porters in town you'll be very lucky to get away the same day.

The population of Humla can roughly be divided into Hindu Chhetris and Thakuris, and Buddhist Bhotias and Nyinbas – Tibetans living in upper Humla. You will find that the Thakuris and Chhetris of Simikot are reluctant to carry loads. They also tend to live at lower altitudes and be more introverted in their communities than the Buddhists, who tend to live in high, open country and are comparatively astute in business and outward looking.

A British charity, The Nepal Trust, has long been working amongst the Nyinbas, building community health-care facilities and micro-hydro plants in outlying villages, as well as a multi-purpose centre in Simikot which serves as a basic restaurant, hotel and information centre. See Nepal OnLine p29.

Simikot to Yari

If you fly in to Simikot, it is sensible to make your first day a short one and walk over the ridge north of town and on down to Masigaon. This is an 800m (2625ft) descent and should give you a better chance of a good night's sleep unacclimatised. There is a small, filthy teashop here run by a friendly old *dhami*, and limited camping space on the terraces below.

The trail to the Nara Lagna and Tibet from Simikot has been a major trade and pilgrim route for many centuries, and walking it today is a cultural education in itself. In the course of a day you will meet white-turbaned *dhamis* with huge gold earrings and billowing *sulpa* pipes, barefoot soot-black ragamuffin urchins herding their flocks to pasture, traders with hundreds of laden sheep and goats (each animal carrying a 10kg load called a *lukal* in small panniers), portly lamas heading for Bodnath or Kailas, almost naked trident-bearing saddhus from India, school-

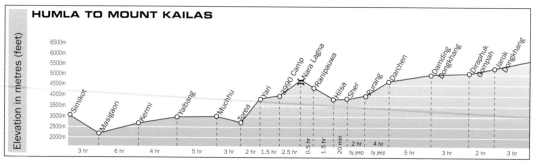

HUMLA TO MOUNT KAILAS

teachers and government officials from all over Nepal, processions of singing village
women carrying firewood
down from the hills and men
spinning wool as they walk.
There's never a dull moment
in Humla.

Allow yourself more than
the minimum five days
required to reach Yari, the
last village in Nepal on this
route. Visit Kermi Gompah
and the Nepal Trust's health-
post at Yangar. Pause at the
vast, verdant meadows by
the Karnali river at Yalbang
and imagine the month-long
mela that used to go on

Nyinba girls at Yalbang village, Humla

there every October. Time
seems to pass at a more natural, primitive pace in
Humla, and to rush through on a tight schedule is
to miss much of what the place has to offer.

The Nepal immigration control is at Muchhu,
and the customs post a day further on at Yari.
There's a dusty camping ground right in front of the
police/immigration post at Muchhu, but a much
nicer spot can be found half an hour beyond, down
by the river. If you've arranged to be met by your
Tibetan or Chinese hosts on the other side of the
Nara Lagna, try to camp above Yari to give yourselves plenty of time for dealing with bureaucracy
the next day. The highest *karkha* on the Nepal side
is at Sipsip (4330m/14207ft), but those not acclimatising so well should camp lower – there is a
meadow at 3950m (12960ft) from which the pass
(4500m/14765ft) can be reached in two hours.

Yari to Tibet
Descending north from the bleak, windswept Nara
Lagna and confronted with Tibet's sweeping vista of
inhospitable and completely barren brown hills, you
may feel like turning tail and fleeing back to Nepal.

The river in the valley before you is indeed the
Humla Karnali, now completely transformed from
the mighty torrent you followed for so long in Nepal.
Here it is a much diminished stream, flowing shal-
low and clear in a desolate wilderness of sand and
stone. A new suspension bridge was completed at
Hilsa (a tiny hamlet at the foot of the Nara Lagna
on the north side – surely the most remote piece of
real-estate in Nepal!) in 1997, and from here it's
just ten minutes walk up to Sher, where a tattered
Chinese flag flies noisily against the perpetual
howling wind proclaiming this the most distant outpost of Chinese rule in Tibet.

The 125km (78-mile) road from Sher to Darchen, starting point for the pilgrim route or *kora*
around Mount Kailas, is rough and difficult for anything other than a four-wheel drive vehicle. The
Chinese do bounce Dong Feng ('Liberation') trucks
along it, but travelling this way is not for the faint-
hearted. Be sure to visit Khojarnath Gompah on
the way, and have a wander around Purang (also
known as Taklakot). The State Bank of China at the
head of Purang's dusty main street, despite its

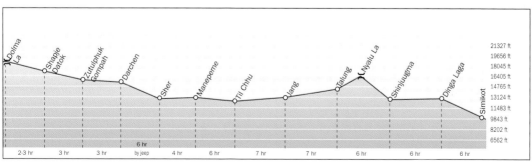

KAILAS KORA

TIBET

0   5   10km
0   5 miles

N

HUMLA TO MOUNT KAILAS

ostentatious facade, does not accept travellers cheques. Exchange procedures are excruciatingly lengthy, so if you are with a group pool all your cash and make one transaction.

You'll probably be obliged to stay in the 'Hotel for Tourists' in Purang. This dusty compound used to be used as accommodation for pilgrims travelling from India across the Lipu Lekh, and facilities are very basic. There are no toilets. Don't be fooled either by the 'Happy Drinking Room' at the entrance – it's a brothel!

The accommodation in Purang may be bad, but the rooms offered at Darchen are much worse. You'll have to stay there on the way in, to arrange yaks to carry your kit around Kailas, though it can easily be missed on the return journey in favour of a camp by the shores of Lake Manasarovar. The food available at these places and provided by the Chinese for trekkers on a trip around Kailas is diabolical (fine if you like noodles), so it's a good idea to have your outfitter in Kathmandu arrange for your Nepali trek crew to accompany you into Tibet.

Tibetan pilgrims make the 52km (33 miles) *kora* around Kailas in a single day (mostly travelling clockwise), leaving Darchen well before dawn and returning late at night. Most foreigners take a more sedate four days, allowing an appreciation of the stunning scenery in the region and a chance to acclimatise to the extreme altitude. Darchen is at 4560m (14961ft); the highest camp used by trekking groups is at Jarok Dongkhang (5210m/17094ft) above Diraphuk Gompah on their second day; and the Dolma La is at 5660m (18570ft). Nowhere is the trail really difficult, and as you slump wearily on a wayside rock to rest you will be cajoled and encouraged by cheery Tibetan ladies twice your age.

Take your time and absorb the wonders of Mount Kailas. This is the spiritual heart of Tibet, the holiest of holies, and witnessing the piety of pilgrims here – both Hindu and Buddhist – will dispel any doubts you may have been harbouring about the resilience of the human spirit. I defy anyone not to be moved by this place.

Walk-out via Limi

Those in search of further adventure may wish to consider a difficult but rewarding diversion on their way back to Simikot. From Sher (on the Tibetan side of the Humla Karnali) a trail heads off into the

TRADE WITH TIBET

Until the Chinese invaded Tibet and sealed its borders with Nepal, major trade and pilgrimage routes wound their way through many of these obscure northern valleys, bringing with them the wealth of merchants and the cultural variety of pilgrims. Their closure was a crushing blow to communities living in the vicinity, precipitating abrupt economic and social decline. Eventually the Chinese relented in the case of Humla, and reopened the border to Nepali traders and pilgrims in the late 1970s. Not until 1993 was an agreement reached between the two governments allowing foreign travellers to make the crossing.

Today Humla is one of the last places in the entire Himalaya where the traditional trade patterns still cling on. By carrying Tibetan rock salt down into the lowlands, exchanging it there for barley, and then returning to Tibet to repeat the process, villagers are able to supplement the meagre yields of their arable land. Because trails in the area are so narrow and precarious, sheep and goats are used as pack animals for these journeys, and passing long trains of them is an unforgettable part of travelling in the region.

Nepali restricted area of Limi. The Bhotias living in this, the most remote of all Nepal's mountain communities, traditionally maintained close links with Tibet, grazing enormous herds of *pashmina*-producing mountain goats on the Tibetan plateau and manufacturing huge quantities of rosewood bowls on stirrup lathes which were highly sought after as far afield as Lhasa.

The rugged trail back this way follows the Takche Chhu east through Limi, turns south at Gumma Yok and Tshom Tso and crosses the 4800m (15749ft) Nyalu Lekh before finally descending the Chhungsa Khola to rejoin the Humla Karnali. Allow at least a week to reach Simikot from Sher by this route. There are many variations possible, and for those properly provisioned and equipped, with sufficient experience of this type of wilderness trekking, Limi is a fantastically rewarding and scenic walk.

KHUMARI KHOLA

One further option near the end of this trek is to follow a little travelled route back towards Rara from upper Humla. From below Muchhu, almost directly across the Karnali from Yangar village, a tiny trail climbs a series of steep *lekhs* to reach the Sankha Lagna (4800m/15749ft), a broad ridge descending from the east face of the Saipal Himal. Passing the remote villages of Puiya and Tsala on its way up, this scenically stunning route then descends into the upper Kuwari Khola at Rani Kharka, and from here the largely uninhabited valley makes a great walk out south to Barchya on the Karnali river. Allow at least nine days to reach Barchya from Muchhu. From here you can either hook up with the western route from Jumla to Rara (see trek 2) at Sinja, or continue southwest to the Kaphtad National Park and the airstrip at Silgarhi.

Mount Kailas, seen across the Plains of Barkha from Chiu Gompah on the shores of Lake Manasarovar.

TREK 5: ACROSS SOUTHERN DOLPO

Ba-Yul, the Hidden Land of Dolpo, was first settled by Rokpa farmers and Drokpa nomads from Tibet in the 10th century. It is one of the highest inhabited places on earth, with scattered fortress-like villages and monasteries nestling amongst mountains of stark, ascetic beauty. Though part of Nepal today, Dolpo remains culturally and economically firmly tied to Tibet. Like Limi in Humla, the people of this desolate area are cut off from their southerly neighbours by snow-covered passes for much of the year. This is fascinating, difficult country to travel in, demanding careful planning and self-sufficiency from parties intending to traverse it.

TREK ESSENTIALS

LENGTH (3 weeks ex Kathmandu.) Walking from Jumla: 4 days to Hurikot, 4 days to Ringmo, 1 day rest at Ringmo, 3 days to Champa Gompah, 4 days to Juphal.
ACCESS *To start* Flight Nepalganj–Jumla. Or local bus Nepalganj–Surkhet then walk to Jumla via Dai Lekh and Tila Khola. *On finish* flight Juphal–Nepalganj.
HIGHEST POINT Highest trekking point: Num La, ±5318m (17450ft) Highest camp: Pelungtang, ±4460m (14630ft).
TREK STYLE Tents and kitchen required.
RESTRICTIONS Permits US$10 per week up to four weeks, then US$20 per extra week; park fee NRs1000.
FURTHER OPTIONS Leave trek near Do Tarap and continue to Jomsom (trek 11).

Brought to the attention of those interested in matters Himalayan and Tibetan by the likes of Tucci and Snelgrove in the 1950s, and then to a wider world by zoologist George Schaller and writer Peter Matthieson, Dolpo is of particular interest today as an enclave of pure Tibetan culture. Situated in the rain-shadow of the Dhaulagiri Himal, this arid high mountain desert does not sustain a dense population. Dolpo is a land of howling winds, open spaces and enormous skies, of blinding sunlight, remote monasteries, yak caravans and the scent of juniper. Dolpo is Tibet in Nepal.

Today much of Dolpo lies within the boundaries of Shey–Phoksundo National Park, the inner core of which is also a restricted area requiring the standard US$700 permit for a ten-day visit. One route does exist, however, which provides a taste of Dolpo and takes in some of the best high mountain scenery in the district without incurring that prohibitive permit fee. This is the trek from Jumla to Juphal via Ringmo and Do Tarap. Along its course you experience all the wonderful variety of landscape and mountain environment that the west has to offer – from grassy *lekhs*, lush meadows, forests of maple and walnut and idyllic clear mountain streams near Jumla, to snow-covered high mountain passes, glaciers and sweeping views of barren, seemingly lifeless hills stretching northwards into Tibet.

September is considered the optimum month for this route, as the monsoon recedes and winter winds and snows have yet to afflict the highlands. Be prepared for sweltering heat, intense humidity and even torrential rain as you hike the first four days to Hurikot. I prefer to go later and endure the cold in order to see the mountains under the crystal skies of October and November.

Jumla to Hurikot

The first eight days, from Jumla to Hurikot and on to the village of Ringmo on the shores of Phoksundo lake via the Kagmara La (5115m/ 6782ft), constitute a challenging enough outing in their own right. Almost immediately this route enters really wild country, and as you stand on the Pattyata Lagna in the afternoon of the long

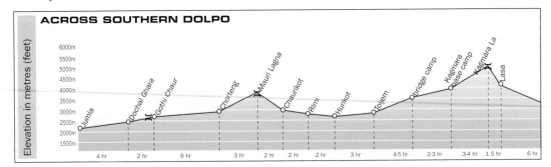

ACROSS SOUTHERN DOLPO

first day heading east from Jumla and look down into the beautiful alpine meadows of Gothi Chaur, your heart will sing. This is trekking country to live for. Sweeping down from the pass is a tree-lined pasture of unbelievable verdure, spangled with bright orchids, forget-me-nots and geraniums. At the bottom of the magnificent basin into which the trail then descends, a gushing spring issues from a series of pools and a more picturesque camping spot could not be imagined.

From Gothi Chaur to Chaurikot across the Mauri Lagna (3960m/12993ft) the trail is fairly gentle, breaking you in slowly and acclimatising you for the rigours ahead. Climb to a small grassy knoll above the pass for a panoramic view east to the distant Dhaulagiri Himal.

The view from the upper Pungmo Khola towards Kagmara.

Just beyond Rimi the trail divides, with a more southerly route heading off over the Balangra La (3750m/12304ft) and on to Juphal and Dunai. The more challenging and rewarding option followed here is to turn left into the valley of the Garpung Khola and make for the sensational Kagmara La (5115m/16782ft) and Phoksundo. A huge amount of potent hashish is cultivated in the area, and in autumn the sweet fragrance of village plantations is discernible on the breeze from miles away.

Hurikot to Ringmo
Just beyond Hurikot, a charming mediaeval village and site of the most important Bon *gompah* in the district, the trail enters the Shey-Phoksundo National Park. Almost immediately the going gets much harder. After a grunt of a climb, an airy traverse and a precipitous descent to cross the Jagdula Khola on a fine cantilever bridge, a police post is reached at Toijem. The carefully tended garden is home to yet more specimens of *Cannabis sativa*. From here the valley climbs with unremitting steepness to Kagmara base camp (±4100m/ 13450ft) and the pass. A rest day before going over is definitely recommended. From camp, you can cross the tiny stream that the Jagdula Khola has by now become, and ascend an easy grassy ridge to the west for sensational views of the entire Kagmara Himal – a range infinitely more impressive than their heights (none top 6000m/ 19690ft) imply.

Set off before dawn to cross the dramatic but straightforward pass. From below the range looks impenetrable without resorting to mountaineering techniques, but in fact the way is not so difficult.

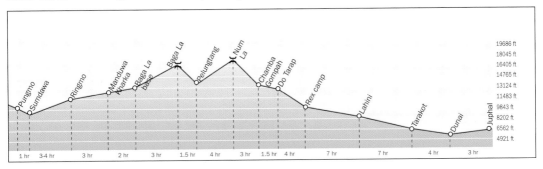

RED RICE ROUTE

At Kaigaon, just beyond Rimi, a lower-lying trail diverges directly towards Juphal. This used to be the way that Jumla's famous red rice (*raato baat*) was carried to Kathmandu during the reign of the Ranas. From Juphal the carriers would continue to Tarakot, Beni and eventually Kathmandu.

From Kaigaon the red rice route leads to the Balangra La – the climb to this pass is through magical forests of conifer, oak, birch, rhododendron and wild rose, all festooned with Spanish moss. On a clear day there are wonderful views east to the Dhaulagiri Himal from the top. Beyond, the route passes through a land of *dhamis* and ancient traditions that date from well before the coming of the Hindu faith. Tiny shrines called *tans*, often in villages but also in dark and secluded woodland grottoes, house bizarre human effigies called *dokpas*, representing protective divinities. During full-moon rituals performed at these primitive temples, *dhamis* go into spectacular trances and speak in unintelligible tongues. From Tibrikot the trail then follows the Thulo Beri river (the name of the Barbung Khola below Tichurong) to the outlandish fortified settlement of Tarakot and on to Beni (see trek 10).

For trekkers, this route offers a mellow alternative to the higher passes of the Dolpo region. It is best walked from east to west, in the form of a trek from Beni to Jumla. As most trekkers in this region take a northern route via the Kagmara La, you will not meet many foreigners on the way.

Head north up valley for thirty minutes from camp, and then turn east into a broad cwm and follow the surprisingly good trail up steepening zigzags for 650m (2133ft) of ascent. The final snow-covered slopes are less steep. After a rest, ascend the ridge rising north from the col to a height of 5380m (17652ft) for a stupendous 360° panorama taking in Kagmara, Kanjiroba, La Shamma, Dhaulagiri, Annapurna and dozens of lesser peaks. A good campsite (4460m/14633ft) is reached after an hour of steep descent.

The Kagmara Himal really marks the boundary of Dolpo on this route. From here onwards the villages are purely Tibetan, consisting of solid, square, stone and timber built houses with prayer-flags fluttering on the rooftops and elaborately decorated *chortens* marking the boundaries. Much accomplished spinning and weaving takes place, but the prices asked, even in remote farmsteads, are very high. As is so often the case in the Himalaya, much of the height so exhaustingly gained on the ascent to Kagmara is lost again before the steep climb to Ringmo begins. Prepare to sweat!

Take a day's rest at Ringmo. Visit the crumbling whitewashed temples of the large Bon *gompah* on the lakeside east of the village, and marvel at the ever-changing azure hues of Phoksundo Tal as clouds scud across the afternoon sky. With

On the summit of Num Ri, with the Kanjiroba Himal on the horizon beyond.

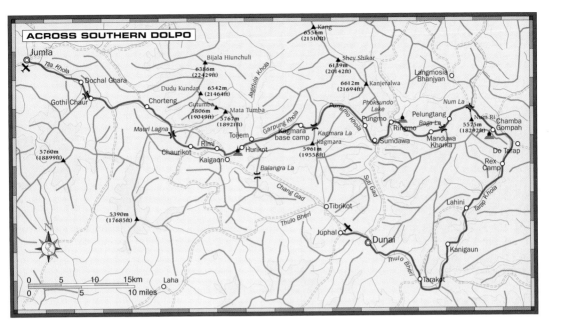

binoculars, watch the progress of yak caravans making their ponderous way northwards along the steep shores of the lake to the Kang La, Shey Gompah and distant Saldang. To follow them you will need to have secured a restricted area permit in Kathmandu.

Ringmo to Champa Gompah

Those with less time may choose to head back to Juphal directly south from Ringmo, but if you want to make your trek in Dolpo really special head east again into the Manduwa Khola. This is the way to Do Tarap via the Baga La and Num La passes, and to reach Juphal this way requires another week at least.

Initially very steep and exposed, the way into this valley is quite sensational, affording breathtaking views of the waterfall where the Phoksundo Khola plunges into the valley south of Ringmo, and back west to the Kagmara Himal. Do not succumb to the temptation to camp at the idyllic Manduwa Kharka, but press on and spend the night at the head of the valley (±4100m/13450ft), immediately below the notch into which the trail steeply ascends towards the Baga La. Eat a big supper and get to bed early, for the next two days are the most strenuous and rewarding of the entire trip.

Reasonably fit and acclimatised trekkers should make the 1100m (3610ft) ascent from this camp to the Baga La (5190m/17028ft) in under three hours. All the way from Jumla the scenery gets increasingly arid, and by the time you make the 600m (1970ft) descent from the Baga La to camp at Pelungtang the transition to high altitude desert is complete. There is not so much as a single stunted juniper bush to be seen, and the diet of the numerous yaks grazing hereabouts consists solely of dry grass and gravel. The mountain views from the camp are more impressive than those from the pass, which is but a narrow cleft in a steep rocky range.

DOLPO TODAY

Dolpo today is an impoverished land. Already well into economic decline, the region was badly hit when the Chinese sealed its borders with Tibet. Traditional winter grazing grounds on the Changtang used by the Drokpas ceased to be available and their huge herds of yaks and *pashmina*-producing *chiang-lu* could no longer be sustained.

The problem has been compounded by the large numbers of Tibetan Khampas who, following the Chinese occupation of Tibet, occupied many remote valleys in northwestern Nepal and mounted a guerrilla campaign against the Chinese. This, coupled with recent Maoist activity in the region, has prevented much of the northwest from sharing the tourism-led economic progress enjoyed by other parts of the country.

The future of Dolpo is far from certain. Assess the political situation carefully before setting off there; excursions in the area are included here in the hope that peace will prevail and the hardy, smiling Dolpo-pa be given every opportunity to live and prosper.

Ringmo Gompah, on the shores of Phoksundo Lake at the heart of Shey-Phoksundo National Park.

The same cannot be said of the Num La. From camp the trail descends a couple of hundred metres before commencing the long, steady pull to this next pass at 5318m (17448ft). A major trail to Saldang and Shey Gompah cuts away north across a vast open mountainside just out of camp, and as you gain height again your descent route from the Baga La is clearly visible behind you, with the Kanjiroba Himal to the northwest. From the windswept col a bleak but breathtaking 180° panorama west, north and east is revealed, though in order to fully appreciate the magnificence of your location a little more energy must be burned. Immediately above the col to the south rises a small peak, Num Ri (5575m/18292ft), and the view from its vast, flat plateau of a summit will have you running out of film before you know it. To the north the desolate brown hills of Dolpo sweep away towards Shey and Tibet. To the west, Kagmara, Kanjiroba and the distant peaks of Humla line up along the horizon. To the south Putha Hiunchuli, the Churen Himal and Dhaulagiri are visible, and to the east the trail to the Chharka La. It is, quite simply, out of this world.

Given time and acclimatisation there is a very tempting ridge-walk around a cirque to the south, finally descending steeply to rejoin the main trail down from the pass into the Tarap Valley. Camp at Chamba Gompah and spend a day or two savouring this wild, Tibetan valley. This is as close to the real Dolpo as you can get without paying for an expensive restricted area permit, and the area is popular with trekking groups. If you have time to linger here and befriend the initially shy village folk, you will soon be sitting by a smoky stove sipping salt-butter tea, or learning to thresh barley in the fields.

Champa Gompah to Juphal
The walk-out to Juphal down the Tarap Gorge takes four days and involves traversing some very airy trails and bridges that would not be out of place in a circus act. Late in the season many of these can be avoided by wading the river. Stop for a *dalbat* feast at the Blue Sheep Lodge in Dunai on the last day, but don't overdo it with the beer and *chang* – the final climb to Juphal is a gruelling three-hour flog. Send a member of your crew on ahead a day in advance to reconfirm your seats, and be prepared for an adrenaline rush as you take off from the shortest of Nepal's STOL airstrips and immediately bank steeply away to avoid the enormous boulder opposite the end of the runway.

WESTERN NEPAL DIRECTORY

REGIONAL FLIGHTS

The main transport hub in western Nepal is Nepalganj. There are several daily flights to Nepalganj from Kathmandu, but whichever way you get there you will have to stay overnight if flying on into the hills, as Jumla, Simikot and Juphal flights leave at the crack of dawn.

The following airlines operate flights to Nepalganj and beyond:

Children at Limithang village in Humla.

Kathmandu–Nepalganj: Nepal Airlines, Buddha Air, Yeti Airways
Nepalganj–Jumla: Nepal Airlines, Yeti Airways
Nepalganj–Simikot: Nepal Airlines, Yeti Airways
Nepalganj–Juphal: Nepal Airlines, Yeti Airways
Nepalganj–Bajhang: Nepal Airlines

It is also possible to charter a plane to the airstrips at Bajhang or Baitadi – inquire well in advance!

REGIONAL ROAD TRANSPORT

Regular night coaches run via the Mahendra Highway from Kathmandu to the outskirts of Nepalganj, and also to Surkhet (Birendranagar). Local buses from Nepalganj serve Surkhet, Salyan, Dipayal and Baitadi.

Kathmandu–Nepalganj: 5 departures daily between 15:00 and 17:00 from New Bus Park at Gongabu; 12–14 hours
Kathmandu–Surkhet: 2 departures daily between 15:00 and 16:00 from New Bus Park; 14 hours
Nepalganj–Surkhet: Several departures daily
Nepalganj–Salyan: Local bus
Nepalganj–Dipayal: Local bus
Nepalganj–Baitadi: Local bus

It is also possible to charter a vehicle or private bus to places like Surkhet or Dandeldhura.

NEPALGANJ

ACCOMMODATION

Accommodation in Nepalganj is limited. Other than the hotels listed below, there are various squalid hotels around Birendra Chowk.

Hotel Sneha, Surkhet Road, Nepalganj, tel (081) 520119, 520487, fax (081) 522573 hotel@sneha.wlink.com.np. The best accommodation Nepalganj has to offer. Call from Kathmandu for airport transfer in an ancient jeep! The food is excellent Nepali.
Hotel Batika, 13, Surkhet Road, Nepalganj, tel (081) 521360, fax (081) 522318. The Batika, located next door to the Sneha, is the only hotel of similar standard.
Hotel Oasis, Surkhet Road, Nepalganj, tel (081) 20827. Moderate standard hotel.
New Hotel Punjabi, Birendra Chowk, Nepalganj, tel 520818. Moderate standard hotel.

TREKKING COSTS

The entire west of Nepal – from Dhaulagiri to the Indian border – is terra incognitae for most of the trekking world, which is a real pity or a blessing, depending on your point of view. Dolpo, Mugu and Humla are remote, difficult areas requiring both official permits and the logistical support of an agent to trek in. This all costs money.

However, the route north into Tibet to Mount Kailas from Humla involves considerably more expense in terms of permits required and trekking agency costs. The Chinese certainly make you pay, and for trekking in Tibet, Kathmandu agents may charge US$135 to US$200 per day per person depending upon the group size and area they want to visit. This includes arranging for the Nepali crew used from Simikot to accompany the group into Tibet (visas, etc).

5

ANNAPURNA REGION

Bounded in the west by the Barbung Khola and Dolpo, and in the east by the Buri Gandaki, the mountains of central Nepal are dominated by the Dhaulagiri, Annapurna and Manaslu Himalaya.

Unlike the peaks in other parts of the country, these ranges are not sheltered from the onslaught of the monsoon by lesser, intervening chains of cloud-snaring hills. Consequently they receive almost double the country's average annual precipitation, and the glaciers tumbling from their snowy heights reach far into the valleys below.

To the north of these mountains lie arid tracts of land which are geographically part of Tibet, inhabited by Bhotias and yet still within Nepal. A circuit of any of the main three ranges is thus not only a varied scenic experience, but a journey through culturally diverse lands.

Dhaulagiri from Poon Hill.

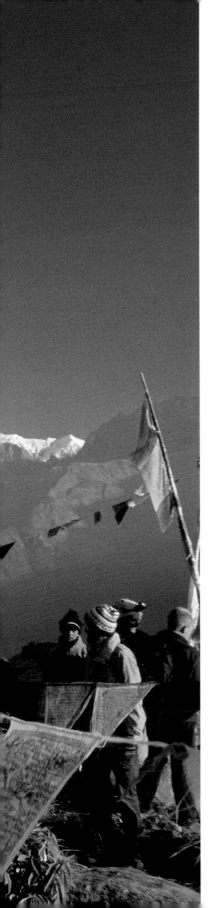

A depiction of the Buddhist deity Yamantaka at Muktinath (trek 7).

Nepal's most celebrated ornithologists, further identify this valley as demarcating Eastern and Western avifauna. The landscape and climate is suitably dramatic for a divide of such importance, with the giant snowfield air-coolers of Annapurna and Dhaulagiri sending ferocious blasts of grit-laden air northwards up-valley towards Mustang every afternoon.

All three main valleys have served as trade routes for centuries. The Kali Gandaki in particular has long sustained large Thakali merchant villages – hence its local name, the Thak Khola. Until the Chinese intervened in 1959, traders regularly brought rock salt, wool, butter and livestock from Tibet and exchanged them for rice, barley, sugar, tea, tobacco and spices from Nepal and India. The trade continues illicitly today, but has been undermined by the growing availability of manufac-tured salt from India (one positive effect of this is that Indian salt contains iodine, reducing the inci-dence of goitre). Although the Thakalis of villages such as Tukche and Marpha have since turned their hands to tourism, fruit growing and other forms of trade, the area has declined economical-ly and many have chosen to move to Pokhara and Kathmandu, leaving their magnificent houses standing empty.

To a lesser extent, the same has happened to Nyeshang in the upper Marsyangdi valley. This area has become popularly known by the name of its largest village, Manang, and businessmen

Annapurna may be the celebrity among the peaks here, but its unsung and loftier neighbours are every bit as sensational. To the north of Manaslu lies Nupri, north of Annapurna lies Manang and north of Dhaulagiri, Mustang. Within a matter of hours you can escape from the most developed, tourist-filled villages and trails in the country and find yourself amongst obscure peaks and valleys on paths that few feet tread.

Dividing the main Himalayan chain in central Nepal are the deep chasms of three ancient val-leys. Rising on the arid Tibetan plateau, the Kali Gandaki, Marsyangdi and Buri Gandaki rivers flow between peaks that exceed 8000m (26248ft). As the valley floors here are at approximately 2200m (7218ft), these are often claimed to be the deep-est gorges in the world, though in reality the word 'gorge' is a misnomer; they are generally vast defiles that only occasionally narrow into what could rightfully be called a gorge.

The Kali Gandaki is of great bio-geographical significance, as it is generally accepted to be the dividing line between the eastern and western Himalaya. To the west plant species are mostly Mediterranean and Eurasian, while to the east they tend to be Southeast Asian. The Flemings,

POKHARA

The main town in the area is Pokhara, and at an altitude of only 827m (2713ft) it feels a good deal warmer and more humid than Kathmandu. With the 64,000 people that set off annually for treks in the Annapurna region, tens of thousands more that come for white water rafting and the tourists who come simply to soak up the stunning panorama of Machhapuchhare and the Annapurna Himal from the shores of Phewa Tal, Pokhara has become a bustling tourist resort. The Pardi Dam, which holds back the waters of Phewa Tal, was con-structed by Indian engineers in the late 1960s to provide hydroelectric power for the town, though it partially collapsed in 1974. The lakeside area today resembles a more tranquil and sprawling incarnation of Kathmandu's Thamel, with book shops, telephone, fax and email bureaus, trekking and rafting agents galore, souvenir stalls and handicraft shops. A strip of lakeside cafes and bars with gardens and terraces overlooks the water, where you can while away your afternoons and listen to live jazz until the small hours. It's a great spot!

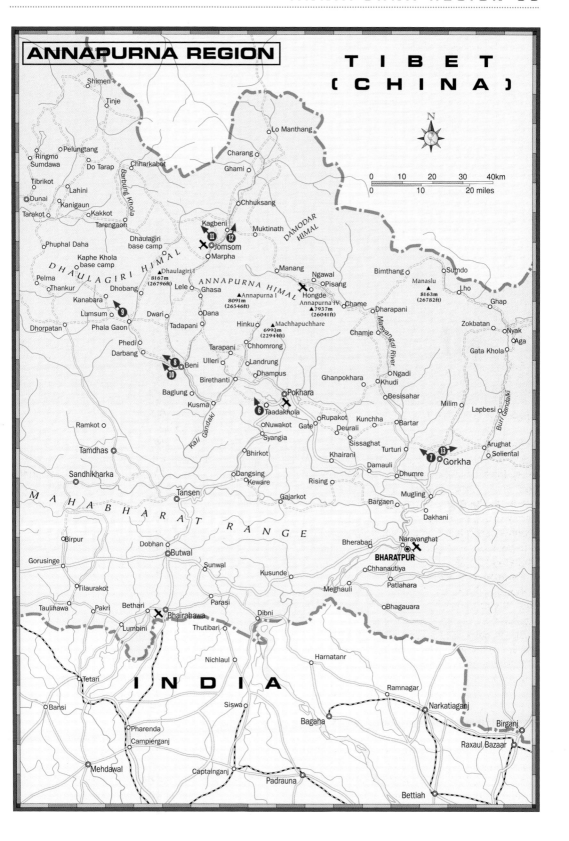

ANNAPURNA REGION

T I B E T
(C H I N A)

Shimen

Tinje

Lo Manthang

Ringmo
Pelungtang
Charang
Sumdawa
Do Tarap
Chharkabot
Ghami

Tibrikot
Lahini
Chhuksang

Dunai
Kanigaun
Kakkot
Tarakot
Tarengaon
Kagbeni
Muktinath
DAMODAR HIMAL

Phuphal Daha
Dhaulagiri base camp
⑪ ✕ Jomsom ⑫
Marpha

Kaphe Khola base camp
DHAULAGIRI HIMAL
Manang
Bimthang
Sundo

Pelma
Dhaulagiri I
8167m
(26796ft)
Lele
Ghasa
ANNAPURNA HIMAL
Ngawal
Pisang
Manaslu
8163m
(26782ft)
Lho

Thankur
Dhobang
Annapurna I
8091m
(26546ft)
Hongde
Chame
Dharapani
Ghap

Kanabara
⑨
Dwari
Dana
Annapurna IV
7937m
(26041ft)
Chamje
Zokbatan
Nyak

Lumsum
Phala Gaon
Tadapani
Hinku
Machhapuchhare
6993m
(22944ft)
Chamje
Marsyangdi River
Gata Khola
Aga

Dhorpatan
Phedi
Tarapani
Chhomrong
Ghanpokhara
Ngadi
Milim
Lapbesi

Darbang
⑧ Beni
Ulleri
Landrung
Khudi
Besisahar

⑩
Birethanti
Dhampus
Ghanpokhara

Baglung
Pokhara
Rupakot
Kunchha
Bartar
Arughat
Soliental

Kusma
⑥ Taadakhola
Gate
Deurali
⑬
⑦ Gorkha

Ramkot
Nuwakot
Sissaghat
Turturi

Tamdhas
Syangia
Khairani
Damauli
Dhumre

Sandhikharka
Bhirkot
Rising
Mugling

Tansen
Dangsing
Keware
Gajarkot
Bargaen
Dakhani

M A H A B H A R A T   R A N G E
Bheralbari
Narayanghat
BHARATPUR

Birpur
Dobhan
Butwal
Sunwal
Kusunde
Chhanautiya
Patlahara

Gorusinge
Meghauli
Bhagauara

Tilaurakot
Parasi

Taulihawa
Pakri
Bethari
✕ Bhairahawa
Dibni
Thutibari
Harnatanr
Ramnagar

Lumbini
Nichlaul
Narkatiaganj

Tetari
I N D I A
Siswa
Bagaha
Birganj

Bansi
Pharenda
Raxaul Bazaar

Campierganj

Mehdawal
Captainganj
Padrauna
Bettiah

N

0 10 20 30 40km
0 10 20 miles

Annapurna I and Annapurna South seen from Ghorepani, the collection of trekkers' hostelries below Poon Hill (trek 6).

from these parts have a long established reputation for being both keen and astute. When
Prithvi Narayan Shah unified the country at the
end of the 18th century, the Nyeshang-pa suc-

ACAP GUIDANCE

The ambitious Annapurna Conservation Area Project was inaugurated in 1986 at the behest of the King Mahendra Trust for
Nature Conservation, and maintains numerous check posts in
the region, as well as an information and environmental education centre in Pokhara (in an alleyway just south of the GPO in
Mahendra Pul, tel 21102). Covering an area of over 7500km^2
(2895 sq miles), ACAP stresses the need for local participation
in a drive to promote environmentally sensitive development
and conservation. To date they have concentrated on educating
trekkers and lodge-owners, encouraging the use of kerosene as
cooking fuel and solar water-heaters, and helping lodge-owners
in various key districts to form committees to standardise
menus and charges for food and accommodation in the face of
persistent, abusive bargaining by many trekkers. Think before
you lose your head totally over the price of a cup of tea. You
may be struggling to keep to a budget, but your air ticket to
Nepal cost over three times the average annual income in this
poor country.

cessfully negotiated a set of unique international trading privileges for themselves. These still
apply today, and have been instrumental in maintaining the pre-eminent position of the Manangis
in commerce. Many own large hotels in
Kathmandu and are involved in trading gold, precious stones and manufactured goods bought in
Bangkok and Singapore. Most of the 'antiques'
hawked to tourists along the trails around
Annapurna were in fact manufactured in southeast Asia – very few real old Nepalese and
Tibetan artefacts are left today.

The immediate vicinity of Pokhara is largely
populated by Chhetris and Brahmin, with a visible Thakali minority, whilst the surrounding hills
are mainly home to Gurungs. British Gurkha
regiments have long recruited here, and consequently the remittance dollars and cosmopolitan attitudes of soldiers returning from abroad
have given the place a greater degree of world-
liness than elsewhere in Nepal. Pokhara may
not have the rich cultural and architectural heritage of the Kathmandu valley, but it is surrounded by lush rural countryside and commands peerless Himalayan views from its lakeside location.

TREK 6: ANNAPURNA SANCTUARY

At the head of the Modi Khola, beneath the fearsome, towering rock walls and snowfields of the south face of Annapurna, lies an incredibly spectacular enclosed basin that has become famous the world over. This is the Annapurna Sanctuary, first discovered in 1957 by Jimmy Roberts, first used as a base camp by Chris Bonington's expedition in 1970, and today visited by thousands of trekkers every year. The hike into the Annapurna Sanctuary is undoubtedly the quickest way to surround yourself with real Himalayan giants in Nepal without facing the twin unpredictables of flights and altitude that a whistle-stop visit to the Khumbu entails.

It is possible to make it into the Sanctuary and back to Pokhara in ten days if you are pushed for time, but really you should devote a good two weeks to this trek in order to fully appreciate its stunning scenery. By far the most popular starting point is a roadside teashop at the bottom of the steep trail that leads to the Gurung village of Damphus, less than an hour from Pokhara by taxi – many groups fly from Kathmandu to Pokhara and make this two hour ascent in the afternoon of the same day. I recommend an alternative approach, however, which will add a couple of days to your trip but give you a much better flavour of the hills around Pokhara before turning north into the Modi Khola. Take a lightweight tent or bivvi-bag if you're not keen on staying in traditional *bhattis*.

TREK ESSENTIALS

LENGTH (2-3 weeks ex Kathmandu.) Walking from Taadakhola: 5 days to Ghorepani via Panchase Lekh, 5 days to Annapurna base camp, 1 day in the Sanctuary, 4 days out to Phedi.

ACCESS *To start* Pokhara. *On finish* taxi Phedi-Pokhara.

HIGHEST POINT Highest trekking point: Annapurna base camp, 4130m (13550ft). Highest camp: Annapurna base camp, 4130m (13550ft).

TREK STYLE Trekkers' lodges and teahouse accommodation available throughout.

RESTRICTIONS No permit required; NRs2000 ACAP fee.

Pokhara to Ghorepani via Panchase Lekh

West of Pokhara town lies a prominent 2500m (8202ft) ridge called the Panchase Lekh, from which there are wonderful views of both the lower Kali Gandaki and the southern aspects of the Annapurna Himal. Begin your walk to the Annapurna Sanctuary by heading in this direction, before continuing towards Ghorepani and Poon Hill and then into the Modi Khola. Many trails criss-cross this stretch of country, so a local guide is definitely an asset. By travelling here you will escape the crowds for a few days, pass through many fascinating villages and give your body ample opportunity to acclimatise for your time in the high-lands. It's probably best to take this route later in

the autumn season, as the trails will be very wet, slippery and leech infested in September.

The starting point is thirty minutes' drive south of Pokhara on the Tansen road, at the hamlet of Taadakhola and the road-head for Kholakhet. From here a steep set of stone steps climbs to the village of Kalapani; your route up onto the Panchase Lekh should then be via Oklai, Bumdi and Baisi Kharka. Camp or bivvi out by the lake just below the highest point for sensational sunrise views, and then continue west to Birethanti, where there is a police and ACAP check post and the beginning of the steep ascent to Ghorepani.

Take your time on this climb! Pace yourself and don't be dispirited by the folk who seem to be

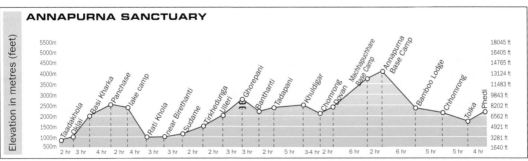

ANNAPURNA SANCTUARY

The reason for making this apparent detour on your way to the Modi Khola will become blatantly obvious when you join the throngs for the forty-minute climb to Poon Hill from the cluster of lodges and shops that nestles on the shoulder of the ridge at Ghorepani. Poon Hill is the westernmost crest of a spur that juts into the Kali Gandaki from Annapurna South, and the rickety wooden platform on the top is the only structure there. Given clear skies, the breaking of dawn over the Dhaulagiri and Annapurna Himal from this bird's-eye viewpoint is undoubtedly one of the finest sights you will ever behold in the Himalaya. If you arrive in good time, go and see both the sunset and sunrise.

Ghorepani to Annapurna Sanctuary

Having witnessed the sunrise from Poon Hill and descended to your lodge or camp for a hearty breakfast, you will be ready to set off on the two-day walk to Chhomrong in the Modi Khola. This used to be a difficult route on a tiny trail through dense forest, but today there is a splendid new path and increasing numbers of folk going this way have prompted the locals to open substantial new lodges, particularly at Tadapani. Another early morning is essential here, to watch the sunrise illuminate Machhapuchhare, Annapurna South and Hiunchuli above a sea of cloud.

Chhomrong, the last village in the Modi Khola, is a large Gurung settlement with many fancy new lodges boasting flagstoned sun terraces, private rooms and panorama-view dining halls. The kerosene depot, shops selling trekkers' requisites and hiring equipment, and the longest established lodges are in the older, lower part of the village.

almost running down from above. Most of them, having crossed the Thorung La, will be in turbo-charged mode as their lungs suddenly encounter the oxygen-rich air of the lowlands again. The trail here is broad and well maintained, particularly between Tirkhedunga and Ulleri where the local Gurungs have constructed a stairway of well over three thousand stone steps. Above Ulleri the hillsides are increasingly forested with rhododendrons and conifers, providing welcome shade. Take a little care on this stretch, as it is notorious for thieving.

Above this village the trail to the Annapurna Sanctuary spends much of its time zigzagging up and down through dense bamboo and rhododendron forest, yielding only occasional glimpses of the majestic peaks ahead. Unlike the trails in the Marsyangdi and Kali Gandaki valleys on the Annapurna circuit, this route has no historical or commercial significance and consequently no real construction work has gone into making it easy and safe. There are several sections which demand care and a sure foot, especially in wet or snowy conditions. After three strenuous days,

On the ridge above Ghorepani, with Dhaulagiri and Tukche Peak beyond.

ANNAPURNA

The unmistakeable form of Annapurna I and Annapurna South as seen from Poon Hill at sunrise.

Annapurna (8091m/26547ft) was the first eight-thousand metre peak to be climbed. The story of the first ascent remains one of the most gripping and disturbing in Himalayan literature.

Very little was known about Annapurna – indeed, very little was known about Nepal – until the kingdom was first opened to mountaineers in 1949. In that year two teams, one of American ornithologists and the other of Swiss mountaineers received permission to enter the country. The following year a French all-star team of nine members, led by Maurice Herzog, set out for the Dhaulagiri–Annapurna area.

1950 Expedition

Initially the French team made exploratory forays onto the flanks of Dhaulagiri, but soon they decided to turn their attentions to Annapurna. The maps were all wrong, and the scouts looking at the northern approaches crossed the West and East Tilcho Passes (the maps showed only one pass, and that was meant to be directly under the north flank of Annapurna) only to find their view of the north face of the mountain blocked by a 7000m (22967ft) ridge they called the Great Barrier.

The north face proved to be the only part of the mountain the scouting teams could not see; so with impeccable French logic, they chose to climb it.

Luck was with them, and almost immediately they found the only reasonable route into the Miristi Khola, containing the North Annapurna Glacier, an event that provoked Lionel Terray to write 'Fortune had favoured us with such a fantastic stroke that it seemed impossible ... that she would abandon us again.'

He was not completely right, although Fortune did favour the French as far as the summit. On the morning of 3 June Maurice Herzog and Louis Lachenal, climbing without bottled oxygen, reached the summit in eight hours. However, the ensuing descent turned into struggle for survival. The summit team and the support climbers were avalanched in the night and lost their boots at camp 3. With terrible frostbite Lachenal and Herzog had to trek out for weeks, carried by strong-backed Sherpas.

Herzog later overcame his amputations to become Mayor of Chamonix, but Louis Lachenal, one of the most brilliant alpinists of his day, never regained his composure, living the next four years in a frenzy which ended with him skiing through a snow bridge into a deep crevasse on Mont Blanc.

As for the support team, Rebuffat turned to other activities, photography and writing, while Terray made the first ascent of Makalu (1955) and died in a tragic climbing accident in 1956, aged 44.

PEAK: THARPU CHULI (TENT PEAK)

The northwest ridge of Tharpu Chuli seen from above high camp, at ±5200m (17061ft)

The accessibility of this peak in the Annapurna Sanctuary makes it an ideal objective for a short expedition, as the necessary acclimatisation is obtained during the walk-in and one or two days' rest at Annapurna base camp. The somewhat diminutive height of the peak in Himalayan terms belies the awesome views from the summit, as among the peaks lining the rim of the Annapurna Sanctuary are eight in excess of 7000m (22967ft) – Annapurna South, Baraha Sikhar, Annapurna I, Gangapurna, Annapurna III, Annapurna V, Khansar Kang and Tarke Kang. Machhapuchhare is perhaps the most beautiful though, at 6993m (22944ft).

CLIMB ESSENTIALS

SUMMIT Tharpu Chuli (Tent Peak), 5663m (18580ft).
PRINCIPAL CAMPS Base camp: across the Annapurna South Glacier from the moraine Annapurna base camp, 4200m (13780ft). High camp: below Rakshi Peak, at ±4900m (16080ft).
GRADE Northwest ridge, Alpine Grade PD; southeast ridge, Alpine Grade AD.

Base Camp and High Camp

To reach the base camp for Tharpu Chuli, descend onto Annapurna South Glacier from the moraine at Annapurna base camp (see trek 6) and follow the cairned trail across the boulder-strewn surface of the ice before climbing the moraine on the other side up a zig-zag trail in the prominent gully visible ahead. There is a flat camping area at the top at 4200m (13780ft).

There are two normal routes on Tharpu Chuli, the northwest ridge at an Alpine Grade of PD and the southeast ridge at AD. Both require a high camp at ±4900m (16077ft) below a subsidiary summit known as Rakshi Peak.

Northwest Ridge

Traverse north below Rakshi Peak and across the glacier ahead to gain the bottom of the ridge. Keep to the right (south) as the peak is approached, and climb 200m (660ft) onto the ridge itself, at 40° at first, steepening to 50° at the top. The broad ridge soon narrows again and steepens to 50° for a short section before easing as the summit is reached.

Descend by the same route.

Southeast Ridge

From the same high camp, make a long but straightforward traverse east beneath Tharpu Chuli to reach a point opposite the large couloir dividing the southeast ridge. Cross a small glacier to gain this couloir, and climb the right-hand side for 150m (490ft), before crossing to the left and ascending through a narrow section. Finally reach a more open snow slope which leads to the ridge itself, and ascend this to the summit. It is narrow and exposed, with a short rocky section which is bypassed to the left.

Descend by the same route.

during which you gain a deceptive amount of height, the trail turns west after Bagar and climbs out of the valley to Machhapuchhare base camp. From this collection of lodges it is a further two hours and 400m (1310ft) up to Annapurna base camp.

Annapurna Sanctuary

In 1986 we found two tiny bamboo shelters in the snow at Annapurna base camp. Today there are five large stone-built lodges offering under-table heating in the dining rooms, pizza and apple pie and private rooms with glass in the windows. At peak season they all get ridiculously crowded, and for this reason I always prefer to camp in such places. A kilometre further on is a flat, sheltered area tucked away from the wind behind the moraine of the Annapurna South Glacier, where the peace of this magnificent spot can be savoured just as Jimmy Roberts found it in 1957.

Spend a couple of nights here if you can, and watch the sunset from the prayer flags that adorn the high-point on the moraine behind base camp. Machhapuchhare is simply breathtaking from this viewpoint, and the immense, brooding presence of the south face of Annapurna com-

PRECIPITOUS WALLS

Just because the Annapurna Sanctuary trek is relatively short does not mean that its seriousness should be underestimated. The smoky bamboo huts that used to serve as lodges may have been replaced with deluxe hostelries, but the trail is still narrow and sometimes dangerous. The walls of the Modi Khola are often precipitous and swathed in dense, damp forests and bamboo groves. Underfoot conditions demand concentration and care, and the upper section of the route, particularly between Hinko's Cave and Machhapuchhare base camp, is prone to devastating avalanches that sweep down from the unseen slopes of Hiunchuli far above. If you are travelling here in early spring or after heavy snowfall at any time, be sure to ask about conditions beyond in Chhomrong before setting off up valley.

pletes a scene that can only be described as pure Himalayan magic.

Annapurna Sanctuary to Phedi

The walk out to Phedi takes four days, though if you walked in from there you really should consider diverting to Ghorepani on your way back.

Annapurna South, Hiunchuli and Machhapuchhare at sunrise from Tadapani; below Machhapuchhare is the deep cleft of the Modi Khola.

TREK 7: ANNAPURNA CIRCUIT

Until 1977 the Nepalese government strictly enforced the status of Nyeshang in the upper Marsyangdi valley as a restricted area due to its proximity to Tibet. The largest village, Manang, remained but a dusty outpost with no facilities and a population renowned for giving outsiders a cool reception. With the lifting of restrictions, however, a route around the Annapurna Himal via the Thorung La became accessible, and word soon spread about this long and rewarding mountain walk. Today it is one of Nepal's classic treks.

TREK ESSENTIALS

LENGTH (3-4 weeks ex Kathmandu.) Walking from Gorkha; 9 days to Manang, 4 days over to Jomsom, 5 days to Birethanti via Ghorepani.
ACCESS *To start* Bus Kathmandu-Gorkha (or Kathmandu-Besisahar via Dumre) *On finish* Walk from Birethanti to Naya Pul; bus Birethanti-Pokhara.
HIGHEST POINT Highest trekking point: Thorung La, 5416m (17770ft). Highest camp: Thorung Phedi, 4404m (14450ft).
TREK STYLE Trekkers' lodges and teahouse accommodation available throughout.
RESTRICTIONS No permit required; NRs2000 ACAP fee.
FURTHER OPTIONS Leave trek at Ghorepani to join route to Annapurna Sanctuary (see trek 6).

Annapurna was the first of the eight-thousand metre peaks to be climbed, in 1950. During the expedition the leader, French mountaineer Maurice Herzog, made a desperate hike down to Manang from his party's base camp at Tilicho in search of food, only to be sent back starving and empty handed. Now even the Manangis warmly welcome tourists. Traditional Nepali *bhattis* have evolved hereabouts into sophisticated and comfortable trekkers' lodges offering varied menus, private rooms and hot showers, with all the environmental, cultural and ecological consequences that these entail.

From a logistical and acclimatisation point of view it makes good sense to undertake this circuit in a counter-clockwise direction starting at Besisahar or Gorkha. I recommend travelling to the town of Gorkha from Kathmandu instead of heading for Dumre and Besisahar as most people do. This will halve your time spent suffering in a Nepalese bus and give you a peaceful first few days' walk through isolated rural countryside. You should be able to arrange to arrive from Kathmandu with sufficient time to visit the splendid Gorkha Durbar before setting off into the valley of the Darondi Khola. It was from this sanctuary atop a hill immediately above Gorkha's main square that Prithvi Narayan Shah sallied forth in the 18th century to begin his successful campaign to unify Nepal.

Gorkha to Manang

Accommodation between Gorkha and Tarku Ghat, where this route joins the main trail up the Marsyangdi valley, consists of primitive *bhattis* so if you plan to start this way and make other detours later it may be wise to carry a bivvi-bag or lightweight tent. To avoid walking on the road (a generous term for this rough track) all the way from Tarku Ghat to Besisahar, cross to the eastern side of the valley at Phalesangu. From here a less travelled path follows the river to rejoin the main trail at Bhulbhule, or if you're feeling really adventurous and have a tent and stove you may consider a five-day diversion up onto the Bara Pokhari Lekh for stunning views of Himalchuli and the Manaslu Himal.

During late spring and early in the autumn, be prepared for sweltering heat and high humidity at

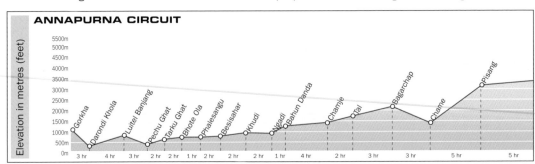

The view towards Annapurna from the Marsyangdi valley north of Besisahar, near the start of the Annapurna circuit.

the lower elevations. As you totter along dripping with sweat between Gorkha and Tarku Ghat and your altimeter tells you you're only 400m (1312ft) above sea level, the 5416m (17770ft) Thorung La will seem almost unattainable. However, the Marsyangdi is a dream of a walk, and by the time you hit 1000m (3280ft) at Bahun Danda at least the evenings will be pleasantly cool. From here on up the scenery just gets better and better, and in autumn the colours revealed in the forests are extraordinary. Waterfalls plummet from vertical cliffs, fed by unseen snows above, and the river roars away in the steep valley below. At Dharapani you pass the valley of the Dudh Khola and the trail from Manaslu and the Larkya La. The next village,

Bagarchap, was obliterated (with many fatalities) by a mud-slide during the apocalyptic storm of November 1995, and there are memorials to the victims.

Beyond this village the trail to Chame, Pisang and Manang is a pine-forested delight, with increasingly spectacular and frequent glimpses of Himalayan giants such as the Lamjung Himal and Annapurna II visible up side valleys. By the time you reach Pisang (3150m/10335ft) the nights will be getting positively chilly. Take the high route from Pisang to Braga via Ghyaru and Ngawal for stunning views of the Annapurna and Lamjung Himal south across the valley, and have a rest day here in the heart of the area known as Nyeshang. This will help your acclimatisation and

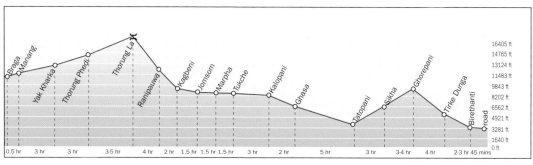

give you a chance to visit Braga's fascinating 900 year-old Kargyu-pa *gompah*. Take your head-torch and peer into the dark and gloomy interior, where you will find a strange and exotic collection of *thangkas*, or Tibetan religious paintings, and artefacts. In the main temple there are 108 terracotta images representing the entire lineage of the Kargyu-pa sect. Braga itself is a fantastic place, set beneath dramatic sculpted sandstone cliffs – though if you decide to go exploring in the village, beware of the dogs!

Most trekkers then continue for the thirty-minute stroll into Manang and stay there, but there are now several lodges at Braga. When choosing which one to patronise, here and throughout the trek, resist the temptation to go for the newest and most fancy. Lodge owners are constantly trying to outdo each other to build the biggest and best in town, and much

PEAK: PISANG

Rising above the Marsyangdi valley, Pisang Peak forms part of the Manang Himal. It was first ascended solo by J. Wellenkamp as part of a German expedition in 1955. The same group also made an ascent of the nearby Chulus during that year.

Base Camp
To reach base camp for Pisang, head north-east from the village of Pisang (see trek 7) on the Marsyangdi River. The usual location for the base camp is at a *kharka* at ±4380m (14370ft) above the village, which may be reached by walking through thinly wooded slopes and fields.

Southwest Face and West Ridge
The route up Pisang Peak is via the south-west face and west ridge, at an Alpine Grade of PD–.

From base camp follow a trail on the broad slopes to a high camp sited at ±5100m (16730ft), where there is a high pasture and some collapsed stone walls. This site may be under snow in cold seasons. Then from high camp continue straight up to the pinnacled west ridge and then the left edge of the southwest face on snow. Follow the snow crest to reach the summit.

Descend by the same route.

CLIMB ESSENTIALS

SUMMIT Pisang Peak, 6091m (19985ft).
PRINCIPAL CAMPS Base camp: *kharka* above Pisang, ±4380m (14370ft).
GRADE Alpine grade PD-.

Pisang Peak seen from the west, with the west ridge in the centre.

unnecessary felling of trees goes on to satisfy this never-ending construction process. There is a health-post in Manang, run by the HRA (Himalayan Rescue Association) and staffed by western doctors during the trekking seasons.

Manang to Jomsom

North of Manang the trail towards the Thorung La starts to gain elevation rapidly, and you should plan for a couple of short days at this stage in order to properly acclimatise. This will also allow you an early

Sunshine streams down on the marvellous *gompah* at Braga.

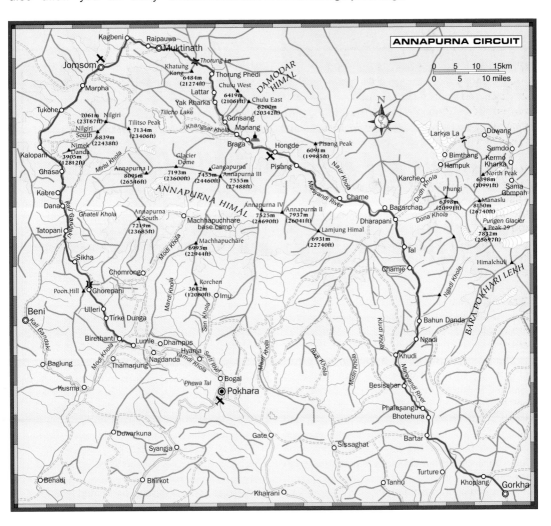

The seasonal teahouse above Thorung Phedi.

the Larkya La or French Pass. By far the best views gained are from a point several hundred metres down on the western side, when Dhaulagiri and Tukche Peak finally reveal themselves and the barren valley of the Keha Lungpa can be seen cutting into the hills to the west of Mustang.

The descent from the pass is steep, losing a knee-crunching 1600m (5250ft) before passing the temple complex at Muktinath and arriving at the village of Ranipauwa, where there are numerous trekkers' lodges, a police checkpoint and an official campsite with cooking shacks. Jomsom, with its up-market lodges, souvenir shops, bakeries and airstrip, is easily reached in half a day from Ranipauwa, but do take the time to visit the fortress village of Jharkot and make a detour via Kagbeni before starting the long walk out down the Kali Gandaki. Beware the afternoon winds that tear up the valley.

Jomsom to Birethanti

Those short of time can arrange to finish their trek in Jomsom and fly out to Pokhara, but I strongly recommend you to continue walking to Ghorepani and Birethanti. No trek in this region is really complete without savouring the hospitality and charm of the Thakali inns at Marpha and Tukche, and taking a dawn plunge in the hot springs at Tatopani. The trail below Jomsom is

arrival at Thorung Phedi, the last accommodation before the pass, and the chance of a bed there if you are not camping, as many people arrive from Manang late in the afternoon. Do not expect any privacy or solitude during this section of the trek, especially at peak season. No matter how early you rise to set off up and over to Muktinath, you will not escape the hordes. When I last walked this way we set off late at 6am, stood on the pass before 9am, and reached the check post at Ranipauwa below Muktinath at 2pm after a leisurely descent. There were already over 250 names in the register of folk coming over that day, and lines of people could still be seen descending from the heights behind us.

The 1000m (3280ft) climb from Phedi to the Thorung La commences steeply, zigzagging off up screes into a foreboding gully above. Thankfully it is not this gruelling all the way, and there is even a seasonal teashop at just over 5000m (16405ft) with great views of the Chulu peaks. It is a long climb though, with several false summits before the lone hut and fluttering prayer flags of the crest appear on the horizon ahead. The views from the pass are sweeping, but the big peaks are hidden or at quite a distance, and it is nothing like as spectacular as

---

RESPONSIBILITY

A sobering incident from October 1997 bears mentioning here in order to stress the absolute moral obligation for trekkers to look after their Nepali staff in high mountain environments. A party a day ahead of us sent back a porter suffering from altitude sickness from the climb to the Thorung La. A young Rai boy of maybe 16 years, he was relieved of his load and sent on his way dressed in only cotton clothes and plimsolls, with a thin blanket against the cold. We had been held up by snowfall at Braga and again at Phedi, and whilst safe enough for properly clothed trekkers, the pass was definitely in winter condition. The unfortunate boy staggered through the snow as far as Yak Kharka, where he collapsed. Fearing for his life, the owner of the lodge there put him in a *doqo* (porter's basket) and immediately set off to carry him down further. He had taken him only about two hundred metres when he died. Covered in just the blanket, the boy's body still lay in the basket by the trail as we passed, a grizzly reminder of how thoughtless people's actions can be. Always treat your staff as well as your companions and look after them!

the busiest in Nepal, with teahouses and lodges at every turn, but the valley is magnificent and should not be missed.

From Tatopani you may wish to continue following the river to the nearest road-head at Beni, but this would be to deny yourself the perfect scenic finale to this classic route. The steep 1700m (5580ft) climb from Tatopani to Ghorepani is easily possible in a day, especially as you will by this time be fit, acclimatised and cruising along. On arrival, set your alarm for 4am the next morning and make the forty-minute hike up to the vantage point of Poon Hill (see trek 6) by torchlight. Gaze westwards as the purple shadows recede and the awesome peaks catch the first dazzling rays of orange sun, and plan your next adventure somewhere further off the beaten track.

PEAKS: CHULU EAST AND CHULU FAR EAST

Occasionally mistaken for one another, Chulu East and Chulu Far East are two neighbouring peaks forming part of the Manang Himal. Several other peaks exist nearby and there is some doubt as to who made the first ascents of these peaks.

Base Camp and High Camp
Access to base camp for both peaks is via Julu near the village of Braga (see trek 7). From here follow a path on the banks of the Chegaji Khola past the band of cliffs with a spectacular waterfall. Base camp is at an altitude of 5334m (17501ft), below the glaciated col between the East and Far East summits, on a grassy meadow.

Either peak may be reached from a high camp two hours higher on snow on the ridge separating the Chulu East and Chulu Far East summits. One route leads from here to Chulu East at an Alpine Grade of PD+, while the other leads east to Chulu Far East at an Alpine Grade of PD−.

Chulu East
Climb the east ridge of Chulu East until it becomes possible to traverse to the right towards the northeast ridge. Climb mixed ground to gain the northeast ridge. Follow the elegant snow ridge above. This is a big, big day.

Descend the same way.

Chulu Far East
Climb the west ridge of Chulu Far East directly towards the summit from the col at 5608m (18400ft), passing two steeper sections, 45° and sometimes icy, and reach the summit without further obstacle.

Descend by the same route.

CLIMB ESSENTIALS

SUMMITS Chulu East, 6200m (20342ft). Chulu Far East, ±6059m (19880ft).

PRINCIPAL CAMPS Base camp: 5334m (17501ft). High camp: 2 hours higher, just below east ridge.

GRADE Chulu East: Alpine Grade PD+. Chulu Far East: Alpine Grade PD−.

Chulu Far East seen from base camp, with the col visible; Chulu East is off-picture to the left.

TREK 8: DHAULAGIRI CIRCUIT

Neighbouring the Annapurna Himal are Manaslu to the east and the Dhaulagiri Himal to the west. Both of these ranges are higher and arguably more spectacular than their celebrated neighbour, but both might as well be on different planets, so far removed are they from the commercial buzz and hype that has been generated regarding Annapurna. People are obsessed with celebrity today, and amongst mountains Annapurna and Everest are the 'It-Peaks'. My mission is to change that.

TREK ESSENTIALS

LENGTH (3 weeks ex Kathmandu.) Walking from Beni: 3 days to Phala Gaon, 6 days to Dhaulagiri base camp, 3 days to Marpha.
ACCESS *To start* Bus Pokhara-Beni. *On finish* Walk from Marpha to Jomsom, flight Jomsom-Pokhara.
HIGHEST POINT Highest trekking point: French Pass, 5360m (17586ft). Highest camp: Hidden Valley, 5050m (16570ft).
TREK STYLE Tents and kitchen essential.
RESTRICTIONS No permit required; NRs2000 ACAP fee.
FURTHER OPTIONS Extend trek at Phala Gaon to continue to Kaphe Khola (trek 9). Or continue from Marpha to Birethanti (see trek 7).

Dhaulagiri is the sixth highest summit in the world, and though its eastern aspects are a familiar sight to those travelling the Annapurna circuit, much of the country surrounding this 60km (56-mile) wide massif remains an enigma. Riven by the deep gorge of the Myagdi Khola, the vast bulk of the Dhaulagiri Himal shelters the barren lands of Dolpo to the west from the moisture-laden winds of the monsoon. There are six principal summits over 7200m (23623ft) and scores of major satellite peaks. Due to its unique position at the western extreme of Nepal's cluster of really high mountains, and the vast valley of the Kali Gandaki which passes right under its highest summit, the Dhaulagiri Himal generates its own unique weather systems.

Crossing the high country to the north is the crux of any circuit of the peak. French Pass has a well-earned reputation for being extremely difficult to navigate in bad weather, especially the final steep descent to Marpha from the second col, Damphus Pass. It is a high and exposed place, known for sudden whiteouts and ferocious winds. Many have been frostbitten and died here. From a fitness and acclimatisation standpoint this route should be tackled clockwise from Beni in the south, but this means tackling the high passes right at the end of the trip, when food and fuel supplies will be low. A retreat at this stage will be a long, hungry hike out, yet decisions made at Dhaulagiri base camp as to whether to go over must be taken rationally. French Pass demands respect.

That said, this is my all-time favourite route in Nepal. The country traversed may be difficult and remote, but the high valleys have a savage beauty and sense of true wilderness. For those seeking a long, adventurous outing into really magnificent highlands the Dhaulagiri circuit is unbeatable.

Beni to Phala Gaon
After flying from Kathmandu to Pokhara, you are likely to arrive in the bus park at Beni in the dark. The plush trekkers' lodges are twenty minutes away to the north. If you have equipment and supplies for three weeks camping with you, you will probably not want to bother having it all

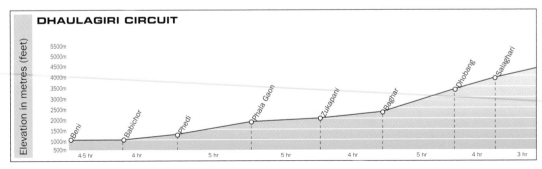

carried up there, and end up piling into the only hotel nearby, making do with a squalid room and *dalbat* on the roof.

The first three days, along the floor of the Myagdi Khola to Phala Gaon, are through classic Nepalese rural countryside, with extensive rice-paddies, banana trees, thatched farmhouses and stone-built *chautaaras* in the welcome shade of enormous pipal or banyan trees. You pass the hot spring at Tatopani on day one, though this is of limited appeal at midday under a blazing sun.

Phala Gaon to Dhaulagiri Base Camp

At Phala Gaon the path forks, with one way continuing up the Dhara Khola,

On the trail in the Myagdi Khola valley.

over a low pass into the Dhora Khola and on to Gurja Gaon – see trek 9 for details of this recommended extension. The other path crosses the Dhara Khola immediately below the village, re-entering the Myagdi Khola valley via Muri.

For a further six days you will toil up the Myagdi Khola, your progress limited by the fact that the trail is so gruelling for porters. At Salaghari the jungle at last begins to thin into coniferous forest, and the hike from here up to Italian base camp is a dream. Amongst the pines, enormous rhododendrons and the delicate green fingers of bamboo sway overhead and the sun is fiercely hot as soon as you step out of the shade. Suddenly, an hour before camp, the awesome sweeping amphitheatre of the Puchhar wall of Dhaulagiri I appears.

From the crest of the moraine at Italian base camp a faint trail plummets down and crosses the snout of the small glacier below, before disappearing into a narrow rocky gorge immediately under the flanks of Dhaulagiri. There is a danger of rock fall and avalanche on this section, so make sure you get an early start. In any case you should aim to be moving before dawn – the day up from Italian base camp is the first of three consecutive marathons that make up the crossing to the Kali Gandaki.

This route is as committing as the Hispar Pass in Pakistan, and feels even more serious on account of the close proximity of Dhaulagiri and Tukche Peak. The glacier travel is not as dangerous, though, and if there is no snow below base camp you will not need to rope up. Once through the vertiginous gorge, which is as bleak and unearthly as any place I know, with scarred black rocks, enormous icicles hanging from cliffs and the constant, brooding, invisible presence of Dhaulagiri towering above, you emerge onto the convoluted snout of the Chhonbardan Glacier and breathe a sigh of relief. All around are peaks of unbelievable ruggedness, reminiscent of the heart of the Karakoram. During the day there is an eerie silence and calm on the glacier, disturbed only by the distant boom and roar of the jet stream buffeting the upper slopes of Dhaulagiri. If you travel this way in December, the wind will torment you for the next three days.

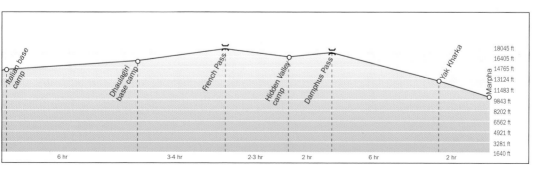

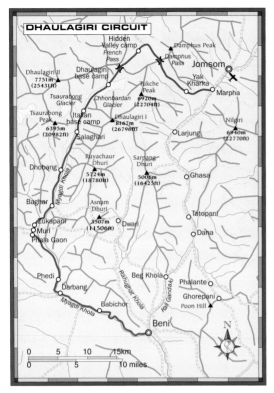

DHAULAGIRI CIRCUIT

Base camp is a lonely and god-forsaken spot on the glacier at 4700m (15420ft), exposed to the full force of the icy blast that rips up the valley from mid afternoon until dawn, with tents buckling and straining against the relentless howl of the wind. Dawn almost comes as a relief in such places. A more spectacular spot would be hard to imagine. To the south, the mighty ice-fall of the Chhonbardan Glacier tumbles in a chaotic mass of seracs and crevasses from the north face of Dhaulagiri I. To the north, Sita Chuchura towers over the camp. To the west, the summits of Dhaulagiri II, III, IV and V form a precipitous barrier that is nowhere less than 7500m (24607ft), and to the east, Tukche Peak dominates the skyline – 360° of dizzying Himalayan giants.

Dhaulagiri Base Camp to Marpha

The way to French Pass from Dhaulagiri base camp is long and steep, stealing up to the head of the Chhonbardan Glacier before turning north to surmount a spur in the middle of the valley and then continuing up its exposed crest to eventually emerge onto the col. From the final snow-covered slopes, a breathtaking view of the

Heading for Damphus Pass across Hidden Valley, with Sita Chuchura and French Pass beyond.

north face of Dhaulagiri I pans out behind you, with the icefall of the Chhonbardan Glacier and base camp still in deep shadow way below. From the windblown cairns and tattered prayer flags on the pass, Tukche Peak and Sita Chuchura literally tower over you, and a new and completely different vista is revealed ahead. To the north the snowy, desolate wastes of Hidden Valley sweep away towards Mustang and Tibet, while to the east Damphus Peak and Damphus Pass are your destinations the following day.

Descend into Hidden Valley and camp below the slopes leading off southeast to Damphus Pass, where there are several large cairns and some almost flat ground. At 5100m (16733ft), this is the highest camp during the trip, and once again you will be exposed to the full force of the wind. If there is snow in Hidden Valley the long march from French Pass will take you many hours, and your porters must be properly clothed and have sunglasses.

A really keen and proficient party might consider an extra day here and an ascent of the technically straightforward Damphus Peak (6035m/19801ft), which gives an eagle's eye view of the whole upper Kali Gandaki, but most will cross Damphus Pass the next day and descend to Yak Karkha, a pasture high above Marpha in the valley. From the wide, gently angled snowfields of the pass, the route stays high for several hours on the crest of an increasingly exposed snowy ridge which juts out east into the Kali Gandaki before plunging away. Given good weather, this is a walk in the sky. At the cairns marking the start of the steep descent you can finally relax as your difficulties are over. To your right are the north faces of Tukche Peak and Dhaulagiri I, straight ahead across the vast chasm of the Kali Gandaki lies Nilgiri, and to your left the brown hills of Mustang recede towards Tibet. Spend one last night out at Yak Karkha and savour the solitude, before hitting the fleshpots of Marpha and the Annapurna circus (see trek 7).

MYAGDI KHOLA

Before walking this way I'd heard all sorts of horror stories about the trail up the precipitous ravine of the Myagdi Khola, but it proved to be a magnificent walk. Uninhabited after the village of Bhagar, it's like something Spielberg dreamed up as a set for a mountain *Jurassic Park*. The trail sneaks its way past the valley's formidable defences, zigzagging up and down through perpendicular jungle and crossing thundering torrents on rickety bamboo bridges, soaked by rainbow dazzling spray from below. It disappears under precariously balanced boulders the size of office blocks and reappears over the rotting trunks of enormous fallen trees. Cliffs are surmounted by way of vertical bamboo ladders, lashed into place with vines, or crumbling stone staircases with dizzying drops into lush foliage below. Tribes of monkeys sit and watch passing humans with detached curiosity while snakes gobble giant frogs at the edges of mossy, tumbling brooks. It's positively primordial.

On the final ridge leading to French Pass, with the north face of Dhaulagiri I beyond.

TREK 9: BUDZUNGE BARRA

By incorporating this scenic and remote diversion into the circuit of Dhaulagiri just described, you will gain an even better insight as to the unsung glories of a vast swathe of the Nepal Himalaya, and complete one of the world's truly great mountain odysseys. This route crosses the gentle but rewarding Budzunge Bara, affording unforgettable views across the southern slopes of the Gurja Himal to Dhaulagiri, Nilgiri and Annapurna, before arriving at the wild Kaphe Glacier.

TREK ESSENTIALS

LENGTH (3–4 weeks ex Kathmandu, including walk to Phala Gaon.) Walking from Phala Gaon: 5 days to Kaphe Khola base camp, 4 days return to Phala Gaon.
ACCESS Walk to Phala Gaon (see trek 8).
HIGHEST POINT Highest trekking point: Budzunge Bara, 4500m (14765ft). Highest camp: Budzunge Bara ridge, 4300m (14108ft).
TREK STYLE Tents and kitchen essential.
RESTRICTIONS No permit required;
NRs2000 ACAPfee.
FURTHER OPTIONS Continue to join trek 10 by descending Kaphe Khola and traversing Phagune Dhuri ridge to Dhorpatan; or by heading northwest to Tarakot and Inner Dolpo via Phuphal Dara.

The possibilities for creative itinerary making amongst these hills are boundless. If you follow the route suggested here and treat this trek to the Kaphe Glacier as an extension of the Dhaulagiri circuit (trek 8), be sure to leave food and fuel at Phala Gaon for the second leg of your journey.

Phala Gaon to Kaphe Khola base camp

From Phala Gaon the trail west follows the Dhara Khola for a day, then climbs out of its northern tributary to cross a ridge at 3280m (10761ft), before descending to the Dhora Khola and the most remote settlement in the area, Gurja Gaon. Under clear skies, the view east from the intervening ridge to the distant Annapurna I is unexpectedly impressive, whilst before you, towering over the

upper reaches of the Dhora Khola, the Gurja Himal constitutes a formidable mountain barrier. Topped with elegant pyramid peaks and graced with perpendicular buttresses and ridges that sweep skyward from forested valleys in deep shadow below, this range will captivate your eye for the next week.

The Chhetri inhabitants of Gurja Gaon lead a hard life. Though a micro hydroelectricity scheme today provides enough power to light a few dim bulbs, their existence has not otherwise changed for centuries. Clothed in coarse homespun jackets with broad sleeves and hoods, knee-length woollen breeches and hand-woven rope shoes, they tend their fields and graze their goats on the high pastures of this secluded valley. Their village is a cluster of flat-roofed dwellings linked by a labyrinth of dank passageways below and a network of notched single-log stairways above.

Beyond the village the trail to the Kaphe Khola traverses farmland for several kilometres before climbing north into the valley of the Darsinge Khola. The trail is not obvious, but there is a bridge over the river about half an hour into this steep defile, and an excellent camping place at Darsinge Kharka. Get an early night after watching the spectacular light-show that sunset plays across the south faces of Ghustung and Gurja Himal from this valley, as the next day is one to make the most of.

Leaving Darsinge Kharka, the tiny trail climbs steeply through dense scrub for an hour before emerging onto the crest of the roller-coaster Budzunge Bara. Often exposed and always airy, this ascent would be a nightmare in snowy condi-

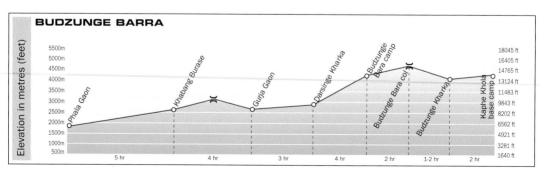

BUDZUNGE BARRA

The stunning high camp on Budzunge Bara ridge, with Nilgiri and the Dhaulagiri Himal beyond.

tions, but given good weather it is sensational. Depending on the availability of water on the ridge and your schedule, you may decide to go all the way over to Budzunge Kharka in a long day, or camp at the high meadow before the pass. If at all possible choose the latter option, as the views from this site are superb.

The col does not become apparent until you reach this campsite at ±4300m (14108ft), the only flat area you pass the whole way. Try to spend at least one night camped here, as the ridge stands clear of everything but the huge mountain wall to the north. On your left, grassy slopes plummet down into the head of the Dhora Khola, while on your right, across the Darsinge Khola, the south face of the Gurja Himal gets more spectacular with every metre climbed.

Budzunge Bara may only be 4500m (14765ft), but it is an immensely satisfying crossing. The trail continues along the crest of the ridge right up to the point where it abuts against the flank of Ghustung, and then makes a rocky traverse left to a steep col that is already almost below you. Arriving at the pass a new vista is suddenly revealed, with the barren Thar Khola leading away west into the Kaphe Khola. Peeping over intervening ridges are the seldom seen summits of the westernmost peaks of the Dhaulagiri Himal – Putha Hiunchuli and Churen. The first sensible camping place is

way down at the confluence of these two rivers, at Budzunge Kharka, and from here it is a steep rocky walk north to the snout of the Kaphe Glacier and base camp for the surrounding peaks.

Plan your itinerary to allow yourselves a couple of days at this wild and remote spot. From various view points on the Kaphe Glacier the full magnificence of these obscure Himalayan giants can be appreciated, especially the vast slopes of Churen West and the west face of Dhaulagiri VI.

Walk-out to Phala Gaon

Allow four days for the retreat to Phala Gaon.

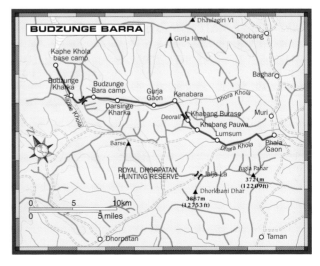

TREK 10: INNER DOLPO

Shey-Phoksundo National Park and the arid, remote highlands of Dolpo are introduced in trek 6 (Across Southern Dolpo). Whilst that route stays south of the country usually referred to as 'Inner Dolpo', this long and sustained outing makes a broad loop right through the heart of it. Crossing a series of high passes, the journey takes in Shey Gompah and the outlandishly exotic villages of Saldang and Chharkabot. Similar to the route taken by George Schaller and Peter Matthieson in 1973 and subsequently known as The Snow Leopard trek after the title of Matthieson's book, it is one of Nepal's classic mountain journeys.

TREK ESSENTIALS

LENGTH (4 weeks ex Kathmandu.) Walking from Beni: 10 days to Tarakot, 3 days to Chharkabot, 6 days to Shey, 4 days to Juphal.
ACCESS To start Bus Pokhara-Beni. On finish Flight Juphal-Nepalganj, flight Nepalganj-Kathmandu.
HIGHEST POINT Highest trekking point: Kang La, 5350m (17553ft). Highest camp: south of the Kang La, ±4600m (15093ft).
TREK STYLE Tents and kitchen essential.
RESTRICTIONS Beni-Tarakot and Ringmo-Juphal: permits US$10 per week for four weeks, then US$20 per extra week; NRs1000 Royal Dhorpatan Hunting Reserve fee + NRs1000 Shey-Phoksundo National Park fee. Tarakot-Ringmo: permits US$700 for first 10 days, then US$70 per day thereafter; liaison officer required.
FURTHER OPTIONS From Chharkabot walk to Kagbeni to join trek 7. Or from Ringmo head northwest to Jumla via the Kagmara La (trek 5), or east across Baga La and Num La to Do Tarap (trek 5) and on to Kagbeni and Jomsom across the Sangda La.

This route is amongst the most ambitious and demanding described in the present volume, for although it does not pass between the real giants of the Nepal Himalaya, it reaches heights in excess of 5300m (17390ft) and traverses some of the most remote territory in Nepal, offering a wonderful variety of both scenery and peoples. From Magar villages with extensive rice paddies and surrounded by abundant, lush jungle in the

sweltering valleys south of Dhaulagiri, to Bhotia fortress hamlets and secluded *gompahs* amid barren, windswept hills on the Tibetan plateau, this trek illustrates perfectly how much more Nepal has to offer than the popular trails to Annapurna, Everest and Langtang. The first ten days, from Beni to Tarakot via Dhorpatan, are memorably described in George Schaller's excellent *Stones of Silence*.

The hills along the way are sparsely populated and the trails through them peaceful and quiet. Particularly beyond Dhorpatan you will traverse remote and rugged terrain, and no facilities are available for travellers. This is definitely a place to be self-sufficient, with a trek crew and tents. Be sure to carry sufficient food and fuel for the duration of your trip, as replenishing supplies usually proves difficult, expensive or impossible.

Beni to Tarakot

Start by travelling from Kathmandu to Beni via Pokhara and set off up the Myagdi Khola as on the Dhaulagiri circuit (see trek 8), walking for three days to reach the village of Phala Gaon. Beyond, where the trail to Deorali and Gurja Gaon climbs into the northern tributary of the Dhara Khola (see trek 9), the broad trail to the Jalja La is clearly visible ascending the opposite hillside to the southwest. Cross the Dhara Khola over an old suspension bridge beyond the village of Lumsum, and start the long climb to the first of many passes on this route. Camp at the huge

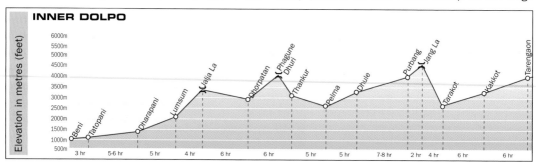

meadows on this broad plateau for sweeping sunset and sunrise views east to Machhapuchhare and north to the Gurja and Churen Himalaya, before continuing to Dhorpatan.

This trail is a major trade route to and from Dolpo, and you will pass many mule trains along the way. Backbreaking work goes into maintaining these key arteries of commerce, and there are some magnificent cantilever bridges spanning side-streams as the path descends to the headwaters of the Uttar Ganga river. The floor of this vast valley is often swampy, with single logs placed strategically over numerous small rivers that snake across the grasslands. Dhorpatan itself consists of a cluster of hamlets around a disused airstrip, while the valley is home to several hundred Tibetan refugees and a few Magar herdsmen and farmers in settlements on the edge of the basin.

There are two trail options at this point, with a low level route heading west to Jajarkot and the valley of the Sani Beri river, and the trail to Dolpo turning north into the highlands. If your lowland porters are expressing reluctance to continue beyond Dhorpatan, you may be able to find new recruits at Chhentung. Should you arrive during the potato harvest, however, every available man will be hard at work in the fields. Note that a little used trail heads north from between Chhentung and Dhorpatan, crossing the Phagune Dhuri east of the main route and continuing along the crest of this ridge before descending into the Ghustung/Kaphe Khola valley to link up with the Dhaulagiri circuit extension (see trek 9).

From Dhorpatan the five-day hike to Tarakot via the Phagune Dhuri and Jang La passes is a sensational way to arrive in Dolpo. The country on this stretch is complex and largely uninhabited, and the few available maps are notoriously inaccurate. Local knowledge is invaluable. If none of your crew have previously travelled here, it would be prudent to engage a guide in Dhorpatan. Schaller and Matthieson got seriously lost amongst these hills.

A young Dolpo-pa at Chharkabot village.

Phagune Dhuri, the prominent system of ridges due north of Dhorpatan, is gained after a long climb up the valley of the Phagune Khola. There is a spectacular false summit way before the actual pass, and from the col a gorgeous vista that includes Putha Hiunchuli, Churen Himal and Dhaulagiri is revealed. The valleys north of here are increasingly devoid of vegetation, and your route for the next few days is through a landscape of stunted juniper and rhododendron scrub, hillsides swept with vast, open screes and lone dwellings nestling in sheltered spots amongst stark mountains. There is an unearthly, captivating beauty in this country. Like all the Buddhist lands of the Himalaya, Dolpo is a powerful, spiritual place. Each prayer flag adorned pass, each way-

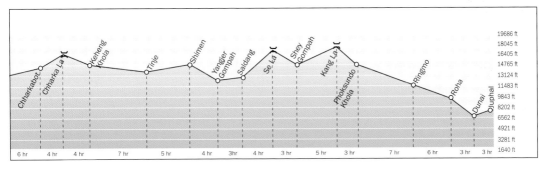

KHAMPAS

Various reasons have been mooted as to why the Nepalese government kept foreigners out of Dolpo for so long, only opening the southern part of the region in 1989 and 'Inner Dolpo' in 1992. The most likely explanation is that after the coming of the Chinese to Tibet in 1950, many valleys in the region were settled by Khampas.

Over sixty thousand Tibetans fled the Chinese occupation, heading south over treacherous mountain passes into India and Nepal. Particularly strident in their opposition to the Chinese occupation were the truculent inhabitants of Kham in eastern Tibet, who mounted a fierce guerrilla campaign against their new oppressors. Reluctant to antagonise their powerful new Chinese neighbours, the Nepalese government denied the presence of Khampas in Nepal, even when they turned their banditry against their hosts. But on several occasions in the 1970s troops had to be sent to calm things down, and to prevent untoward incidents foreigners were banned from the border areas.

More recently Dolpo was the source of a wave of Maoist unrest as the democratic government in Kathmandu was increasingly perceived as corrupt and ineffectual during the 1990's. This situation now appears to have been resolved – see p11-12

side shrine and *mani* wall a testament to the faith of those that preceded you along the way.

The last two days to Tarakot, over the Jang La, are the hardest of the trip so far and you may want to take a rest here before continuing. Like so many passes in the Himalaya, the Jang La does not yield its secrets easily, and there is a cairned false summit (the Maja La) before the real pass, which is marked by more cairns and flags at a prominent rocky outcrop. The views north into Dolpo from this wind-ravaged spot are exquisite, with the distant snows of the Kanjiroba Himal and numerous peaks in Tibet and Mustang soaring in the sky above vast swathes of bleak, intervening hills. This is the gateway to 'Inner Dolpo', and standing here looking north you really do feel as if the world is at your feet.

Descending from the Jang La into the valley of the Barbung Khola, you enter the region known as Tichurong. Tarakot, lowest of the fourteen villages here, is the fortress on a ridge near the river. You may now turn west to Dunai and Ringmo (see Red Rice Route box, trek 5), or east for Chharka and routes north of Dhaulagiri through Dolpo towards Mustang and Tibet.

Amongst these arid hills the Dolpo-pa eke out their precarious living against a backdrop of

Leaving the outlandish village of Chharkabot in Dolpo for the Chharka La and the Keheng Khola.

relentless desert stone and rock. Tiny patchworks of fields briefly burst into iridescent verdure each year with the coming of the rains. While the women tend their flocks and work the land, the men take their yak caravans to Tibet and continue the trans-Himalayan trade that has sustained these isolated communities for countless generations. Harvest time is perhaps the best to travel here, as everyone is working in the fields winnowing, threshing and singing harvest songs. The incantations and mantras of Bon-po and tantric Buddhism accompany every deed of these pious folk, and their villages and monasteries are testaments in stone to the resilience of the human spirit in the face of overwhelming odds.

Tarakot to Chharkabot

From Tarakot to Chharkabot, the highest village in the Barbung Khola valley, takes three long but intensely rewarding days, passing remote hamlets and providing glimpses of distant snowy Himalayan giants. This is the major trade route from Tichurong east to the Kali Gandaki, and northwards into Tibet via the Keheng Khola valley. The trail is wide and often elaborately constructed, staying well above the narrow gorge through which the river mainly flows. After the grain harvest in autumn many heavily laden yak caravans pass this way heading for upper Dolpo and Tibet.

Chharkabot is undoubtedly one of the highlights of this trek. Remote, mediaeval and thoroughly exotic, this fortified cluster of ancient stone houses sits spectacularly poised atop a cliff above the rushing Barbung Khola, set against a panoramic backdrop of bleak, snow-capped peaks. Outlandish whitewashed *chortens*, decorated with terracotta and ochre panels, bear the icons of Buddhist faith and stand in vibrant contrast to the desolate surrounding country. On flat roofs piled with brushwood and in dusty yards, women weave their distinctive narrow strips of dark, striped woollen cloth for blankets and shawls on primitive back-strap looms. Huge mastiffs lie chained in the midday sun while eagles and vultures soar overhead.

Chharkabot to Shey

The Chharka Pass is your next challenge on this route, leading northwest into the head of the

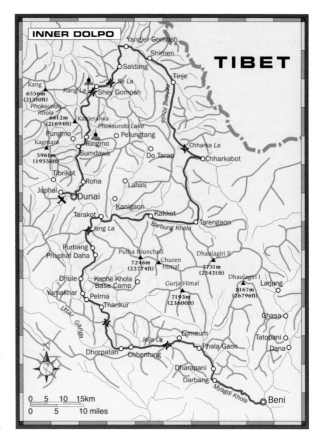

Keheng Khola, down which you travel for three days to Shimen and Yangjer Gompah. Should you be disposed to venture beyond this point in the valley, and relish the uncertainties of travelling

---

CRYSTAL MOUNTAIN

Standing over the gorge leading to the Kang La from Shey Gompah, the Crystal Mountain is a relatively small, bulky grey peak that takes its name from the veins of crystal that crisscross its walls. Before the grain harvest, on the July full moon, pilgrims come from all over Dolpo to circumambulate this sacred peak. In *Stones of Silence* George Schaller relates the legend of the Buddhist ascetic Drutob Senge Yeshe, who vanquished the fierce mountain spirit of the area in a contest of magic, whilst mounted on a snow lion. He turned the spirit into a 'thundering mountain of pure crystal'. In Drutob's words

I flew through the sky on a snow lion
And there, among the clouds, I performed miracles.
But not even the greatest of celestial feats
Can equal once rounding on foot this Crystal Mountain

Villagers thresh barley against the background of Chharkabot's mediaeval stone dwellings.

through one of the most difficult defiles in the entire Himalaya, you might wish to consider attempting to follow the river all the way to Mugu. Very few people have successfully completed this route, which skirts north of the Kanjiroba and Sisne Himalaya to enter the Mugu Karnali at Kimri before finally reaching Gum Ghari on the trail from Rara Lake to Humla (see trek 3).

At Yangjer Gompah the route followed here finally turns south for Saldang and Shey. Resist the urge to cover this last section quickly. Though you should by now be fit and acclimatised, these are some of the most interesting places on the trek and to hurry would be to deny yourself appreciation of the jewels at Dolpo's heart. After days in the Keheng Khola valley it is a joy to climb out of the Nagung Khola south of Saldang and make for the Se La and Shey. From this pass more pieces of the complex jigsaw puzzle of Dolpo's hills fall into place, as spectacular views are revealed east to Mustang and Tibet and west to Kanjiroba, Kagmara and the holiest mountain in Dolpo, Riu Dhukta, the Crystal Mountain. Shey Gompah is regarded as the spiritual heart of Dolpo.

Shey to Juphal

From Shey, Ringmo is only two days away across the Kang La to the south. This is the highest point on the trip, and prone to snowfall even early in the autumn. From the final, open slopes leading to the col an increasingly impressive vista opens behind you to the north, and as you reach the cairns at the crest the Churen Himal, Putha Hiunchuli and the Dhaulagiri Himal appear on the skyline south and east. It is now a matter of descending into the valley of the Phoksundo Khola and camping by the first water, before following the broad but often very exposed trail along the shores of Phoksundo Lake the next day to reach the village of Ringmo. After weeks amongst such arid hills the sight of Phoksundo Lake's vivid turquoise waters is a shock, so intense is their glistening, sparkling hue.

The airstrip at Juphal can easily be reached in two days from Ringmo.

TREK 11: NORTH OF DHAULAGIRI

From Do Tarap in eastern Dolpo, a little used route cuts southeast across three high passes to emerge into the Kali Gandaki at Jomsom. By flying into Juphal and arriving at Do via the Tarap gorge, this stunning trail can be accessed with relatively little difficulty. Some rest days are required first to allow for acclimatisation before heading off across the north of Dhaulagiri, via Chharkabot.

If you commence your journey from Juphal as suggested, allow five days to reach Do Tarap (see trek 5). After toiling through the dark and precipitous confines of the Tarap Chhu gorge walking from Juphal via Tarakot, the valley opens suddenly and dramatically at Do, revealing sweeping vistas of brown hills and barren ridges running north towards Tibet.

Tarap is the name given to this entire valley system, and the houses in its windswept upper reaches are solid affairs of typical Tibetan stone construction, clustered together like fortresses against the cruel winter elements and having tiny windows in their sloping walls. Allow yourself at least two days resting here or exploring the hamlets and monasteries in the vicinity.

Do Tarap to Chharkabot

The first section of the trek from Do Tarap crosses the Chharkula Banjang to Chharkabot. An obvious trail leaves the village in an easterly direction, immediately entering the steep defile of the Doto Chhu beneath towering limestone cliffs. The path is not difficult to follow – indeed it is visible all the way to the pass from the Num La some 20km (13 miles) to the northwest. Early on you pass two small *gompahs*, one Bon and one Nyingma-pa, both of which are worth seeing. Camp at a small pasture approximately 500m (1640ft) below the pass after a relatively short day's walk.

Locals generally reach Chharkabot in a single day from here, but you should plan to take two,

climbing the steep screes immediately above camp to cross the Chharkula Banjang and spending the next night high in the upper reaches of the Keheng Khola. Savour the views on both these days, particularly the second as you turn southeast and head for the Chharka La (also known as the Mohala Banjang). The trail is not steep, and after a gentle climb stays above 5000m (16405ft) for more than 5km (3 miles) before descending to Chharkabot. Ascend some of the small hills either side of the trail along this stretch for sensational views of the Mukut and Dhaulagiri Himalaya.

TREK ESSENTIALS

LENGTH (4 weeks ex Kathmandu, including walk from Juphal to Do Tarap). Walking from Do Tarap: 3 days to Chharkabot, 4 days to Sangda, 2 days to Jomsom.
ACCESS *To start* Flight Kathmandu-Nepalganj, flight Nepalganj-Juphal, walk from Juphal to Do Tarap (see trek 5). *On finish* Flight Jomsom-Pokhara.
HIGHEST POINT Highest trekking point: Sangda La, ±5400m (17717ft). Highest camp: before Sangda La, ±4900m (16077ft).
TREK STYLE Tents and kitchen essential.
RESTRICTIONS Permits US$700 for 10 days, then US$70 per extra day; liaison officer required; NRs2000 ACAP fee.
FURTHER OPTIONS Begin by walking from Jumla to Do Tarap (see trek 5). Or begin by walking from Beni to Chharkabot (see trek 10).

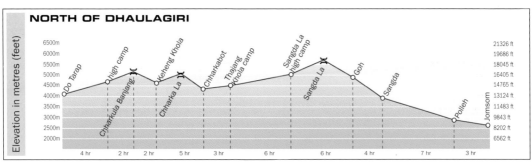

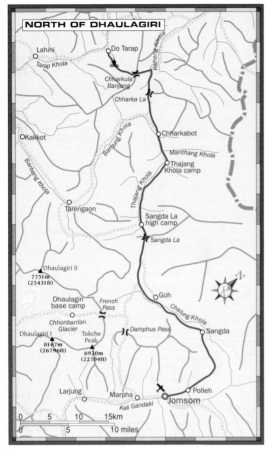

NORTH OF DHAULAGIRI

AROUND DO

In the upper reaches of Tarap, yaks are the preferred beast of burden and work, being extensively used for load carrying and ploughing. Men here braid their hair with red tassels in the style of the Khampas of Tibet, and the women adorn themselves with extravagant Tibetan turquoise, coral and amber jewellery and sport distinctive silver headgear. Both Bon and Nyingma-pa *gompahs* can be found in the vicinity, though none is particularly active. Definitely worth a visit though is the striking whitewashed edifice of Ribo Bhumba, visible from far and wide on the hillside north of Do. Next to this *gompah* is an unusual *chorten* supposedly containing the remains of a demon vanquished by Guru Rimpoche. Adorning the walls are paintings representing both Bon and Buddhist deities.

Chharkabot to Sangda

At Chharkabot this route connects with the trail from Tichurong via the Barbung Khola (see trek 5), which would have to be your line of retreat should the Sangda La be blocked by snow. Spend a day in spectacular Chharkabot (see trek 10), which sits in a strategic, elevated location at the point where the Thajang Khola meets the Jagkhel to become the Barbung. Then to reach Jomsom, leave Chharkabot and head southeast up-valley. A good plan is to set off late and walk for approximately a couple of hours to camp just beyond the second major tributary valley joining the Thajang from the east, as you are then perfectly poised for the three stages to Sangda.

The Thajang Khola runs down from the south at this point, and the walk up it towards the Sangda La is a real joy. As you traverse steep, grassy hillsides and contour above the valley to reach a high point before descending back to the river, there are clear views north to the Chharka La. This is an alpine wonderland of stunning, sweeping vistas and high pastures used by the villagers of Chharkabot for

The distinctive silver head-dress favoured by ladies from the Tarap valley.

grazing their yaks. There are several walled enclosures towards the head of valley, and the Sangda La is best tackled from a camp at the highest of these.

A guide from Chharkabot would certainly be an asset at this stage, as there are two different routes over the Sangda La. The lower alternative involves a potentially dangerous trail through an unstable gorge to reach the head of the Chalung Khola (also known as Keha Lungpa) valley. Safer, and far more scenic, is the high route which ascends a drovers' trail to cross a ridge to the north at just over 5400m (17717ft). The views from this col are outstanding, and certainly make the effort required to reach it worthwhile. Beyond the Mukut Himal to the south Tukche Peak, Dhaulagiri I and Dhaulagiri II are clearly visible, while to the east the distinct notch of the Thorung La can be seen north of Damphus Peak. Beyond this col the trail drops into a beautiful hidden valley before ascending to a second pass with views across the upper Chalung Khola towards the Khamjung Himal and Brikhuti in Mustang. The switchback descent towards the tiny village of Goh is steep, and there is a campsite with water by a terracotta *chorten* overlooking the village.

Nearing the crest of the Chharkula Banjang between Do Tarap and Chharkabot.

Sangda is visible down valley from this camp, and looks deceptively close. However, the valley sides here are steep and the trail tortuous, descending to cross the river and climbing again to avoid sections of vertiginous gorge. It is at least a short day from the campsite at Goh to Sangda.

Sangda to Jomsom

Carry plenty of water during the day here, as these slopes are devoid of streams and springs. The views from the trail as it contours airily around the flanks of steep hillsides high above

the Chalung Khola get better all the way, with marvellous panoramas northwards across upper Mustang. Finally, from a prominent cairn where the trail turns to the south, the entire Annapurna Himal appears beyond the chasm of the Kali Gandaki. Make the most of this fantastic path; stay high, and continue skirting the hillsides opposite Kagbeni to descend only at the last instant, directly to the airstrip at Jomsom. From the final ridge the awesome north faces of Dhaulagiri I and Tukche Peak stand before you in all their ice-plastered vertical magnificence. Savour your solitude here awhile, before descending.

TREK 12: JOMSOM TO MUSTANG

At the head of the Kali Gandaki, north of the Annapurna and Dhaulagiri Himalaya, lies one of the most culturally interesting and scenically dramatic regions in Nepal. Known by its inhabitants as Lo and by the rest of the world as Mustang (probably a mispronunciation of the name of the capital, Manthang), this tiny principality remained shrouded in mystery until the Nepalese government finally opened it to foreigners in 1992.

TREK ESSENTIALS

LENGTH (2 weeks ex Kathmandu.) Walking from Jomsom: 5 days to Lo Manthang, 4 days return to Jomsom.
ACCESS Flight Pokhara–Jomsom.
HIGHEST POINT Highest trekking point: leaving Lo Manthang, 4070m (13354ft). Highest camp: Lo Manthang, 3735m (12255ft).
TREK STYLE Tents and kitchen mandatory.
RESTRICTIONS Permits US$700 for 10 days, then US$10 per day; liaison officer required; NRs2000 ACAP fee.
FURTHER OPTIONS Walk out from Lo Manthang to Muktinath via Tange and Tetang.

Historically, much of this region's prosperity derived from its position on the Kali Gandaki/Thak Khola trade route to Tibet, and under the patronage of its rulers many *gompahs* and other religious edifices were constructed. Manthang, the capital, is a walled city of medieval splendour, set amid a lunar landscape of wind-eroded hills and cliffs. The browns, yellows, greys, reds and pinks of the sands and screes in upper Lo add a surreal element of colour, especially at sunrise and sunset. During summer the fields around the villages become patchworks of intense, almost miraculous, green.

In the face of the recent tourist invasion, various conservation and development projects have been set up in the area by Nepalese and overseas agencies, though the Lo-pa themselves are certainly no innocent tribe in need of protection from the outside world. For generations they have been

accomplished traders and travellers, and, like the Manangis on the other side of the Annapurna Himal, many are today involved in important businesses in Kathmandu and southeast Asia.

Should you fly into Jomsom to begin your walk, spend a day at this dusty trading post to acclimatise and complete the formalities attendant with a visit to Lo. Jomsom is actually the capital of Mustang, and on arrival you will have to register with the police and tourist information office, who will check your equipment, stoves and fuel.

Jomsom to Lo Manthang

You will be subjected to further checks and registration when you pass through Kagbeni on your way up-valley. Clearly Tibetan in character, with flat-roofed stone houses huddled around a distinctive monastery, Kagbeni marks the start of the restricted area. Similar settlements are passed on the way to Lo Manthang, becoming more and more outlandish as the valley climbs and the surrounding hills become increasingly arid and spectacular.

North of Kagbeni the Kali Gandaki assumes truly epic proportions, as the trail enters a stark wilderness of towering conglomerate cliffs, eroded into fantastic pillars and shapes by the wind which howls up the valley every afternoon. Between these multi-coloured pastel walls of shale, the braided river snakes its way across a flat bed of stones, with the trail running along it at first. In spring, the volume of water increases dramatically due to snow-melt and forces travellers on to a higher path.

From various crests on the high path stunning panorama views are revealed, especially on the

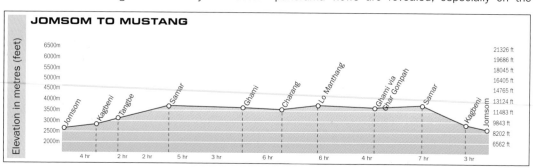

JOMSOM TO MUSTANG

Charang village, surrounded by the wind-eroded hillls and cliffs that typify the region.

first day as Nilgiri and Dhaulagiri rise like gargantuan sentinels either side of the Kali Gandaki to the south. Do try to take in some of the villages that lie off the main trail. Tangbe and Chhuksang, the first villages after Kagbeni, are mostly inhabited by Thakalis, but beyond the valley is populated by Lopas of Tibetan origin. The trail to Lo Manthang is a major highway due to its historic importance as a trade route, and nowhere is it really difficult. After Chhuksang it crosses to the west of the valley and stays there all the way to Lo Manthang. Chele is the first village on the west, reached after crossing a steel suspension bridge and ascending a high bluff above the river.

The manicured stacks of juniper and brushwood that adorn the roofs of orange and white houses in Chele and many other villages in the area are not winter firewood but auspicious displays of wealth. Clusters of *chortens* in the centre of villages testify to the Buddhist faith of the inhabitants, while numerous wayside hostelries, complete with courtyards and stables for mules, are further reminders of the commercial thoroughfare that the valley once was. None of these inns have metamorphosed into the deluxe trekkers' accommodations found lower in the Kali Gandaki at villages like Marpha and Tukche, but they are certainly interesting. The one at Ghami contains a small monastic cell, and you can eat your *dalbat* to the sounds of chanting, the ringing of bells and the clash of cymbals. This

establishment, and a similar one at Charang, belong to members of the Lo royal family.

High on the bizarrely sculpted cliffs that tower overhead you will spot numerous seemingly inaccessible caves and hermitages, many of which are used by monks as meditation retreats. The way to Lo Manthang also crosses several minor passes as it skirts around the hillsides on the west of the Kali Gandaki, and from each the views are tremendous, with the Annapurnas, Tilicho Peak and Nilgiri to the south and the brown hills of Tibet to the north.

Take your time on the last couple of days, and soak up the fantastic scenery, architecture and culture of this unique place. Your permit allows you ten

LO

Lo was originally part of the loose federation of states in far western Tibet known as Ngari. By the 14th century much of this territory had fallen under the jurisdiction of the Malla kingdom with its capital near Jumla. The current king or Gyelbu of Lo is a direct descendant of Ame Pal, who is credited with the founding of the state in 1380, and for 25 generations this dynasty ruled their mountain kingdom until King Tribhuvan came to power in Kathmandu in 1951. Like Dolpo to the west, the more recent history of Lo has been affected by the Chinese occupation of Tibet and Khampa activity in Nepal (see box on page 86).

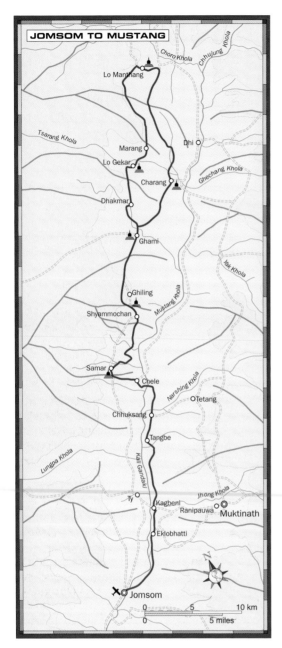

climb onto the roof of one of the inns. Within the 10m (33ft) high city walls are approximately 150 private dwellings, several monasteries and the Gyelbu's palace. Visible a short distance to the north is a prominent hill topped by two ruined forts, and from there it is possible to look south across Lo Manthang to the distant Annapurnas.

Walk-out via Ghar

The cost of simply being in Lo Manthang precludes spending any real time in the area, and most people turn tail and walk out after two nights. Vary your route on the way back, and take the westerly trail to Ghami via Lo Gekar and Ghar Gompah. According to legend the great saint Guru Rimpoche visited Ghar. The tiny rooms inside are decorated with paintings depicting him, and on the walls many brightly painted carved stones are arranged in wooden frames. Descending from the next spur into the village of Dhakmar is idyllic, with a stream running by and a massive red eroded cliff standing in dramatic contrast to the surrounding yellow-grey hills. Camp at Ghami and Samar before leaving the restricted area again at Kagbeni. There is another wild and difficult alternative eastern route out from Lo Manthang to Muktinath via Tange and Tetang, which may enable you to sneak out unnoticed if your permit has expired, but it involves many river crossings and some long, waterless days.

days for the journey from Kagbeni to Lo Manthang and back, and though you could easily complete it in less you may wish you had more time.

A couple of hours beyond Charang the trail reaches a crest and suddenly, set in a wide depression known as 'the plain of aspiration', the exotic walled city of Lo Manthang lies before you. There is only one entrance to its maze of streets – in the northeast corner, sheltered from the wind. The best way to orientate yourself once inside is to

South to Nilgiri from the trail up the Kali Gandaki north of Kagbeni.

TREK 13: AROUND MANASLU

If you would like to sample both extremes of the trekking experience in Nepal, and really get to see what all the fuss is about in terms of the most awesome mountain scenery on earth, then look no further than the circuit of Manaslu via the Larkya La. Like Nyeshang at the head of the Marsyangdi, the Tibetan enclave of Nupri, north of Manaslu at the head of the Buri Gandaki, was closed to foreigners for years on account of its proximity to Tibet. The area was surreptitiously opened in 1991, but it took several years for the word to get out.

I was fortunate enough to walk this route in 1996, and after twelve years of wandering the most obscure and unfrequented valleys of Nepal, discovered a quiet mountain Eden right next to the most heavily trekked part of the country. Whilst large numbers of trekkers walk up the Marsyangdi from Besisahar at the start of the Annapurna circuit, the deep defiles cutting into the Manaslu Himal from it are virtually unheard of. Separated from its illustrious but lower western neighbour, the Annapurna Himal, by the Marsyangdi valley, Manaslu (8156m/26760ft) is the ninth highest summit in the world.

Here are precipitous ravines, thundering rivers and soaring peaks every bit as spectacular as the Annapurnas, yet the trails that snake their way up into the mountain paradise above are quiet, secluded and untrodden. Here are villages devoid of garish hoardings advertising soft drinks, imported beers and cigarettes, of trekkers' lodges vying for passing trade with sun terraces, nightly video shows and elaborate menus.

Gorkha to Sama Gompah

Start your walk from Gorkha. Plan to arrive there mid afternoon, hire your porters, and walk the first hour up past the Durbar, Prithvi Narayan Shah's fort, to camp at Ghodakali. Sunrise over the Annapurnas and Manaslu from this ridge-top camp, with tongues of mist lapping at the shadowy valleys below whilst the first rays set the peaks aglow in flaming colour, is a sight to warm the stoniest heart. A more stunning backdrop to a first morning on the trail you will not find.

Big descents early on during an approach to the high Himalaya are always disconcerting, as the valley floors are like saunas and any height lost will only have to be regained later at considerable cost in terms of perspiration and the consequent deterioration of any sartorial elegance you may have been trying to maintain. This trek has one of the biggest descents, as the trail immediately plunges down the hillside to Khanchok and Arughat Bazaar at the steamy and

TREK ESSENTIALS

LENGTH (3 weeks ex Kathmandu). Walking from Gorkha; 9 days to Sama Gompah, 1 day rest, 4 days to Dharapani.
ACCESS *To start* Bus Kathmandu–Gorkha. *On finish* Walk from Dharapani to Besisahar, bus Besisahar–Kathmandu.
HIGHEST POINT Highest trekking point: Larkya La, 5135m (16848ft). Highest camp: Duwang, 4460m (14633ft).
TREK STYLE Tents and kitchen mandatory.
RESTRICTIONS Permits Sept – Nov US$90 per week, Dec – Aug US$75 per week; NRs2000 ACAP fee for Manaslu and NRs2000 ACAP fee for Annapurna; Liaison officer required.
FURTHER OPTIONS Extend trek at Dharapani by joining trek 7.

dauntingly low altitude of 500m (1640ft). From here the route north follows the valley of the Buri Gandaki, and unless you are feeling adventurous and opt for the more demanding route into the valley via the Rupina La (4600m/15100ft), you will stay the night at Arughat.

The Buri Gandaki, separating the Manaslu Himal from the Ganesh to the east, is spectacular. Longer than almost any of the other trans-Himalayan defiles in Nepal, it is so dramatic it could be intimidating, with long sections of vertiginous, light-excluding gorge, and waterfalls so high and steep that their entire issues dissipate over wide areas as fine spray, casting rainbows against the shadows rather than falling to the ground and joining the main river as tributaries.

The trail constantly ascends to cross ridges that sweep down from unseen heights above, only to drop back to the river that thunders deafeningly away on the valley floor. Level ground is almost non-existent, and on occasion you may have to clear space in the undergrowth for tents. In many places the monsoon rains will have washed the trail into the river, necessitating careful route-finding through debris and fallen trees. Seemingly interminable stone stairways surmount imposing cliffs, log bridges span bottomless chasms, and the dense forest is alive with screeching birds and

Trekking in the valley of the Buri Gandaki near Arughat.

of the way. Entering Nupri at last, the *mani* walls, *chortens* and prayer flags of Tibetan Buddhist culture began to appear with growing regularity. The cliffs that have been towering over you for days retreat to a more respectful distance, permitting glimpses of mighty snow-capped peaks and enormous swathes of blue sky overhead. The valley becomes the classic U-shaped product of previous glaciation, and deciduous forest gives way to bamboo, conifer and rhododendron.

From Lho the trail to the Larkya La via Sama (Rö in Tibetan) and Sumdo meanders through a landscape more glorious than anything on the Annapurna circuit and all the more enjoyable because it is so

exhibitionist monkeys. It's huge, it's wild and it's absolutely wonderful.

It takes several days to get through the steepest part of the gorge, where the only signs of human endeavour are the trail upon which you walk and the occasional *bhattis* in which the Gurung inhabitants of the lower valley ply a tenuous trade. Though the way is difficult, the upper Buri Gandaki does lead to two important trade routes to Jongka Dzong in Tibet, and the route has been in use for centuries. Your porters will be slow here, so plan short days, look after them, and go back with torches if some have not made camp when darkness falls.

After five sweltering but highly entertaining days, you will reach the village of Ghap at 2100m (6890ft) and at last the evenings will start to become deliciously cool. From here the climbing really begins, and the next day is an eight-hour pull up a thousand metres to Lho. It may be a strenuous walk, but the effort expended is offset by the magnificent scenery that reveals itself at every turn

peaceful and unspoiled. Here you may be called by families working in the fields to join them for salt tea and delicious boiled potatoes, which are eaten dipped in a paste made by grinding chillies, onions and rock-salt together on a stone. I have been serenaded by inebriate minstrels, given filthy babies to hold, dressed in flea-ridden *chubas* and introduced to uncles, cousins and grandmothers in the dark interiors of mediaeval homes.

Just beyond Lho, in the ravine of the Shara Khola, there is a fork in the trail, with the main path going ahead to Sama, and a small path heading off left. This worthwhile diversion heads steeply up through dense rhododendron forest to Honsansho Gompah and the hamlet of Kyunbun. From there it is a short climb onto the lateral moraine of the Pungen Glacier, from which there is a heart-stopping view of Manaslu and Peak 29. Continue along the moraine to Ramanan Kharka for more. The diversion yields some of the best

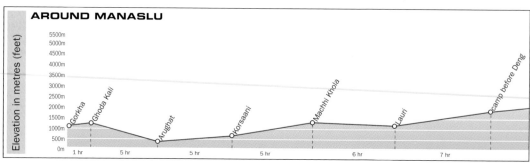

AROUND MANASLU

Elevation in metres (feet)

5500m
5000m
4500m
4000m
3500m
3000m
2500m
2000m
1500m
1000m
500m
0m

Gorkha · Ghoda Kali · Arughat · Korsaani · Machhi Khola · Lauri · camp before Deng

1 hr · 5 hr · 5 hr · 5 hr · 6 hr · 7 hr

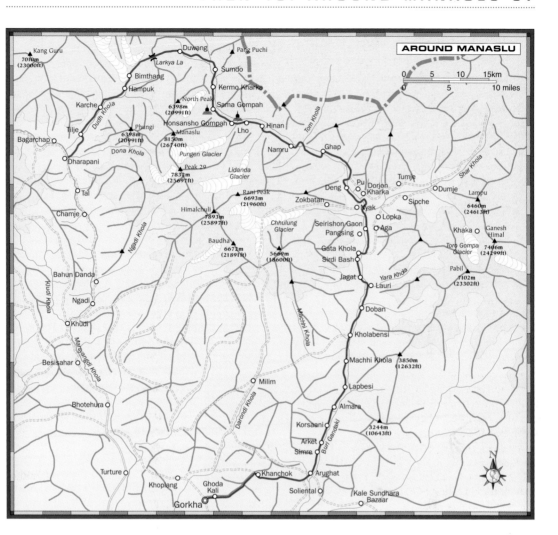

views of the trip, and is easily missed so ask someone from Lho to put you on the right path.

Sama

Manaslu and Himalchuli are now constantly on the skyline ahead, drawing the eye to their dizzying grandeur and graceful symmetry. Take a rest at Sama, and camp in meadows by the picturesque

gompah there. The women of the village sit out in the warm autumn sunshine weaving cloth on backstrap looms, the gay sounds of their chatter and laughter rising on the breeze. Goats sunbathe and bare-bottomed children scamper about. Get up early and go for the thorny and burr-coating scramble to the crest of the ridge above the village to the west and watch the sun perform its daily light show

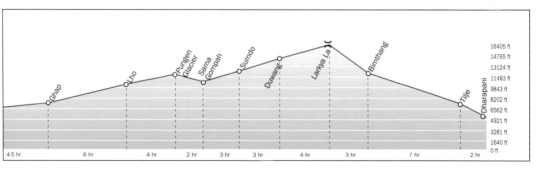

CARVERS' VILLAGE

There is a village called Bih, high above the trail between Ghap and Lho, which is home to some of the finest stone-carvers in the country. From their chisels come exquisite renderings of scenes in stone that are unique to the upper Buri Gandaki and Nupri. Many feature the legendary Tibetan saint Milarepa, who is supposed to have retreated to meditate in caves near here, and at the tiny *gompah* in Lho there are some really accomplished carvings, comparable almost to *thangkas* (Tibetan canvas paintings). On one occasion I met a rotund and rosy-cheeked lama who had travelled all the way from Pemayangtse in Sikkim to teach here.

as it creeps skyward, painting the summits apricot and orange against the deep blue ether.

Sama to Dharapani
Sumdo, the last permanent settlement in the valley, is really only a half-day walk away, and lies at the confluence of the Buri Gandaki and Shyāle Khola valleys, beneath Pang Puchi's awesome ramparts. A community of some two hundred Tibetan refugees eke out an existence here, despite nature's attempts to thwart them, maintaining tenuous trading links with their kinsfolk across the border to the north. Two passes lead to the Tibetan trading village of Riu from Sumdo. Most cross-border trade has ceased since the occupation by the Chinese (the once thriving Larkya Bazaar lies in ruins just up valley), but Tibetan pilgrims heading for Bodnath in Kathmandu and the occasional smuggler still come this way, and Chinese merchandise can be found in village shops down-valley.

Beyond Sumdo the trail to the Larkya La turns to the west and finally leaves the valley of the Buri Gandaki, now barely a trickle in a barren wilderness, to climb steeply into a land of boulders, frozen streams and even more dramatic views. To the east, the elegant snow-pyramid of Ganesh I sits perfectly framed by the valley below. The pass itself, at 5135m (16848ft), is a good deal lower than the Thorung La on the Annapurna circuit, but much more spectacular, as it sneaks between the Manaslu and Cheo Himalaya. From the lonely stone shelter at Duwang (4460m/14633ft) it is a long but sensational day's walk over to the idyllic meadows of Bimthang on the other side, 1700m (5580ft) down from the col. Arriving at the cairns and wind-torn prayer flags on the crest of the Larkya La one is confronted by a breathtaking array of peaks and hanging glaciers, all of which tower over the pass and fully justify its growing reputation as one of Nepal's most sensational crossings.

After then descending the valley of the Dudh Khola for three days to emerge at Dharapani – in the valley of the Marsyangdi and on the main drag towards the Annapurnas (see trek 7) – you will be faced with a dilemma as you sit outside one of the tea shops there, furtively eyeing the chocolate bars and rolls of pink Chinese toilet paper and feeling like a tramp in Harrods. Do you turn left and head for the road, or right for Manang and the Thorung La? I would strongly advocate the latter.

Manaslu, seen towering over the roof of Sama Gompah in the upper Buri Gandaki.

ANNAPURNA REGION DIRECTORY

REGIONAL FLIGHTS
Pokhara is served by numerous daily flights from the capital, and flights to Jomsom and Manang originate here.

Kathmandu–Pokhara: Nepal Airlines, Buddha Air, Gorkha Air, Yeti Airlines, Cosmic Air, Sita Air
Pokhara–Jomsom: Nepal Airlines, Yeti Airways, Cosmic Air, Sita Air
Pokhara–Manang: Nepal Airlines

Breakfast alfresco at Manang in the Marsyangdi valley (trek 7).

REGIONAL ROAD TRANSPORT
Travellers arriving in Pokhara from Kathmandu by public bus will find themselves disembarking at the bus station on Shreejana Chowk just north of the airport, whereas most of the tourist coach services have stops on the lakeside. Buses from Pokhara to Baglung leave from their own bus station at the junction of Bhairab Tole and the main Pokhara–Baglung highway.

Kathmandu–Gorkha: 3 departures daily between 07:00 and 09:00 from New Bus Park, Gongabu
Kathmandu–Pokhara: Tourist bus, 5 departures daily between 07:00 and 11:00 from New Bus Park, Gongabu. Local bus, 5 departures daily between 12:00 and 20:00 from New Bus Park, Gongabu. Also Green Line & various other coach services which run on to Chitwan (If you're planning on heading straight out on the Annapurna Circuit from Kathmandu, change buses at Dumre for Besisahar). Greenline services depart from their depot on Tridevi Marg, others from Kantipath. Book in advance! Numerous agents in Thamel will arrange tickets for you.
Kathmandu–Besisahar direct: 2 departures daily between 07:00 and 08:00 from New Bus Park, Gongabu
Pokhara–Beni: Local bus

It is also possible to travel by chartered/reserve bus from Kathmandu to Gorkha, Dumre, Besisahar etc or on from Pokhara to Phedi or Beni.

POKHARA ACCOMMODATION
Pokhara's tourist accommodation and facilities are concentrated in the Dam Side and Lakeside areas of town, south of the main bazaar areas. Accommodation and food are available to all tastes and budgets.
Fishtail Lodge, PO Box 10, Lakeside, Pokhara, tel (061) 520071, , 520984 fax (061) 520072. An oasis of tranquillity, reached by ferry across the lake. The oldest and most luxurious in town. Prince Charles stayed here! www.fishtail-lodge.com
Hotel Hungry Eye, Baidam, Lakeside, Pokhara, tel (061) 520908, 523096, fax 523089. A revamped old travellers' favourite.
Hotel Lakeside, Baidam, Pokhara, tel (061) 20073. Almost opposite the Fishtail. Cheap, comfortable and clean.
Hotel Stupa, PO Box 322, Baidam, Pokhara, tel (061) 22608. Cheap, clean and popular.

TREKKING COSTS
Much of the Annapurna region is an open zone, requiring no trekking permit (Annapurna Conservation Area Project fee applies). However, Inner Dolpo, Mustang and Nupri are restricted areas, and involve high trekking fees.

LOCAL ACTIVITIES
Sunrise Ballooning **Balloon Sunrise Nepal**, *PO Box 1273, Lazimpat, Kathmandu, tel (01) 4424131, fax (01) 4424157, www.catmando.com/balloon*

TRADITIONAL STRUCTURES

During the course of a trek in Nepal you are likely to encounter various distinctive stone structures. Many of these have both practical purpose and spiritual significance, and by understanding the basic concepts of their design you can appreciate their value and treat them with due regard.

Chautaaras

Few sights are more welcome, as you toil up the relentlessly steep trails of lowland Nepal, sweating buckets and suffering with the heat and humidity, than a *chautaara*. These stone-built resting platforms, with ledges for porters to set down their loads, are usually strategically placed on ridges or promontories to catch the rising breeze. Such places also almost invariably command fine views.

Chautaaras are often built by local people in memory of a departed soul, and the Hindu custom is to plant a pipal and a banyaan tree beside them, symbolising the harmony between male and female. These grow to enormous sizes over hundreds of years, and their massive limbs and broad leaves provide plenty of delicious shade. Deluxe versions may incorporate a water spout, and often form the venue for impromptu cook-ups, drinking sessions and meetings.

Stupas

These ubiquitous reliquary shrines, known as *chortens* in Tibetan, are as fundamental an icon in the Buddhist world as the cross is in the Christian. Stupas evolved in prehistoric India from burial mounds, and have been adapted to local architecture with the spread of the Buddhist faith. Some are bare, whitewashed simplicity, while others, such as the funeral stupas of the Dalai Lamas in the Potala in Tibet are clad in gold and exquisitely decorated with precious stones. Yet, from the elegant pagodas of Japan and Burma to the squat bulk of Bodnath Temple in Kathmandu, the essential components in the design remain.

The longest *mani* wall in Nepal, between Geling and Charang on the trail to Lo Manthang in Mustang (trek 12).

The structure symbolises the five elements. At the base is a square platform representing earth, above which rises a round, dome-shaped section representing water. Next is a stepped pyramid or shaft representing fire, usually comprised of thirteen layers symbolising the thirteen steps to enlightenment. On top of this is a half moon for air and finally a sun for infinite space.

Mani stone at Mount Kailas in Tibet (trek 4).

Stupas may be built for a variety of reasons – to hold the ashes of incarnate *rimpoches* or lamas, to house sacred objects and scriptures, to commemorate significant or auspicious events or to mark the place where a saint or deity lived or meditated. Devout Buddhists always pass to the left of these sacred sites or circle them clockwise, and as a mark of respect you should follow suit.

Mani Stones

In Buddhist upland areas of Nepal, as throughout the Himalaya, you will come across *mani* stones, either individually placed at strategic points beside the trail, or built into walls often hundreds of metres long and occasionally inset with prayer wheels that are vigorously spun in passing. All *mani* stones bear the Tibetan inscription *Om mani padme hum* ('All hail the jewel in the lotus'), and wherever possible the trail will pass both sides of *mani* walls, allowing the devout to pass on the left as they do with stupas.

Stupa at Charang in the upper Kali Gandaki valley, Mustang (trek 12).

6

LANGTANG REGION

As you descend from the plane onto the tarmac at Kathmandu's Tribhuvan International Airport and breathe your first lungfuls of fresh mountain air, your eyes will immediately be drawn to the spectacular snowy summits that rear to the north above the green hills enclosing the Kathmandu valley.

These are the peaks of the Ganesh, Langtang and Jugal Himalaya, the most accessible ranges from the capital and popular with trekkers on account of this proximity and the fact that most of the routes are liberally scattered with tea-houses and trekkers' lodges.

Organising a trek here is logistically straightforward, as you are not dependent on the anarchic schedules and fickle weather that often afflict internal flights in Nepal.

Gang Chenpo (6387m) from Tserko Ri.

Clearing a roadblock on the road to Syabru Bensi

waters of the Langtang Khola and Bhote Khosi below Syabrubensi. The latter stream should not be confused with the mighty river of the same name that flows into Nepal at Kodari. The name *Bhote Khosi* means 'river from Tibet', and like the Karnali and Arun these torrents predate the Himalaya.

The trails to Langtang are nowhere as busy as those to Everest and Annapurna, probably because of the absence of eight-thousand metre peaks in the area. There are, however, a host of delectable mountains reaching almost 7000m (22967ft), approached from the south on trails that snake along some of the most exhilarating ridges in the country. The hike out from Paldor along the Tiru Danda is as fine an outing as any in the country. The accommodation available may be a little less sophisticated than that in the more popular regions, but it is perfectly adequate and trekking independently is feasible.

In 1971 Langtang became Nepal's first National Park, and, as in the ACAP area, lodge owners have formed committees to standardise their menus and tariffs in order to counteract the ruthless bartering and concomitant sense of humour failures that some trekkers insist on indulging in.

Gosainkund, largest of a group of high-altitude lakes west of the Laurebina La, was formed, according to Hindu mythology, when Shiva thrust his trident (*trisul*) into the ground to create the

Bounded in the west by the Buri Gandaki and in the east by the Bhote Khosi, this stretch of the Nepal Himalaya marks the point where the Tibetan border converges on the main Himalayan chain sufficiently to preclude the wonderful circuit treks possible around the likes of Manaslu and Annapurna. Indeed immediately northeast of the Langtang Himal lies Shishapangma, the only one of the world's 14 eight-thousand metre peaks which lies entirely within Tibet.

It was to the Ganesh and Langtang Himalaya that Bill Tilman turned in 1949, having been refused permission to approach Everest from the south. Tilman is widely credited with being the first to explore the Nepal Himalaya, though as he points out in the introduction to his book of the same title, 'One of these pleasing traits of the Westerner or Paleface is to assume that what is not known to him cannot be known to anyone.' Tilman was drawn to Langtang by the appearance on his map of the area (one of a set of quarter-inch scale maps of the entire country, made between 1924 and 1927 by the Indian Survey Department) of the magical word 'unsurveyed'. And by the fact that beyond Pemthang Ri across the Nyanam Phu Glacier lies Gosainthan, more commonly known as Shishapangma. During his explorations with Peter Lloyd that year he climbed Paldor and crossed a number of remote and difficult passes at the head of the Langtang Glacier close to the border with Tibet.

The principal river draining the Langtang Himal is the Trisuli, the name given to the combined

TRISULI BAZAAR

Trisuli Bazaar used to be the trail-head for excursions into Langtang, but nowadays a rough road leads beyond to the sprawling town of Dhunche and on to Syabrubensi. Whichever way you choose to travel along this route, you will surely sweat, be it toiling up the sweltering valley on foot from Trisuli Bazaar or jammed into a packed local bus threading its way along the unmaintained and often hair-raising road. To minimise the trauma of the journey, consider starting your walk from Bodnath on the outskirts of Kathmandu or Sundarijal in the Kathmandu valley and from there reaching Langtang via Helambu, the Laurebina La and Gosainkund.

headwaters of the Trisuli River. Every August some tens of thousands of pilgrims congregate here to perform *puja*. The area is populated by Tamangs and Bhotias, and even a short trek here provides a wonderful insight into the rural mountain lifestyles of upland Nepal and the colourful cultural contrasts of Buddhist and Hindu villages.

Southeast of the Laurebina La and the Chimisdang Lekh, the upper reaches of the Malemchi Khola comprise a prosperous area known as Helambu, populated by a distinctive clan of Sherpas that call themselves Yolmo. A rewarding circuit trek can be made here, from Sundarijal to Malemchi Pul via Tarke Gyang, which can easily be extended by heading east from Tarke Gyang to the Panch Pokhari Lekh for a magnificent ridge-walk finale to the Kathmandu–Kodari highway.

It should be noted that Helambu's accessibility from Kathmandu has heralded a period of rapid development, with the growing influx of relatively wealthy tourists encouraging begging by village children, the hawking of 'antique' trinkets and even daylight robbery.

TREK 14: LANGTANG AND GANESH

Given that there is now a road as far as Syabrubensi in the valley of the Trisuli Khola, the best way to reach Langtang on foot and achieve sufficient acclimatisation on the way to enable you to safely visit the high country is from Sundarijal via Helambu and the Laurebina La. This is a rare opportunity to experience a walk into the high Himalaya as the explorers of old did, walking all the way from Kathmandu. The route suggested goes on to visit the upper Chilime Khola and Paldor base camp before turning south and walking out along the sensational Tiru Danda ridge.

TREK ESSENTIALS

LENGTH (3 weeks ex Kathmandu.) Walking from Sundarijal:
7 days to Syabrubensi, 1 day rest,
5 days to Sanjung Kharka and back to Thangjet,
5 days to Pansing Banjang via Paldor base camp,
4 days out to Trisuli Bazaar.
ACCESS *To start* Walk to Sundarijal from Bodnath; or local bus Kathmandu–Sundarijal. *On finish* Bus Trisuli Bazaar–Kathmandu.
HIGHEST POINT Highest trekking point: Laurebina La, 4610m (15125ft). Highest camp: Paldor base camp, 4580m (15027ft).
TREK STYLE Trekkers' lodges and teahouse accommodation available to Syabrubensi; tents and kitchen required for walk out-along Tiru Danda ridge.
RESTRICTIONS No permit required; NRs1000 park/conservation fees.
FURTHER OPTIONS Leave trek at Thare Pati and walk either to Malemchi Pul via Tarke Gyang or on to join trek 15 at Laghang Gompah. Or leave trek at Syabru and continue to Kyangjin Gompah and beyond (trek 15).

This trek features a succession of ridges, and the views towards the east across the complex terraced valleys of Helambu are an unforgettable treat on the first few days. Various scattered Hindu shrines, Buddhist *mani* walls and *chortens* passed along the way act as constant reminders of the ethnic diversity of this fascinating tract of hill country.

Sundarijal to Syabrubensi

If you walk from Sundarijal, your first climb is to the Shivapuri Lekh, the ridge that forms the northern rim of the Kathmandu valley. Exercise due caution on this early part of the trail, as lone trekkers have been robbed and assaulted here. From the crest above Mulkharka there are excellent views of the Ganesh and Langtang Himal, and from the first camp at Chisapani similarly wonderful sunrise panoramas, from Everest to Annapurna.

As the trail works its way northwest, the ridges crossed get progressively higher, with the Phagu Danda and Thare Danda offering particularly fine walking. The country gets wilder also, with the trail ascending and descending steeply through dense rhododendron and coniferous forest, occasionally emerging into beautiful *kharkas* with temporary monsoon shelters called *goths*. Make your days short at this stage to maximise your acclimatisation while you climb through the 3000m (9840ft) line onto the Thare Danda. From Magengoth the Gosainkund Lekh and the route to the Laurebina La are visible, and it's a classic, airy ridge walk from here to Thare Pati and the apparently impassable headwall of the Thadi Khola. The vegetation that thrives along the crest of this ridge is a fragrant and delicate cloud forest consisting of a mixture of berberis, juniper and spruce, all draped with lichen and interspersed with deep beds of luxuriant moss.

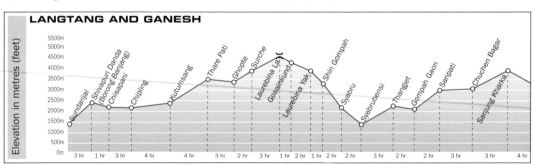

Beyond Thare Pati the trail becomes a roller coaster track through landscape reminiscent of a Chinese watercolour painting, rounding a series of stark rocky promontories and spires and disappearing between them into dark, misty, forest-cloaked ravines. Navigate with caution if there is any snow on the ground, as some sections are seriously exposed and potentially lethal. Cross the Laurebina La (also known as the Surjakund La) either from the primitive teahouse and cave at Ghopte, or from camping places hewn out of the steep mountainsides at Surche or Bheragoth.

From a point a few minutes beyond the Laurebina La a truly breathtaking vista is revealed across the Langtang valley to Langtang Lirung, with Gosainkund below and a host of Himalayan giants including the Annapurnas, Manaslu, the Ganesh Himal and countless distant peaks in Tibet along the horizon. Descend past the lakes, pausing to make your ritual ablutions if you wish to acquire the karmic merit associated with such acts of hypothermic exhibitionism, and spend the night recovering at Laurebina Yak. This small collection of lodges on a ridge just below the 4000m (13125ft) mark also commands a stupendous view.

If you are considering travelling from the Laurebina La to the upper Langtang valley (see trek 15), under no circumstances attempt to follow the direct trail indicated on some maps between Laurebina Yak and Ghore Tabela. It has long fallen into disuse; indeed large sections have fallen into

The Ganesh Himal from above Syabrubensi.

the river and at least one trekker has died attempting to pass this way. The only feasible route into the main valley is the knee-cracking 3200m (10500ft) descent from the pass to Syabru and Syabrubensi. On emerging at last from sub-tropical forest to arrive at this town your ears will be buzzing with the increased air pressure as if you had just stepped from an unpressurised aircraft.

Syabrubensi to Sanjung Kharka

The trail to the Ganesh Himal and Sanjung Kharka leaves Syabrubensi to the north and almost immediately turns east to cross the Bhote Khosi and enter the valley of the Chilime Khola. Here you suddenly leave behind the buzz and ballyhoo of the teahouse trekking scene and enter a quiet, unspoiled valley of magnificent proportions. By now you should be storming along, perfectly acclimatised and ready for the rigorous trails ahead.

The three-day hike to Sanjung Kharka is a real treat for your trekking feet, passing idyllic hamlets with terraced barley fields, dotted with white-washed *chortens* and *mani* walls. At Tatopani you can indulge in a luxurious hot wash and look back with incredulity on your temporary insanity at Gosainkund. The vast outwash plain below the Sangjung Glacier then provides as spectacular a campsite as you could wish for, strongly reminiscent of Ramze on the southern side of Kangchendzonga, with the snow-plastered east face of Ganesh I towering over the meadows. The trail does continue beyond Sanjung Kharka to the

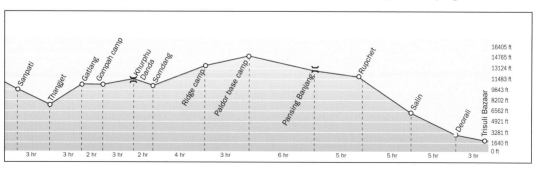

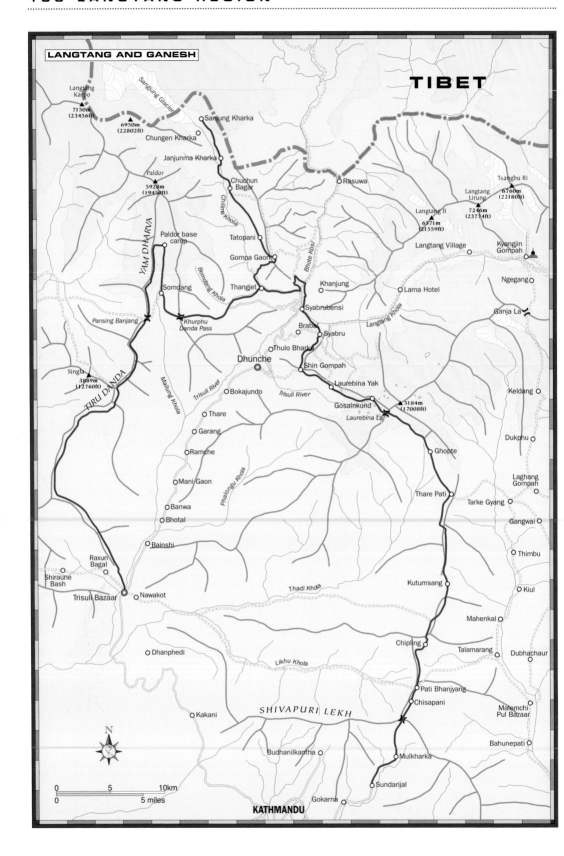

LANGTANG AND GANESH

TIBET

Langtang
Karpo
7150m
(23456ft)

Sangjung Glacier

Sanjung Kharka

6950m
(22802ft)

Chungen Kharka

Janjunma Kharka

Paldor
5928m
(19450ft)

Chuchun
Bagar

Rasuwa

Tsangbu Ri

Langtang
Lirung
6760m
(22180ft)

Langtang II
7246m
(23774ft)
6371m
(21559ft)

Chilime Khola

Tatopani

Langtang Village

Kyangjin
Gompah

YAM DHARVA

Paldor base
camp

Gompa Gaon

Ngegang

Bhote Kosi

Bamdang Khola

Somdang

Thangjet

Khanjung

Lama Hotel

Langtang Khola

Ganja La

Pansing Banjang

Khurphu
Danda Pass

Syabrubensi

Brabal

Syabru

Thulo Bharku

Dhunche

Shin Gompah

Singla
3989m
(12760ft)

TIRU DANDA

Mailung Khola

Trisuli River

Bokajundo

Trisuli River

Laurebina Yak

Gosainkund

5184m
(17008ft)

Laurebina La

Keldang

Thare

Garang

Ramche

Ghopte

Dukphu

Mani Gaon

Phalongu Khola

Thare Pati

Laghang
Gompah

Banwa

Tarke Gyang

Bhotal

Gangwai

Bainshi

Thimbu

Raxun
Bagal

Shiraune
Bash

Trisuli Bazaar

Nawakot

Thadi Khola

Kutumsang

Kiul

Mahenkal

Dhanphedi

Chipling

Talamarang

Dubhachaur

Likhu Khola

Kakani

SHIVAPURI LEKH

Pati Bhanjyang

Chisapani

Malemchi
Pul Bazaar

Budhanilkantha

Mulkharka

Bahunepati

N

Sundarijal

Gokarna

0   5   10km
0   5 miles

KATHMANDU

'ONE PEN!'

This is fast replacing '*Om mani padme hum*' as the preferred mantra chanted to trekkers by children in villages along the more popular routes in Nepal. Several variations may be encountered, such as '*Mithai!*' ('Give me sweets!'), 'Balloon!' or 'Rupee!' ('Give me money!').

Handing out gifts to children along the trail may make you feel good, but it does little to further the self-esteem of the children, and promotes the already ubiquitous image of tourists as affluent gift-horses in the minds of those inhabiting the busier trekking areas. You only have to venture a short distance away from the trekkers' highways to find out how wonderful the children were before begging became a major pastime. Resist this insidious practice, and give your donations instead to the many organisations struggling to counteract the effects of the crushing poverty which afflicts so much of rural Nepal.

glacier, but the best views are from the *kharka* and the summit of a small peak (4980m/16340ft) to the east.

Sanjung Kharka to Paldor Base Camp via Thangjet

To complete this trek with a visit to Paldor base camp in the upper Mailung Khola and the walk south along the Tiru Danda to Trisuli Bazaar, retreat down the Chilime Khola to the hamlet of Thangjet. From here a four-day hike into the Bemdang Khola and across the Kurphu Danda leads towards Paldor base camp. A rough road, built to service an army post and a series of mines in the Mailung Khola, also runs this way, cut through virgin forest past Gatlang as far as the village of Somdang. The trail suggested here joins the road before reaching Somdang.

Two short but steep days heading north from Somdang bring you past the rocky peak of Ned's Thumb to a sheltered base camp site in a steep barren valley directly beneath the Paldor glaciers and the peak itself. From this spectacular spot the winding ridge of the Tiru Danda can be seen twisting away south, down into the blue ridge-country of the foothills.

Paldor Base Camp to Trisuli Bazaar

To reach the Tiru Danda, take the magnificent direct route onto the Yam Dharva out of base camp, threading your way along the crest amongst rocky towers and ridges and crossing precipitous gullies and ravines to reach Pansing Banjang. The views are tremendous both east and west from this seldom travelled trail. South of Pansing Banjang the ridge is less sharp, but the trail is an absolute joy, snaking back and forth along the spine of the country as it drops away south towards Trisuli Bazaar. Often above a sea of cloud in the valleys below, this section truly feels like a walk in the sky, with Paldor constantly dominating the horizon behind you. On the morning of your fourth day south of Pansing Banjang you will make the final steep descent from Deorali to Trisuli Bazaar, where you can eat a massive *dalbat* and down a few beers to fortify yourself and steady your nerves for the switchbacks of the road across the Luchhe Danda back to Kathmandu.

The view from base camp north towards Paldor in the upper Mailung Khola.

PEAK: PALDOR

During his explorations in 1949, Bill Tilman first climbed Paldor along with Peter Lloyd, Tenzing Sherpa and Da Namgyal, by the northeast ridge. The peak affords spectacular views all round, especially of Shishapangma and Ganesh Himal.

Base Camp

To reach base camp (see trek 14), walk northwards from Somdang up the Mailung Khola via Lari mine (possible camp) and beyond for about three hours, ascending steeply above the river gorge between rocky outcrops. Base camp is directly below the summit of the mountain, at 4200m (13780ft), best situated on the left of the obvious moraine.

CLIMB ESSENTIALS

SUMMIT Paldor, 5928m (19450ft)
PRINCIPAL CAMPS Base camp: upper Mailung Khola, 4200m (13780ft). High camp: due east of Fang, 5200m (17061ft).
GRADE Alpine grade AD, AD+.

Northeast Ridge

Climb northwards up to the obvious moraine and follow the path on the crest to Paldor tarn. Then cross rocky slopes below the south ridge of Fang to gain Paldor Glacier East, and boulder slopes. Follow the glacier which soon becomes a large glacial bowl. A possible high camp is at 5200m (17061ft) due east of Fang. From high camp follow the glacier, now complicated by crevasses, to Windy Col, on the northeast ridge of Paldor. There are steep snow slopes above the bergschrund.

From Windy Col skirt the rocky pinnacle on the left (south side). A horizontal snow ridge leads to an exposed rocky crest, ascending over several loose pinnacles with awkward steps. The latter section used to be snow-covered, but is now the point of return for many if not most parties, due to the extremely unstable loose rock exposed by the retreating snow and ice. The crest then leads to another horizontal snow ridge, narrowing dramatically as it reaches the 150m (94ft) headwall. Ascend this on steep snow to junction with southeast ridge. Continue easily to the summit.

Descend by the same route.

The route across Paldor Glacier East to Windy Col and along the northeast ridge to the summit of Paldor, seen from high camp.

TREK 15: LANGTANG AND JUGAL

Easily accessible from Kathmandu, the valley of the Langtang Khola above Syabru is spectacular and rewarding enough in its own right to justify an excursion. By continuing beyond the last accommodations in this valley to Langshisa Kharka and glaciers further on, it is possible to leave the crowds behind. Combined with an exit south across the Jugal Himal via one of several challenging passes to Helambu, this makes for an unexpectedly adventurous journey through a popular part of Nepal.

Today many of the 'settlements' in the Langtang region are no more than collections of trekkers' lodges, and as you hike up-valley you may find yourself wondering what it must have been like before. As the route suggested here shows though, there are still quieter trails to be explored.

Dhunche to Lanshisa Kharka
Begin by walking from Dhunche to Syabru. From Syabru, the trail to the upper Langtang valley descends past a line of lodges before crossing the Chopche Khola and following the southern bank of the Langtang Khola until just before Lama Hotel. The valley sides hereabouts are steep, densely forested with oak and enormous bamboo and prone to monsoon landslides. Frequent diversions should be expected and care taken late in the season, when water cascading from cliffs and gullies above freezes, rendering odd sections of path treacherous with boiler-plate ice. Keep your eyes peeled through the foliage ahead as you walk, both for glimpses of Langtang Lirung and Langtang II towering above the head of the valley, and for the wildlife in the woods. You should certainly see troops of langur monkeys, and if you are very lucky you might spot an elusive red panda.

Beyond Lama Hotel the bamboo rapidly becomes more stunted, and the lush oak woods give way to rhododendrons before disappearing altogether shortly after Ghore Tabela. Here the valley widens at last, resembling the classic U-shaped product of massive previous glaciation. The surrounding peaks may not be of the same stature as those above Manang or Namche Bazaar, but they are scarcely less beautiful. Although neither Gang Chhenpo, Kimshun nor Yangsa Tenji reach 7000m (22967ft), gazing at their majestic summits you realize that height is nothing but a number. More impressive still is the south face of Langtang Lirung, especially as seen from Kyangjin Gompah – as awesome a piece of Himalayan mountain architecture as you will ever see.

There are two small *gompahs* in the upper Langtang valley, both belonging to the Buddhist

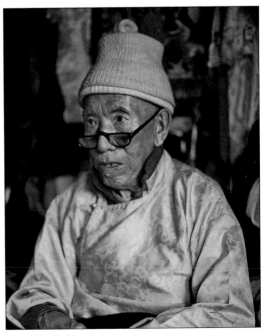

Lama at Kanjin *Gompah*, Langtang

The south face of Langtang Lirung as seen from camp II.

Nyingma-pa sect. Kangtangsa is half an hour below what has become known as Langtang village, and Kyangjin is tucked away on an old alluvial plain beyond the terminal moraine of the Ledrup Lirung glacier a couple of hours further on. There are now many lodges at Kyangjin, which was once a peaceful summer grazing ground. Standards vary, but prices are consistently high. These are the furthest accommodations in the valley, and to continue to

---

AROUND KYANGJIN

Immediately above Kyangjin Gompah to the north is a hill known as Kyangjin Ri. The first summit, with its many cairns and prayer flags can be reached up steep slopes in an hour, and from here the second summit becomes visible, at least another hour away at 4665m (15306ft). Alternatively, Tsergo Ri is the prominent hill ahead as you approach Kyangjin Gompah. This can be ascended by any of its ridges in four hours, and from the summit at 4985m (16356ft) there is a stunning panorama which includes Langtang Lirung, Naya Kanga, Dorje Lakpa, Langshisa Ri and the summit of Shishapangma.

Langshisa Kharka or Morimoto Peak base camp you will need tents and kitchen equipment.

Leave the teahouse scene behind and head off into the wild country for a couple of days. Even if you don't venture onto the glaciers beyond, the view of Pemthang Karpo Ri from Morimoto Peak base camp is unforgettable. A hike up onto the Langshisa Glacier from Langshisa Kharka for a closer look at the stupendous west face of Dorje Lakpa is highly worthwhile.

Lanshisa Kharka to Laghang Gompah

Several adventurous options are available for those seeking to return to Kathmandu by crossing the Jugal Himal into Helambu. All are serious propositions, and only one, the Ganja La, is feasible for groups travelling with porters. Even this requires much care, as the steep upper slopes may require step cutting and the fixing of ropes. In perfect conditions the Ganja La is a reasonably straightforward pass, but in winter or after snowfall it is a place for competent, experienced mountaineers only. The descent route is far from obvious, and ideally a local guide should be engaged at Kyangjin Gompah. The range has been crossed by mountaineers in other places, most notably by Tilman in 1949 via the steep col between Dorje Lakpa and Kangsurum. Tilman's route has been repeated, but by fit, acclimatised and properly equipped parties. Like the crossing of Sherpani Col from Makalu base camp to the Khumbu, it is not a route to attempt with porters.

To cross the Ganja La, set off from Kyangjin Gompah with tents and sufficient food and fuel for at least five days – double this if, as suggested, you plan to walk out via the Panch Pokhari Lekh. Cross the pass in a long day from a high camp at Ngegang (±4400m/14436ft), to the roofless *goths* at Keldang on the other side. Depending on the

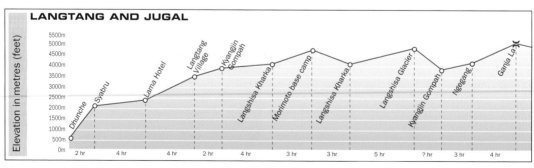

LANGTANG AND JUGAL

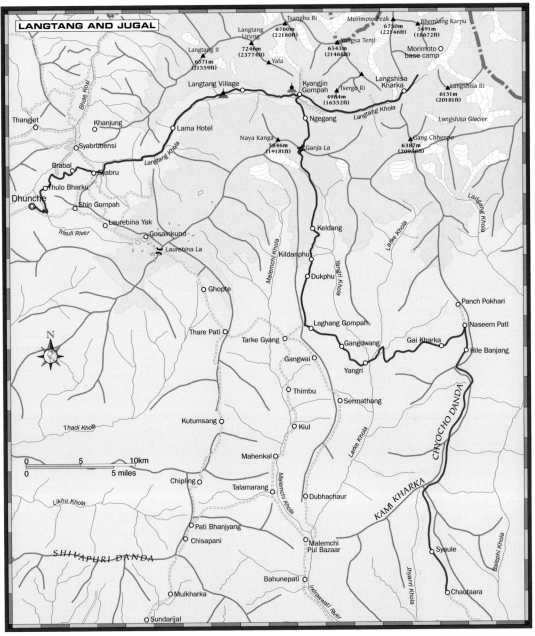

LANGTANG AND JUGAL

Tsangbu Ri · Morimoto Peak · Bhemlang Karpu
6760m (22180ft) · 6750m (22146ft) · 5691m (18672ft)
Langtang Lirung · Yangsa Tenji · Morimoto base camp
Langtang II · 7246m (23774ft) · 6543m (21468ft)
6571m (21559ft) · Yala
Langtang Village · Kyangjin Gompah · Tsergo Ri · Langshisa Kharka · Langshisa Ri
4984m (16352ft) · 6151m (20181ft)
Thanglet · Khanjung · Lama Hotel · Ngegang · Langtang Khola · Langshisa Glacier
Syabrubensi · Naya Kanga · Gang Chhenpo
5846m (19181ft) · Ganja La · 6387m (20956ft)
Brabal · Syabru · Langtang Khola · Laddang Khola
Thulo Bharku
Dhunche · Shin Gompah · Keldang · Larke Khola
Laurebina Yak · Gosainkund · Kildanphu · Yangri Khola · Panch Pokhari
Trisuli River · Laurebina La · Dukphu · Naseem Pati
Ghopte · Laghang Gompah · Hile Banjang
Thare Pati · Tarke Gyang · Gangdwang · Gai Kharka
Gangwai · Yangri
Thimbu · Sermathang
Kutumsang · Kiul · Larke Khola
Thadi Khola · Mahenkal · CHYOCHO DANDA
Chipling · Talamarang · Dubhachaur · KAMI KHARKA
Likhu Khola · Pati Bhanjyang · Malemchi Pul Bazaar · Syaule · Balephi Khola
SHIVAPURI DANDA · Chisapani · Jhyanri Khola · Chautaara
Bahunepati
Mulkharka · Indrawati River
Sundarijal

0 5 10km
0 5 miles

N

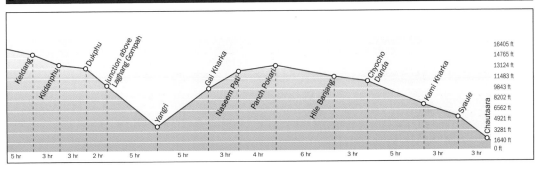

16405 ft
14765 ft
13124 ft
11483 ft
9843 ft
8202 ft
6562 ft
4921 ft
3281 ft
1640 ft
0 ft

Keldang · Kildanphu · Dukphu · Junction above Laghang Gompah · Yangri · Gai Kharka · Naseem Pati · Panch Povan · Hile Banjang · Chyocho Danda · Kami Kharka · Syaule · Chautaara

5 hr · 3 hr · 3 hr · 2 hr · 5 hr · 5 hr · 3 hr · 4 hr · 6 hr · 3 hr · 5 hr · 3 hr · 3 hr

availability of water it may be possible to camp earlier. The views to the north from the col on a clear day are stupendous, particularly of Shishapangma. Many expeditions use this route as an exit after climbing Naya Kanga (the peak west of the pass) from a high camp at ±5100m (16733ft) on a glacial shelf north of the peak.

The initial descent from the col is potentially treacherous, and even much further down care should be taken to avoid descending east into the difficult Yangri Khola valley. The trail stays high on the crest of the ridge all the way to Keldang and on past Dukphu, only cutting off west to Tarke Gyang

or east to Laghang Gompah a couple of hours beyond Dukphu.

Laghang Gompah to Chautaara

At the trail junction near Tarke Gyang you have more than one option. To reach the Panch Pokhari Lekh as suggested, descend east and cross the Larke Khola via Laghang Gompah and Yarsa before ascending once more to Gai Kharka and Naseem Pati. The road at Chautaara is at least eight days away by this route. Alternatively you could continue south along the Palchok Danda or head for Tarke Gyang and the main trail back to Sundarijal.

PEAKS: YALA AND NAYA KANGA

Part of the Langtang Himal, Naya Kanga rises dramatically above the Ganja La. It is often combined with Yala, on the other side of the Langtang Khola, as they share the same base camp. Though comparatively minor, Yala affords surprising views of Shishapangma.

CLIMB ESSENTIALS

SUMMITS Yala, 5500m (18046ft). Naya Kanga, 5846m (19181ft).
PRINCIPAL CAMPS Base camp: Kyangjin Gompa. Yala high camp: beyond Yala. Naya Kanga high camp: below the Ganja La, at ±5000m (16405ft).
GRADE Yala: Alpine Grade F. Naya Kanga: Alpine Grade PD+.

Base Camp

The base camp for both peaks is at Kyangjin Gompah (3749m/12300ft), some 6km (4 miles) east of Langtang village (see trek 15).

Yala: East Face and Northeast Ridge

From base camp follow a trail to the shepherds camp of Yala; a high camp can be placed on grass, half an hour higher. Climb a subsidiary ridge above base camp, descend to a boulder field, and then follow a rocky ridge to the summit snowfield, and the final narrow snow crest.

Descend by the same route

Naya Kanga: East Face and Northeast Ridge

From base camp cross the Langtang Khola to Chhona and follow the trail towards the Ganja La, passing Branchen Kharka at 4100m (13452ft). At about 5000m (16405ft) below the Ganja La (high camp), a glacial shelf runs diagonally rightwards across the east face from the La towards the northeast ridge. The route runs in the same direction as the crevasses – take care.

Either climb the central couloir in the east face or follow a tiny little couloir to gain the northeast ridge, which is broad at first. A steep section then leads to the knife-edge summit ridge.

Descend by either route.

Naya Kanga seen from the east, with the Ganja La just in the left of the picture.

LANGTANG REGION DIRECTORY

REGIONAL FLIGHTS
The Langtang region is easily accessible from Kathmandu, so domestic flights are not necessary.

REGIONAL ROAD TRANSPORT
Regular bus services run from Kathmandu to the main trail-heads at Sundarijal, Trisuli Bazaar and Dhunche.

Kathmandu–Sundarijal:
Local bus departs from Old Bus Park (Ratna Park)
Kathmandu–Trisuli Bazaar:
Local bus departs from New Bus Park (Gongabu)
Kathmandu–Dhunche:
Local bus departs from New Bus Park (Gongabu)

Across the Langtang valley from Tserko Ri (5033m)

Alternatively it is possible to charter a minibus or hire car to Sundarijal or Trisuli Bazaar. For travel beyond Trisuli Bazaar to Dhunche, 4WD can be hired. Trekking agents in Kathmandu will do this for you.

KATHMANDU ACCOMMODATION
There are literally hundreds of hotels of all standards from flea-pit to five-star in Kathmandu. During peak season, it is important to book your accommodation beforehand and reconfirm just before you depart from home if you want to stay in an international tourist class hotel. There are also many smaller guest-houses and lodges not mentioned here, often with gardens and excellent restaurants on the premises.

Hotel Ambassador, Lazimpat, Kathmandu, tel (01) 4414432, 4419432, fax (01) 4413641. Close to British Embassy, international standard hotel.
Hotel de l'Annapurna, Durbar Narg, Kathmandu, tel (01) 4221711, fax (01) 4225236, http://www.annapurna-hotel.com One of the oldest and most expensive in town.

Hotel Vaishali, Thamel, Kathmandu, tel (01) 4423934, 4413968, fax 4414510 www.vaishalihotel.com. Large new hotel.
Hotel Yak & Yeti, Durbar Marg, Kathmandu, tel; (01) 4248999, 4240520, fax (01) 4227781, www.yakandyeti.com The most famous and expensive in town. Deluxe!
Kathmandu Guest House, Thamel, Kathmandu, tel (01) 4700800, 4700632, fax (01) 4700133, www.ktmgh.com Old travellers' favourite, always busy, but there are nicer places today.
Hotel Vajra, Near Swayabhunath, Kathmandu tel (01) 4271545, fax (01) 4271695 www.hotel-vajra.com My absolute favourite place to stay in Kathmandu – paradise!
Nirvana Garden Hotel, Chhetrapati, Kathmandu tel (01)4256200, 4256300, fax (01) 4260668 www.nirvanagarden.com One of the quieter and more pleasant places to stay in Thamel – popular with expeditions & trekking groups.

TREKKING COSTS
The whole of the Langtang region is an open zone for trekking, and requires no special permit. However, several park fees are payable, including entry into Lantang National Park and Shivapuri Wildlife Reserve.

LOCAL ACTIVITIES
Mountain biking The potential for two-wheeled adventure is simply vast. Here are a couple of the best agencies for bike hire and guides:
Dawn til Dusk Kathmandu Guest House Compound, Thamel tel (01) 4700286, 4700617 fax (01) 4412619 www.nepalbiking.com
Himalayan Mountain Bikes PO Box 12673, Kathmandu tel (01) 4212860 fax (01) 4212861 www.bikeasia.info

7

EVEREST REGION

The Mount Everest region is second only to the Annapurnas in terms of the number of trekkers visiting it annually, and it would surely be the most popular destination in the country were it not slightly more difficult to get to.

Home to the famous Sherpa people, the Solu–Khumbu is a paradise of unparalleled mountain splendour, boasting four of the worlds' 14 eight-thousand metre peaks – Everest, Lhotse, Lhotse Shar and Cho Oyu – and a host of others in excess of 7000m (22967ft).

This region is arguably the jewel in Nepal's mountain crown.

Ama Dablam from Tengboche and Everest.

Morning sunlight on the *gompah* at Tengboche, with Everest beyond.

Strictly speaking, the Everest region, or Solu—Khumbu, is divided into three distinct districts. The southerly part is Solu, with an average altitude of 3000m (9843ft), and its principal villages are Junbesi and Phaphlu. The fruit grown in carefully tended orchards hereabouts is superb, particularly the pears and apples. North of Solu, in the valley of the Dudh Khosi, lies the intermediate district of Pharak, and finally at altitudes in excess of 3500m (11484ft), there is the Khumbu valley, which descends from the mighty Khumbu Glacier on Everest itself. Khumbu is bounded in the west by the Tesi Lapcha pass and the Rolwaling Himal, and in the east by Baruntse and the massive watershed dividing the Imja Khola from the Barun and Hongu basins.

It is from the Khumbu and its principal villages of Namche Bazaar, Thame, Kunde, Khumjung and Pangboche that the legendary Sherpa mountain guides and porters hail. Of all the highland people in Nepal whose livelihoods suddenly evaporated in 1959 when the Chinese sealed the borders and cut these economic lifelines, it is the Sherpas of the Khumbu who most successfully adapted to and benefited from the new invasion of tourists, trekkers and mountaineers.

Nevertheless, the Sherpas are relatively recent arrivals in Nepal, having migrated from Kham in Tibet some three hundred years ago. Pangboche is their oldest village, and Tengboche monastery their cultural stronghold. Situated atop a prominent forested spur north of Namche Bazaar, the most renowned Buddhist *gompah* outside of Tibet commands breathtaking views south to Tramserku and Kang Tega, east to Ama Dablam and north to Nuptse, Lhotse and Everest itself. Built in 1916, Tengboche was destroyed by an earthquake in 1934 and a catastrophic fire in 1989, which also claimed much of the priceless library of ancient Tibetan texts. It has recently been lavishly rebuilt with generous donations from all around the world. The monks here follow the Nyingma-pa tradition of tantric Buddhism, and their annual festival of masked dances and drama, Mani Rimdu, takes place over the full moon of the ninth month in the Tibetan calendar, which is usually in November. Tourists flock from all over the world to witness this spectacular and colourful pageant, and securing a bed or tent space in the area during the festival can be difficult. A similar festival, also called Mani Rimdu, takes place at the *gompah* in Thame village, usually in the month of May.

Behind the square red edifice of the *gompah*, the current *rimpoche* has overseen the construction of a cultural centre containing displays on al

LUKLA AIRSTRIP

By flying to and from Lukla it is possible to sample the remote splendours of the Khumbu within a week of leaving Kathmandu. As well as an extra risk of inadequate acclimatisation, however, this involves a degree of unpredictability. The often frantic scene of trekkers scrambling for seats on flights at Lukla has generated its own legends and folklore. Some of it is apocryphal, but most has a basis in truth. Plane-loads of police have been flown in from Kathmandu to restore order.

In the early 1990s, several private Nepalese aviation companies acquired fleets of powerful Russian Mi17 helicopters capable of flying to heights in excess of 7000m (22967ft), which did much to alleviate the bottleneck of tourists at this spectacular mountain hub. However, the era of reliable, cheap helicopter services in Nepal was short-lived. In 1995 a dearth of spare parts and lack of service facilities in Kathmandu forced the Nepalese aviation authorities to rescind the passenger licences of these ageing craft, and the entire fleet was grounded.

Today once more, it is upon fixed-wing aircraft that the services rely, and, flying without radar or other instrumentation, the pilots have to be able to see their way down in order to land. As a sign above the check-in counter at the old Kathmandu domestic terminal used to read; 'Passengers Please Note: In Nepal we do not fly through clouds, as here they often have rocks in them!'

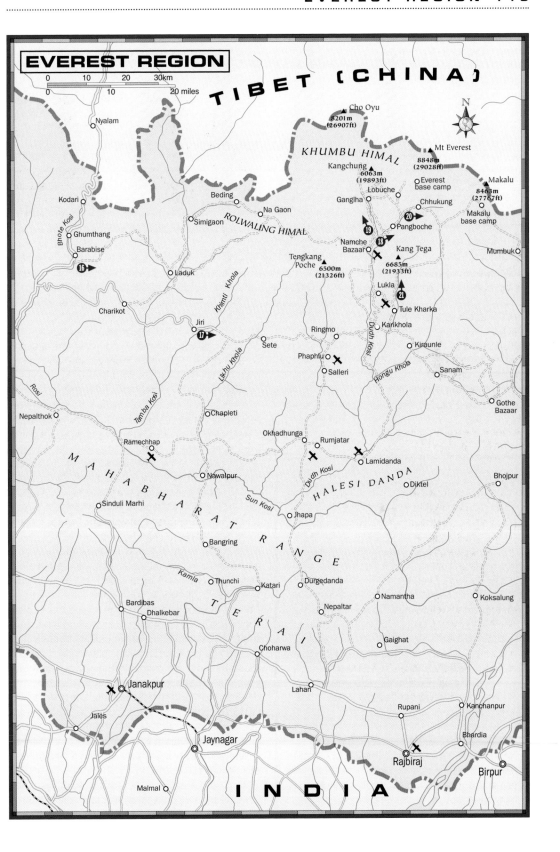

EVEREST REGION

0   10   20   30km

0   10   20 miles

TIBET (CHINA)

Nyalam

KHUMBU HIMAL

Cho Oyu
8201m
(26907ft)

Mt Everest
8848m
(29028ft)

Kangchung
6063m
(19893ft)

Makalu
8463m
(27767ft)

Kodari

Beding

Na Gaon

Ganglha

Lobuche

Everest
base camp

Chhukung

Makalu
base camp

Bhote Kosi

Ghumthang

Simigaon

ROLWALING HIMAL

Pangboche

20

Mumbuk

Barabise

Namche
Bazaar

18

19

Kang Tega
6685m
(21933ft)

16

Laduk

Tengkang
Poche
6500m
(21326ft)

Lukla

Charikot

Jiri

17

Sete

Ringmo

Karikhola

21

Tule Kharka

Kiraunle

Khimti Khola

Phaphlu

Salleri

Dudh Kosi

Hongu Khola

Sanam

Likhu Khola

Gothe
Bazaar

Nepalthok

Chapleti

Tamba Kosi

Rosi

Ramechhap

Okhadhunga

Rumjatar

Lamidanda

Bhojpur

MAHABHARAT

Nawalpur

Dudh Kosi

HALESI DANDA

Diktel

Sun Kosi

Sinduli Marhi

Jhapa

RANGE

Bangring

Kamla

Thunchi

Katari

Durgedanda

Namantha

Koksalung

TERAI

Bardibas

Dhalkebar

Nepaltar

Choharwa

Gaighat

Janakpur

Lahan

Rupani

Kanchanpur

Jales

Bhardia

Jaynagar

Rajbiraj

Birpur

Malmal

INDIA

aspects of Sherpa customs and religion. Amid the growing influx of affluent foreign travellers and their materialist, all pervading culture, this new building and the monastery itself are oases of *darma* and timeless tranquillity. Even today most expeditions heading for Everest and the surrounding giants pause at Tengboche and have a *puja* conducted by monks there to bless their ascents – the high peaks of the Khumbu Himal are revered as sacred by the Sherpas.

The colourful history of expedition climbing in the area, and more recently of commercial trekking and mountain tourism, began in 1950 when the American climber Oscar Houston managed to wangle permission to visit the Solu–Khumbu through some diplomatic friends. His party, the first westerners ever to approach Mount Everest from the south, included his son Charles, and the legendary British mountaineer Bill Tilman. From Tengboche Charles Houston and Tilman scurried off up to the Khumbu Glacier, anxious to reconnoitre possible approaches to the mountain, just as the international race to the highest summit on earth was hotting up.

Despite later describing their outing as 'a picnic', the famously laconic Tilman and his companion turned back after a brief look at the bottom of the Khumbu icefall and a partial ascent of Kala

Sherpani porters carrying loads en route to Ama Dablam.

Pattar. They were the first of thousands to ascend this way too quickly and be forced to retreat by the rapid onset of acute mountain sickness.

Had Tilman and Houston gone but a couple of hundred metres higher on that occasion, they would have discovered what Eric Shipton and Edmund Hillary observed from a buttress on Pumori above Kala Pattar in September the following year – namely that there was indeed a route from the icefall to the head of the Western Cwm, and from there up the Lhotse face onto the snowy saddle of the South Col. It was this revelation that abruptly switched the focus of the worlds' climbing community away from the previously favoured route on the Tibetan side of the mountain, and ushered in a new era of fame and fortune for the Sherpas of the Khumbu. In 1953 Hillary and Tenzing succeeded in climbing Everest via this new route, and the rest, as they say, is history.

Hillary has since bequeathed a generous legacy to his indomitable Sherpa climbing companion and his people. Various schools, hospitals and welfare facilities run by his organisation, the Himalayan Trust, have made a significant contribution to improving the lot of a people without whom even the hardiest of mountaineers would not even reach base camp, let alone scale the heights. It was to facilitate access to their hospital at Khunde that the Himalayan Trust constructed the first primitive airstrip at Lukla in 1965. Today this is the third busiest airport in Nepal (after Kathmandu and Pokhara), and from here the vast majority of trekkers begin their odyssey amongst the highest peaks on earth.

However you decide to get to Namche Bazaar – be it by plane to Lukla and then on foot, or via one of the longer trekking routes described in this book, you are bound to find the land of the Sherpas utterly beguiling and breathtakingly spectacular.

NAMCHE BAZAAR

Namche Bazaar, the administrative centre of the Khumbu region, sits on a steep hillside at 3440m (11287ft), above the confluence of the Bhote Khosi and Imja Khola rivers. Once upon a time it was merely a staging post for the trading expeditions mounted by Sherpas across the Nangpa La to Tingri in Tibet, and were it not for adventure tourism the place would undoubtedly have suffered the economic decline wrought on similar towns elsewhere in Nepal in the wake of the Chinese occupation of Tibet.

There are now bakeries serving fresh cinnamon rolls and sticky buns cooked in electric ovens, lodges offering nightly video shows, satellite dishes on house roofs, telephone and fax links to the capital and beyond and internet cafes. There is a police post, post office, airline offices, bank and money changers. The headquarters of the Sagarmatha National Park are in town, as is a dental clinic staffed by Canadians, plus numerous shops crammed with 'Tibetan' artefacts (brought in from Kathmandu!) and trekking and mountaineering equipment for rental and sale. Do not expect to find bargains though – the Sherpani proprietors are astute business women and know the value of their stock.

TREK 16: BARABISE TO NAMCHE BAZAAR

The Rolwaling Himal lies to the west of the Khumbu across one of the most serious passes described in this book, the 5750m (18866ft) Tesi Lapcha. As a route into the Khumbu, the Rolwaling valley and the crossing of this glaciated and potentially dangerous pass offer properly equipped and experienced parties a challenging and unspoiled trek through some of the wildest mountain scenery imaginable in Nepal or anywere else. This is not a route for novices.

TREK ESSENTIALS

LENGTH (3-4 weeks ex Kathmandu.) Walking from Barabise: 6 days to Simigaon, 3 days to Na Gaon, 1 day rest (4 days to ascend Ramdung), 5 days to Namche Bazaar.

ACCESS *To start* Bus Kathmandu–Barabise. *On finish* Join treks 18 or 19.

HIGHEST POINT Highest trekking point: Tesi Lapcha, 5750m (18866ft). Highest camp: Tesi Lapcha Phedi, ±4700m (15420ft).

TREK STYLE Tents and kitchen required.

RESTRICTIONS Permission to cross the Tesi Lapcha only possible in conjunction with a NMA climbing permit for Parchamo (6187m/20300ft) or Ramdung (5925m/19440ft).

FURTHER OPTIONS Shorten trek by 3 days, by taking bus to Kathmandu - Dalanka via Charikot, then walking to Gongar up Tamba Khosi valley. Exit via the Yalung La to the Khare Kola and Charikot on the road to Jiri.

The rewards of this seldom travelled trail are quite stupendous, with rare close-up views of Gauri Shankar (7145m/23443ft) and Menlungtse (7181m/23561ft) and stunning panoramas east to Everest and the peaks of the Khumbu. The villages are unspoiled, the forests pristine, and the people encountered spontaneous and hospitable.

It is possible to complete this route without even contemplating the ascent of one of the peaks in the area, though officers manning the police checkposts on the way have long been wise to the ruse. When my companions and I passed by in 1988, carrying only light packs and masquerading as the British Ramdung Expedition, our permits were in order but we were closely questioned as to exactly where our equipment was!

Barabise to Simigaon

The most commonly used route to the Rolwaling valley commences at Barabise on the Arniko Highway. After crossing the 3319m (10890ft) Tinsang La to Bigu Gompah, it descends the northern slopes of Sangawa Khola to enter the main Tamba Khosi above Laduk, north of which the valley is known as the Bhote Khosi. A camp high on the Tinsang La affords excellent morning views east to Gauri Shankar, and the short diversionary climb from the main trail beyond to visit Bigu, a Kargyu-pa nunnery which is home to thirty or so Sherpanis, is well worth the effort. The long white building in front of the temple is the living accommodation for the nuns – it's an idyllic spot, surrounded by ancient juniper woods and commanding fine views.

Entering the Bhote Khosi from Bigu via Laduk, the trail becomes a major highway and descends to the river at Gongar. There are magnificent views of Gauri Shankar ahead, and careful route finding is necessary as the path winds its way through intensively cultivated and terraced farmland. Continuing northwards through an impressive gorge, the valley of the Rolwaling Chhu is then entered to the east after a steep climb to the large village of Simigaon.

Descending from the Tinsang La to Bigu Gompah, as a paraglider takes the easy way down.

Simigaon to Na Gaon

Simigaon is the last major settlement until Beding (3694m/ 12120ft), which is reached after two days of jungle-bashing in the precipitous and diffi-cult Rolwaling gorge. In the monsoon season this section of trail can be impassable due to washed-out bridges, forcing a tortuous diversion along tiny paths on a higher route to the south. The leeches hereabouts are huge and voracious, making passage in wet conditions a real ordeal for the squeamish.

An hour and a half of gentle climbing beyond Beding brings you to the crest of a ridge, beyond which the character of the valley abruptly changes. The dark forested gorge is behind you now, and ahead the scenery opens dramatically, revealing a stunning array of peaks. The elegant snow-fluted summit of Chobutse (6689m/21947ft) is particularly unforgettable, and the remaining half-hour walk to Na Gaon is along the almost flat bed of a classic U-shaped glacial valley.

A day or two acclimatising at this barren spot is advisable, and it is from just above Na that the route south to the Yalung La and Ramdung heads off up a steep rocky hillside. Whether or not you are intending to climb Ramdung, a trip to the Yalung La (5310m/17422ft) will certainly aid your acclimatisation prior to a crossing of the Tesi Lapcha, and there are several other adventurous excursions possible in the area, including an ascent of the lesser Yalung Ri (5630m/18472ft). This is best attempted from the place known as Ramdung base camp, beside the highest small lake on the north side of the Yalung La at an altitude of 4850m (15913ft). There are actually two summits on this challenging little peak, and the routes to both are obvious from camp – the one to the left is a fairly straightforward snow climb with an interesting technical summit ridge, while the

---

BEDING

The houses of Beding are clustered on a hillock above the village *gompah*, which contains some particularly fine murals. There is little farmland hereabouts, and the place gets practically no sunshine on account of the precipitous valley walls. Edmund Hillary's Himalayan Trust has constructed a school in the village, and during the summer months the inhabitants still conduct their traditional trading expeditions across the Menlung La (5510m/18078ft) into Tibet, where they exchange rice and barley for Tibetan rock-salt. Those with time who are sufficiently acclimatised may wish to make the three day round trip to this isolated col from Beding. The trail heads off north from a point ten minutes beyond the village, and from the pass there are awesome views of Menlungtse.

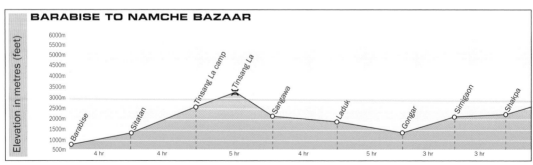

BARABISE TO NAMCHE BAZAAR

PEAK: RAMDUNG

Although technically straightforward at an Alpine Grade of PD−, the ascent of Ramdung, the most popular trekking peak in the Rolwaling, demands careful logistical planning and adequate acclimatisation.

Base Camp
To reach base camp, follow a path along the south side of the Rolwaling Chhu from the village of Na Gaon (see trek 16) until you are opposite Kabuk. From here follow a trail south towards the Yalung La (5310m/17422ft) to ±4900m (16077ft) where base camp can be situated on a grassy plateau by a small lake fed by clear streams.

North Face from Yalung La
Above base camp follow the cairned trail to the east, cross the ridge behind base camp and gain the west side of the glacier above. Then follow this glacier to a plateau west of Point 5766m (18918ft). High camp is at around 5550m (18210ft).

Climb a steepish slope to the short snow ridge running south to ±5665m (18587ft), then continue southwest towards the summit. Final steep slopes

CLIMB ESSENTIALS

SUMMIT Ramdung, 5930m (19456ft).
PRINCIPAL CAMPS Base camp: below Yalung La, at ±4900m (16077ft). High camp: plateau west of Point 5766m (18918ft), at ±5550m (18210ft).
GRADE Alpine grade PD-.

lead to the summit, which is large and flat, with awesome views.

Descend by the same route. This is a long summit day.

Leaving high camp for the summit of Ramdung, with Point 5766m (18918ft) on the left.

one to the right offers a long and difficult rock scramble along an alpine ridge. Note that as the Rolwaling valley is now an open area it is possible to exit via the Yalung La and cross into the Khare Kola valley before trekking out to the Jiri road at Charikot.

Na Gaon to Namche Bazaar
Only when you are sure you have achieved sufficient acclimatisation should you consider setting off for a crossing of the Tesi Lapcha. Most parties send back their Barabise porters at Beding and take on local men (and women) from

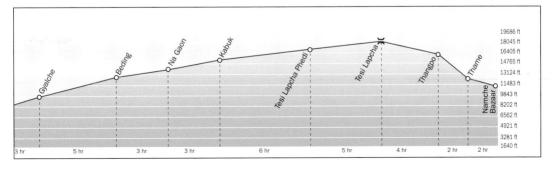

Beding for the crossing, as they are more accustomed to the cold and know the difficult approach route onto the pass from the west. As always in these situations, a little up-to-date local knowledge can make all the difference between a successful crossing and a disastrous one.

Traditionally, parties heading for the Tesi Lapcha went beyond Na and made a camp at Chobu, north of the enormous glacial lake of Tsho Rolpa before climbing to the high camp at Tesi Lapcha Phedi and crossing the pass in a long day from there. More recently an alternative route to the south has been favoured, camping at a place known as Kabuk and then moving up to Tesi Lapcha Phedi. From Kabuk the newer route climbs a steep ridge to avoid the hideous-

ly contorted and boulder-strewn lower reaches of the Trakarding Glacier, before descending to the ablation valley and on down to the surface of the glacier via a steep 50m (164ft) gully. From here it is a gruelling four hours northwards to a collection of excavated tent platforms at Tesi Lapcha Phedi, immediately below the fearsome Drolambu icefall.

Start well before sunrise for the actual crossing, as it is a long, long way to the first decent camp on the other side, and it is essential to complete most of the ascent before the warmth of the sun loosens the rocks above. The route climbs the rock to the right (true left) of the Drolambu icefall. The start, reached in 45 minutes from camp, is the right-hand end of the last and most prominent buttress beyond the icefall. Don't be tempted

PEAK: PARCHAMO

Forming part of the Rolwaling Himal, Parchamo rises high above the Tesi Lapcha. The peak, with its elegant snowy summit, was first ascended by Dennis Davis and Phil Boultbee in 1955, during the course of

a highly successful expedition relying on information gained from Shipton's 1951 exploration. Shipton examined appoaches to Cho Oyu, reached the Tesi Lapcha from Thame, but was turned back by the steep ice step just 100m (330ft) below the top – possibly because his party chose to climb without crampons.

Base Camp
Base camp is normally at Tesi Lapcha, 5755m (18882ft) (see trek 16), where it is usually windy. However, there are other possible sites to the east of the col below the glacier at ±5200m (17060ft).

North Ridge from Tesi Lapcha
From the La the route is the broad glacial ridge leading south to the summit, at an Alpine Grade of PD. There are some crevasses and, in particular, a serac step about 100m (330ft) below the top which can often give real problems.

Descend by the same route.

The snowy peak of Parchamo seen from the Tesi Lapcha.

An awkward section on the Drolambu icefall heading for the Tesi Lapcha.

by the gully to the right, but scramble up to a leftwards traverse across the rock. If you have porters it is necessary to fix ropes up the first 10–15m (33–50ft). Beyond this, a path weaves its way up easy angled gullies of scree amid steep rock. You may have to fix part of the route or cut steps if ice has formed here. It is two hours to the end of the steep ground, after which the route emerges into a level valley beside the Drolambu glacier. Ahead to the right is Parchamo, and the pass is immediately north. Continuing along this valley, the route passes beneath a series of seracs before finally ascending the snow slopes which rise above them to the rocky crest of the Tesi Lapcha.

If for any reason you arrive at these upper slopes late in the day, it is possible to take a sheltered camp 60m (66yd) beyond the crest on rock ledges beneath protective overhangs. Be sure to position yourselves well under these, as during the afternoon and evening the area becomes a shooting gallery from above. The views west from the col to the Rolwaling are sensational, but east into the Khumbu they are limited to Tengkang Poche 6500m (21327ft). Those intent on climbing Parchamo will be rewarded with a more comprehensive panorama of Khumbu giants from the summit.

The descent route then continues down a clear track which traverses left across some broken crags to a gully. Below this a scree slope leads to a small glacier, and after crossing the moraines you can cruise down the smooth central ice to a stream which in turn leads to more icy moraines and a boulder slope beyond. A good trail then descends to pastures and a camp at 4750m (15585ft). If you have the time and energy there is a teashop at Thangpo approximately 40 minutes further on down, and from here you can finally find yourself sitting on a terrace sipping a cold beer in Namche within five hours.

TESI LAPCHA

First crossed at the end of the seminal 1951 Everest reconnaissance expedition by New Zealanders Earle Riddiford and Edmund Hillary, the Tesi Lapcha is no light undertaking. The western approach is prone to stone fall and demands great care, even by the most experienced of parties. Helmets should be worn, ropes may have to be fixed and steps cut for porters, who should certainly be adequately clothed and equipped for such a high and spectacular crossing.

TREK 17: JIRI TO NAMCHE BAZAAR

This is the classic expedition approach to the Khumbu, and it is a scenically magnificent and tough hike. The major valleys draining the highlands in this area run north–south, and the trail cuts across the grain of the land from west to east before finally turning north into the valley of the Dudh Khosi at Jubing. There are many lung-busting ascents and knee-crunching descents, and by the time you reach Namche Bazaar you will already have more than climbed Everest in terms of the total amount of climbing done.

TREK ESSENTIALS

LENGTH (1-2 weeks ex Kathmandu.) Walking from Jiri: 4 days to Junbesi, 1 day rest, 4 days to Namche Bazaar.

ACCESS *To start* Bus Kathmandu–Jiri. *On finish* Join treks 18 or 19.

HIGHEST POINT Highest trekking point: Lamjura Banjang, 3530m (11582ft). Highest night: Namche Bazaar, 3440m (11287ft).

TREK STYLE Trekkers' lodges and teahouse accommodation available throughout.

RESTRICTIONS No permit required; NRs1000 Sagarmatha National Park fee.

FURTHER OPTIONS Fly Kathmandu–Lukla and join trek at Lukla (see box on page 128).

The walk from Jiri will get you into good shape to fully enjoy your time amongst the high peaks and valleys of the Khumbu, and serves as a wonderful introduction to the rural villages of highland Nepal. To miss out on this beautiful route for the sake of flying to Lukla and saving a week is to devalue your whole mountain experience. If you have time, take my advice and walk in. The benefits of all the effort involved in this trek will become apparent on the steep final 600m (1970ft) climb from Jorsale to Namche Bazaar when, even at a relaxed pace, you will effortlessly overtake the hordes of breathless people on only their second day out from Lukla.

Many people take only seven days to reach Namche from Jiri, but this is too fast to really

appreciate the surrounding country. Resist the temptation to see just how fast you can walk, and relax into your trekking days.

Jiri to Junbesi

Allow yourself four days to reach Junbesi, especially if you are carrying a heavy pack, and break the 2000m (6562ft) climb from the Tharo Khola to the Lamjura Banjang by spending a night at Sete. When I walked this way in 1984, there were only the most primitive *bhattis* providing tea and *dalbat* to travellers between the main villages on the trail, but today you will find frequent and substantial lodges, built by Sherpas who have migrated from the north. The deforestation that occurred as a result of all this construction and the subsequent cutting of firewood to cook food for trekkers and provide them with hot showers is truly shocking.

The crossing of the Lamjura Banjang from Sete to Junbesi on the fourth day of this walk is quite magnificent, as the trail passes through the least populated and highest stretch of country between Jiri and Namche Bazaar. The path climbs steadily into dense cloud forest, with gnarled maple and birch trees and enormous rhododendrons completely swathed in lichen and moss. If you are of an ornithological persuasion, dally here and have your binoculars at the ready, for you may catch sight of various flycatchers, minavets and sunbirds. You will no doubt hear the marvellously melancholy notes of the whistling thrush's call before you catch sight of

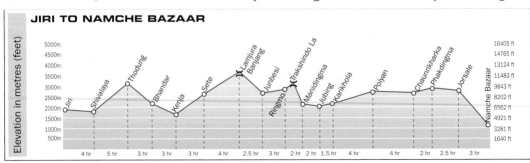

JIRI TO NAMCHE BAZAAR

this dark blue apparition flitting away throught the shadows.

A rest day in Junbesi is highly recommended, if only to visit the school of *thangka* painting nearby at Phugmochhe. This makes a charming side trip, and on the way you can also call in at the impressive monastery of Thubten Chhuling, which is home to a large community of exiled monks and nuns from Rongbuk on the north side of Everest in Tibet. The walk to Phugmochhe up the Junbesi Khola from the village is absolutely idyllic, and the school itself is situated in an incredible position atop an enormous rock, with stunning views back down the valley.

Beautiful Junbesi village makes a fine resting place on the walk-in to the Khumbu.

Junbesi to Namche Bazaar

Beyond Junbesi you are in Sherpa country the whole way to Namche, and the trail gets wilder every day. Given clear weather, from the crest of the ridge above Junbesi at Khurtang you will get your first look at Everest on the trek, though from this perspective it appears diminutive amongst the neighbouring peaks of Thamserku, Kang Tega and Kusum Kangru ('Cousin Kangaroo' in trekker-speak). The river crossed below this viewpoint – the Ringmo Khola – is the last you will encounter in which you can comfortably bathe. From here on in the waters are quite unfeasibly cold.

Possible diversions along this section of the route are many. The once famous cheese factory at Trakshindo has now closed, but just beyond the Trakshindo La is the wonderful Trakshindo *gompah*, one of the finest examples of Sherpa

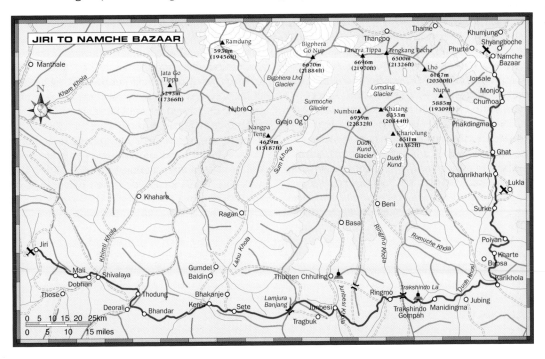

A RNAC Twin Otter taking off from Lukla.

this point the route frequently climbs high above the river and affords sensational views to the snow-capped peaks ahead, especially Cho Oyu.

Beyond Chaunrikharka, at Chablung, you join the trail descending from the airstrip at Lukla, and instantly realise just what bliss the past week has been, as the number of wayside shops and restaurants quadruples, prices leap upwards and the trail is suddenly teaming with trekkers in spotless clothes carrying rucksacks with airline baggage labels still attached. On my first ever trek, I sat in the shade wearing shorts and a T-shirt, cooling off from the sweltering heat during the final steep climb to Namche, watching processions of newcomers in woollen breeches, lumberjack shirts and double plastic expedition boots, wielding two ski-poles apiece, toiling away upwards, their faces scarlet, veins bulging on their foreheads. Welcome to the Khumbu circus!

monastic architecture you will see. Most trekkers spend a night below this place at Manidingma, where there are numerous lodges and a traditional paper-manufacturing centre. At Jubing, a Rai village in the heart of Sherpa country, the trail finally crosses the Dudh Khosi and turns north for the last stretch to Namche Bazaar. Beyond

FLYING TO LUKLA

Flying in to the tiny airstrip at Lukla is by far the most popular way of reaching the Khumbu, particularly with commercial treks and expeditions. However, various factors should be borne in mind when contemplating reliance on air transport in this sector. The planes used by airlines serving Lukla are small, and the altitude of the airstrip prevents them operating with full payloads. Baggage allowances of 15kg (33lb) per passenger are strictly enforced.

Airlines here operate a reservation system whereby those with confirmed seats for a given flight are given priority, no matter how big the backlog or how long those on the waiting list have been waiting. Even if you have a 'confirmed' seat for your return journey on a given date, it is prudent to check that your name is actually on the reservation list when you first arrive. Be sure to arrive back in Lukla no later than 4pm the day before to present your ticket at your airline's office office for reconfirmation. Many trekking agents maintain staff in Lukla for the sole purpose of doing this for their clients. Failure to fulfil this essential requirement will result in your booking being cancelled. Even then, should your flight fail to operate – for any reason – you will be put at the bottom of the waiting list, and at the peak of the season this typed sheet often has 300 names on it. Extra flights – sometimes fifteen in a day – are laid on as soon as conditions permit, but given bad weather and cancelled

flights, you should be prepared for a long wait or to walk out. Similar problems can afflict any mountain airstrip in Nepal – Lukla is just the busiest and most intense. There is absolutely no point in getting stressed out about it!

Once you have disembarked from your flight at Lukla and regained your composure after the shock of the steep approach and landing on a runway that's 50m (165ft) higher at one end than at the other, it is a two-day hike to Namche Bazaar. The trail is broad and busy, descending into the valley of the Dudh Khosi and joining the path from Jiri at Chablung. Lodges and teahouses of all standards are particularly abundant hereabouts, but the most popular overnight spot between Lukla and Namche is Phakdingma. Note that commercial trekking and mountaineering outfitters use yaks to transport food and equipment to Namche (and the valleys beyond). These animals, the HGVs of the Himalayan haulage business, do not naturally live below 3500m (11484ft), and the comparative heat of the valleys often puts them in a foul temper. Though naturally docile, they have enormous horns and should be always be given a wide berth on the trail. Particularly on steep sections, try to stand uphill of them as they pass. They have absolutely no conception of the width of their loads and are apt to unintentionally bounce you off the path.

MOUNTAIN NO XV

It was during the years 1849-1850 that No XV was first observed by the Survey of India, from a distance of approximately 180km (113 miles). Two years later as a result of these observations No XV's height was determined to be 8839m (29002ft). It was not an easy calculation and took time as early computations had to be corrected for refraction as the light passed from the thin cold air above Tibet to the dense Indian plains below Darjeeling. And there was the curvature of the earth to take into account.

Later Measurements

Realising they had a very high mountain indeed, the computers (people, not machines, in that day) reworked the calculation and corrected the figure to 8882m (29141ft) in 1907. It was revised again in 1922 when the figure became 8884m (29149ft). But still one important correction was missing, and it was only in the 1920s that the correction for the difference between the spheroid (the assumption that the earth is a perfect sphere) and the geoid (the actual shape of the earth, which has a larger diameter across the equator than across the poles) was calculated at the base of the mountain. This gave a new height of 8863m (29079ft) – nearly back to the 1852 figure. The current figure is the result of re-computation in 1954 and stands at 8848m (29028ft).

Mountain 'No XV' seems to have had no original native name, though its locality or massif may have had one. Various suggestions have been put forward as to an original name, but none has withstood close examination of its pedigree. To add to the complexity of naming the peak, it lies on the border between Tibet and Nepal. Thus, whilst it was observed and surveyed under British direction, it lies partly under the political control of Nepal and partly that now of the Chinese. All the above have contributed conflicting names.

Naming the Peak

The mountain's many aliases include:

Chha-mo-lung-ma ('Valley or District of the Birds'). Used by the Tibetan government in passports for the 1921 expedition.

Tchomolungma (probably a corruption of Chomo Lobzangma, meaning 'Liberal Minded Goddess'). Used on a map in 1733 by Capuchin Friar d'Anville.

Mount Everest (named after Sir George Everest, Surveyor General of India). Formally adopted in 1865 by the Government of India.

Qomolangma Feng (probably a Sinofied version of Chomolungma). Official name used by Beijing.

Sagarmatha (derived from Sanskrit, meaning 'Sky Head'). Used by the Nepalese government.

A sensational view of Everest from camp I on Pumori.

TREK 18: APPROACH TO EVEREST

At the head of the Khumbu valley, behind the Khumbu icefall and the Western Cwm, lies the highest mountain on earth. Symbolic of mankind's struggle to overcome the forces of nature and an icon of mountaineering achievement for decades, Mount Everest is today the focus of commercial expeditions and the aspirational high point of many people's journeys to Nepal. Surrounded by a host of only marginally lesser peaks, Everest has never yielded its secrets easily. However, by trekking beyond the last shelters at Gorak Shep and ascending to the vantage point of Kala Pattar you can experience for yourself the awesome grandeur of this, the ultimate mountain.

TREK ESSENTIALS

LENGTH (Minimum 2-3 weeks ex Kathmandu, including trek 17 to Namche Bazaar). Walking from Namche: 1 day to Tengboche, 5 days to Kala Pattar, 3 days return to Namche.

ACCESS *To start* Walk from Jiri to Namche Bazaar (trek 17). *On finish* Walk from Namche to Lukla (see trek 17), flight Lukla–Kathmandu.

HIGHEST POINT Highest trekking point: upper Kala Pattar, 5623m (18449ft). Highest camp: Gorak Shep, 5184m (17009ft).

TREK STYLE Trekkers' lodges and teahouse accommodation available throughout.

RESTRICTIONS No permit required; NRs1000 Sagarmatha National Park fee.

FURTHER OPTIONS Begin trek by flying Kathmandu–Lukla or walking from Tumlingtar to Lukla (trek 22), then walking from Lukla to Namche (see trek 17). Or begin by walking from Barabise to Namche (trek 16).

Few people that visit the Khumbu do so without seeking a viewpoint from which to gaze upon the summit of Everest. Whilst the view from Gokyo Ri is arguably more spectacular, that from Kala Pattar is the more famous and it is along this trail that the vast majority of trekkers in the area head. The route is well serviced by trekkers lodges, and even the highest of these now stay open practically all winter, such has been the increase in traffic recently. Preferably begin by walking to Namche Bazaar from Jiri (trek 17) – otherwise take extra rest days at Namche and Tenboche to acclimatise.

Namche Bazaar to Tengboche

The first day of this trek, from Namche to Tengboche, offers a couple of options at the start. The easiest, but least interesting, heads out of town along the reasonably level main trail that begins at Chhorkung and traverses around the hillside into the valley of the Dudh Khosi. The route suggested here, however, is slightly

Tengboche under snow with Everest just visible in the background.

more strenuous, climbing to the airstrip at Shyangboche (built to service the Everest View Hotel – www.hoteleverestview.com) before crossing a low ridge and descending through Khunde and Khumjung to join the main trail near the collection of teahouses and 'antique' stalls that has become known as Sanasa. From Shyangboche, and the trail to Khunde, superb panoramas that include peaks such as Thamserku, Kwangde, Kang Tega and Ama Dablam are revealed. For those staying in the area, Khunde and Khumjung provide a welcome alternative to the kitsch and hype of Namche. Both villages have maintained a far more traditional feel than their famous neighbour below, and the surrounding hills and ridges offer fine day hikes.

From Sanasa, the trail to Gokyo climbs away north, whilst the trail to Tengboche and Everest base camp descends to cross the Dudh Khosi at Phunki. This is the lowest place in the Khumbu – worth remembering if you do have the misfortune to come down with serious altitude problems. Beyond Phunki the route climbs again to reach Tengboche, where you may wish to spend a couple of nights, to acclimatise, soak up the stunning views and visit the monastery. Be particularly thorough with your water purification here, though, as peak season traffic far exceeds the accommodation available and what sanitation facilities there are simply cannot cope. The water source is below the ridge-line, and it should be considered polluted.

Tengboche to Kala Pattar

Most people travelling this way spend nights at Periche and Lobuche on their way from Tengboche to Gorak Shep. The stages are meant to be short to help you acclimatise, and at least one other rest-day should be incorporated in your hike to Gorak Shep and base camp. This is particularly

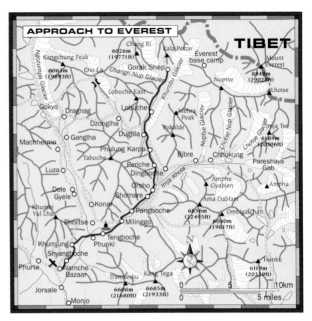

PACE

It is important to pace yourself carefully on trek and not to lose sight of the fact that you are doing it for pleasure! Struggling up towards the Ngozumpa Glacier (trek 19) alone on my first ever Himalayan trek, I found myself slumped on a rock in the mist, shivering with cold and exhaustion just below Gokyo, when I spied three figures advancing slowly towards me through the murk. To my surprise, it was an elderly Australian couple heading down with their Sherpa guide. Their cheerful, spirited conversation soon made me ashamed of my own miserable demeanour. They inquired as to where I had walked from that day, and when I told them - Machhermo - they were incredulous, saying that it had taken them three days to cover the same stretch!

Even today, I remember that happy couple and feel so lucky for the encounter. Enjoy the magnificent scenery at your own pace and rejoice.

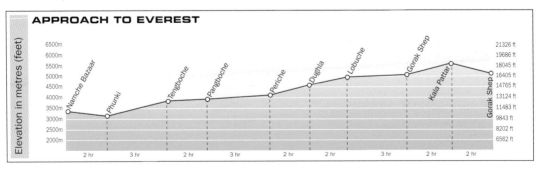

true if you are intending to cross one of the high passes in the area. At Periche the wind howls relentlessly, making it among the coldest places in the Khumbu. Periche-ing cold! There is a trekkers' health post here, run by the Himalayan Rescue Association (HRA), providing informative daily lectures on altitude physiology and other trek-related medical issues.

Many people stay no higher than Lobuche and climb Kala Pattar in a long day from there, but, assuming you want to be on the top at sunrise or as soon afterwards as possible, a night's discomfort at Gorak Shep may be worthwhile. If struggling out of your sleeping bag in the dark and staggering off up by the light of a head torch is as much an ordeal for you as it is for me,

PEAK: LOBUCHE EAST

The climb described here follows the south ridge of Lobuche just as far as a subsidiary summit before Lobuche East (6119m/20076ft). The trekking peak is connected to the 'expedition peak' of Lobuche West (6145m/20162ft) by a long ridge. The East summit is often mistaken for the West, and this is because most parties do not in fact complete the route to the main summit of Lobuche East, but return from the subsidiary summit (which is separated by an awkward notch from the main summit) or from the

CLIMB ESSENTIALS

SUMMIT Lobuche East, 6119m (20076ft).
PRINCIPAL CAMPS Base camp: near Lobuche Village. High camp: above Tsho La Tso, ±5000m (16405ft).
GRADE Alpine grade PD.

shoulder at the junction of the east ridge and south ridge.

Base Camp
Base camp for Lobuche East is normally sited near the village of Lobuche (see trek 16).

South Ridge
The high camp for the south ridge is above a small lake called Tsho La Tso (±5000m/16405ft) at the beginning of the rock slabs under the southwest face of Lobuche. From here there are superb views of Ama Dablam, Taweche and others.

Climb the slabs, terraces and ramps leading to the south ridge to the junction with the south-southwest Ridge. Above this follow the edge of the snow by the rocky east flank to the shoulder (where the east ridge joins). Then follow the narrow southeast ridge proper to the subsidiary summit, which is sometimes referred to as Lobuche Far East. Alpine grade PD+ thus far. The main summit can be gained by rappelling down the notch and following steep snow/ice on the far side. (Alpine grade D+)

Descend by the same route.

Lobuche East from the southeast; the subsidiary peak is just right of the main peak.

A stunning view northwest across the Cho La to Cho Oyo (far right) from high on Lobuche.

sleeping that bit higher and staying warm in bed for an extra couple of hours may be irresistible. This strategy works best if you are camping, though, as the 'lodges' at Gorak Shep are pretty rudimentary.

ACCLIMATISATION

However you've reached Namche Bazaar, but especially if you've flown into Lukla, you should proceed with great caution when ascending further. The trails above this town climb rapidly, and it is all too easy to move too fast and come down with altitude sickness. By taking the suggested rest days and drinking sufficient fluid to prevent dehydration, you can maximise your chances of getting up to Kala Pattar or Gokyo Ri without so much as a headache, but always be prepared to heed the signals your own body gives you. No two people acclimatise at the same rates, so keep an eye on your companions and be ready to slow down if they find it harder than you. Don't continue ascending if you have a headache. Breakdowns in communication between even the best of friends can lead to dangerous situations developing and getting out of hand. If you are feeling unwell, tell your friends. Don't bottle it up for fear of appearing weak or less competent!

Unless you're a connoisseur of piles of garbage on glaciers, there is not much to recommend going beyond Gorak Shep to Everest base camp at the foot of the Khumbu icefall. The mountain itself is actually hidden from this cold and squalid spot, and most people forgo the dubious pleasure of the six-hour round trip, preferring instead to head off up Kala Pattar. It takes two hours to reach the top from Gorak Shep, and only from the slightly higher summit of Upper Kala Pattar is the South Col visible. From either top, however, there is an array of awesome Himalayan giants that more than makes up for the lung-bursting climb up there. Immediately east across the Khumbu Glacier, Everest soars like a great black pyramid beyond the jagged white fang of Nuptse, complemented by a 360° panorama that includes Ama Dablam, Kang Tega, Thamserku, Pumori and Changtse. Carry spare film and batteries for your camera!

Walk-out to Namche Bazaar
You'll make much better time on the return leg to Namche (two days is easily possible) – though why come all this way to walk straight to Gorak Shep and back? Carry the superb Schneider map of the Khumbu Himal.

TREK 19: GOKYO AND CHO LA

The Gokyo or upper Dudh Khosi valley offers a fine and arguably even more spectacular route into the heart of the Khumbu than the popular direct trail up the Khumbu valley, especially when combined with a crossing of the Cho La to Lobuche. As with the conventional approach to Everest base camp, the stages recommended on this trek are purposely short to give you time to acclimatise.

TREK ESSENTIALS

LENGTH (Minimum 2-3 weeks ex Kathmandu, including trek 17 to Namche Bazaar.) Walking from Namche: 4 days to Gokyo, 2 days climbing Gokyo Ri and exploring, 3 days to Periche.
ACCESS *To start* Walk from Jiri to Namche Bazaar (trek 17). *On finish* Join trek 18 at Periche or Lobuche.
HIGHEST POINT Highest trekking point: Cho La, 5420m (17783ft). Highest camp: Cho La high camp, ±5000m (16405ft).
TREK STYLE Trekkers' lodges and teahouse accommodation available except at Cho La high camp.
RESTRICTIONS No permit required; NRs1000 Sagarmatha National Park fee.
FURTHER OPTIONS Begin trek by flying Kathmandu–Lukla or walking from Tumlingtar to Lukla, then walking from Lukla to Namche (see trek 17). Or begin by walking from Barabise to Namche (trek 16). Or leave trek at Gokyo and walk to Namche via challenging Renjo pass, Bhote Khosi and Thame.

Preferably begin by walking to Namche from Jiri (trek 17). If you begin your trip with a flight to Lukla, however, be sure to spend at least a couple of nights in Namche Bazaar before setting off up, and include at least one extra rest day before reaching Gokyo. Though less travelled than the trail to Kala Pattar from Namche, the Gokyo valley has become increasingly busy, and at Gokyo itself there is now a veritable lakeside resort with large, comfortable lodges, a library and the ubiquitous litter sadly associated with trekkers today.

Namche Bazaar to Gokyo

To reach the Gokyo valley, leave Namche on one of the two trails mentioned at the start of trek 18, and walk as far as Sanasa. If you're travelling this way on a Saturday there is likely to be a raucous party atmosphere at the collection of teahouses here, as women from surrounding villages stop to gossip and imbibe kettles of *chang* on their way home after the market in Namche. From here the Gokyo route heads off northwards above the Khumbu valley and climbs steeply to a prominent *stupa* at the Mong La (3900m/12796ft) before descending to the Dudh Khosi at Phortse Tenga.

Take your time as you make your way up this valley. The ascent is steep and it's all too easy to get ahead of your body's acclimatisation. It is also a stunningly beautiful place with waterfalls cascading from above, peaceful groves of rhododendron and birch trees, and occasional summer grazing pastures or *yersa*. There are many more lodges along this section of trail than there were when I first walked it, allowing you plenty of tea-stops and a greater degree of flexibility when planning your overnight halts.

Beyond Machhermo, the trail climbs the ridge above the Yeti Lodge, before briefly descending to Phangor and then beginning the final steep ascent up the terminal moraine of the Ngozumpa Glacier to Gokyo. By the time you reach the first lake at 4650m (15257ft) your travails are almost over, as the path then levels out and enters the ablation zone on the west of the longest glacier in Nepal. The views get increasingly breathtaking as you ascend, with Kang Tega to the south and Cho Oyu

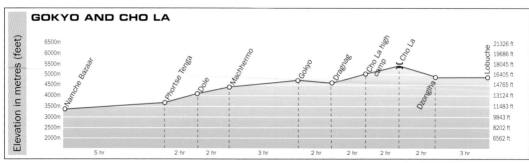

GOKYO AND CHO LA

to the north particularly drawing the eye. Be sure to ascend to the crest of the lateral moraine for a look at the chaotic, boulder-strewn surface of the Ngozumpa Glacier and to contemplate your way across a couple of days hence. Gokyo is reached in less than an hour from the first lake, beyond the second on the shores of the third.

In 1984 I huddled with a few other trekkers in a converted yak-shelter at Gokyo. This was the best accommodation on offer. Today, there are five lodges here, and the manager of the largest, the Gokyo Resort (headhunted from the now defunct Everest View Hotel), proudly shows prospective guests his glassed-in conservatory!

Spend a couple of days soaking in the phenomenal views around Gokyo. Beyond the lodges a faint trail continues up-valley, eventually passing a couple of other lakes and affording perhaps the most dramatic perspective of Everest from any trekking route in the Khumbu, and almost overpowering close-up views of Cho Oyu and Gyachung Kang. This makes an excellent acclimatisation hike, and may be followed up by an ascent of Gokyo Ri the following day.

For most people visiting Gokyo, an ascent of Gokyo Ri (5483m/17990ft) is not to be missed. Its summit affords perhaps an even finer panorama of peaks than that seen from Kala Pattar. The peak rises above the northern edge of Dudh Pokhari (also known as the 3rd Gokyo Lake). Set off before dawn to watch the sun rise from the top. The climb is simple enough if there is no snow, and a well cairned but steep path reaches the first summit in a couple of hours. Beneath, the Ngozumpa Glacier lies recumbent in deep shadow along the valley bottom like an enormous slumbering ice-serpent. Beyond, high peaks catch the first rays of the sun and glow like dazzling pink sentinels against the receding night sky. Cho Oyu, Gyachung Kang, Everest, Lhotse and Makalu are all visible from here, but it is the view of Everest that really draws the crowds. It's slightly further away from here than Kala Pattar, but more of the mountain is visible, and the surrounding peaks are simply incredible.

If then you still haven't had enough of the views this way, you may wish to consider ascending one of the Nameless Towers – three fingers of rock that rise between the fourth and the fifth lakes. The lowest (5500m/18046ft) is an enjoyable rocky scramble (Alpine F) to an airy summit best tackled via its southern ridge – allow 5 to 6

Camping high on the Ngozumpa Glacier, with Cho Oyu beyond.

hours for the climb and 2 to 3 hours down. The highest finger (5800m/19030ft) is a fine mixed climb at around Alpine TD on its northern side.

Trekking along the lateral moraine of the Ngozumpa Glacier with Gokyo beyond.

From both of those described here there are superb views of the Cho Oyu massif and of Everest.

Gokyo to Lobuche

Having reached Gokyo and seen the sights, you have a couple of options for further travel. To the west the seldom used but fantastically spectacular Renjo Pass (5345m/17537ft) offers a challenging crossing into the valley of the Bhote Khosi and a return to Namche via Thame in two days. The route suggested here, however, is to the east, where the more popular Cho La provides a fairly straightforward but visually stunning crossing to Dzonglha in the upper Chola Khola and thence to either Lobuche or Periche on the main trail to Kala Pattar.

CHO OYU

Also known as 'The Turquoise Goddess', Cho Oyu (8201m/26907ft) is the easiest of the eight-thousand metre peaks; its northwest face (the original route on the Tibetan side of the mountain) is subject to a large number of commercial ascents annually, with as many as 15 expeditions and 200 climbers occupying the base camp terraces in busy seasons. The first ascentionists, H. Tichy, S. Jochler and Pasang Dawa Lama, crossed into Tibet without permission by way of the Nangpa La to establish their base camp in September 1954. This was an exemplary lightweight outing, and all three reached the summit without using fixed ropes or oxygen 22 days later.

This route is perfectly feasible for acclimatised and properly equipped parties in good weather, but in cloud route-finding is problematic and after snowfall underfoot conditions can be treacherous. Local guides and porters are definitely advisable. To reach the pass you first have to cross the Ngozumpa Glacier. A cairned yak trail heads across the debris on the surface from just above the first lake and makes for the teahouses of Dragnag beyond the eastern lateral moraines. It's an easy 45 minutes across on this path – or a desperate couple of hours if you don't find it.

Some people stay at Dragnag and cross the Cho La from here, but if you have a tent and stove it's much better to head for a high camp at ±5000m (16405ft) just below the first boulders on the pass. Above Dragnag the trail climbs the valley until it opens out, at which point there is an ancient lateral moraine ahead. Climb to the large boulder and cairn at the lowest point, from where the Cho La is visible, and make a point of identifying the way ahead from this spot. The route climbs scree slopes through a prominent band of iron red rock to the col. The pass is *not* the rather tempting snow-covered glacier to the north. From the boulder, descend to the narrow ablation valley and over the next ancient moraine ridge to arrive at a reasonable campsite below a static boulder field. There is good water a few minutes further down.

Leaving this camp, a good trail climbs up and over the boulders to the scree slopes below the pass, and from these screes the way can be seen zigzagging away up towards an obvious breach in the band of red rock. Beware of rockfall on this section, especially if you are travelling late in the day. The descent eastwards follows the southern (true right) side of a fairly level glacier at first. Usually there's a trench made by previous trekkers to follow through the snow, though you should be roped together here. After a short way a cairned trail sneaks off down through a series of rock bands and on to the teahouse at Dzonglha, from which there is a magnificent, if somewhat intimidating, view of the immense north face of Chola Tse.

TREK 20: PERICHE TO IMJA GLACIER

This visually stunning little detour from the main trails in the Dudh Khosi valley is well worth the effort. The valley of the Imja Khola is the classic U-shaped product of previous glaciation, and as it tends to run east–west it gets more sun than its westerly neighbour. Particularly memorable are the views of the north face of Ama Dablam, an unnamed peak flanking the Amphu Lapcha just to the west – the snow-fluted summit of which completely defies superlatives – and the outrageous southern aspect of the Nuptse–Lhotse wall.

There are sufficient possibilities for excursions in the Khumbu to keep anyone busy for at least a couple of weeks. Although increasingly busy over recent years due to the popularity of commercial expeditions to climb Imja Tse (Island Peak), the Imja Khola is bypassed by many visitors to the region. Don't be one of them! This diversion makes an excellent acclimatisation interlude on your way to Kala Pattar (see trek 18).

Periche to Pareshaya Gab

Depending on where you're coming from, set off up the valley from either Periche or Dingboche. The latter is slightly higher, but gets considerably more sun. If you have time here, you can take the opportunity to wander amongst the only fields of barley in the Khumbu, made possible by irrigation, or follow a two-hour hike west up to Nangkartshang *gompah* for views to Makalu.

Both stages from Dingboche to Imja Tse base camp are fairly short, giving you plenty of scope for afternoon explorations. The going is easy and the valley broad and long, with a real sense of open space. Arriving at Chhukung alone in a snowstorm when I first journeyed this way, I found one hovel of a lodge with no-one else staying there. Today there are several comparatively sophisticated modern lodges. Do make time while at Chhukung for an

TREK ESSENTIALS

LENGTH (3 weeks ex Kathmandu, including trek 18 to Periche). Walking from Periche: 2 days to Pareshaya Gab.
ACCESS Trek 18 to Periche/Dingboche.
HIGHEST POINT Highest trekking point: Chhukung Ri, 5559m (18239ft). Highest night: Imja Tse base camp, ±5000m (16405ft).
TREK STYLE Trekkers' lodges/teahouse accommodation available in Periche/Dingboche and Chhukung. Tents required above.
RESTRICTIONS No permit required; NRs1000 Sagarmatha National Park fee.
FURTHER OPTIONS Leave trek at Chhukung and walk out via Pokalde base camp to Lobuche and then join trek 18.

Ama Dablam and Lhotse Glacier seen from near Imja Tse base camp.

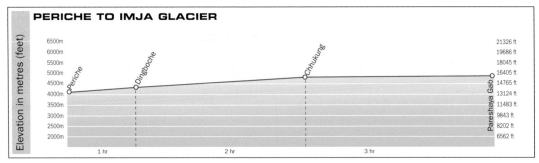

PERICHE TO IMJA GLACIER

PEAK: IMJA TSE (ISLAND PEAK)

The mountain is logically an outlier on the south ridge of Lhotse Shar, and enclosed by the giant Lhotse and Imja Glaciers. In 1952 Eric Shipton saw Imja Tse rising from the sea of glacial ice and named it Island Peak. The compelling name has stuck with western parties ever since.

Imja Tse was climbed the next year by Charles Evans, Alf Gregory, Charles Wylie, Tenzing Norgay and seven sherpas during the preparations for the first ascent of Everest. The team was testing their bottled oxygen equipment, so it would appear the first ascent of Imja Tse was achieved in less than perfect style.

The views from the summit of Imja Tse are quite spectacular, surrounded and dwarfed as it is by Nuptse (7879m/25851ft), Lhotse (8501m/27892ft) and Lhotse Shar (8383m/27505ft). The eastern horizon is dominated by Makalu (8475m/27806ft) and Baruntse (7720m/25329ft) while just across the valley to the south rises the shapely Ama Dablam (6856m/22495ft).

Base Camp

Base camp is often at Pareshaya Gab 5078m (16661ft), easily accessible from Chhukung (see trek 20), but note that the grassy slopes above here are prone to avalanche after heavy snowfall. It is generally safer and less dusty to place base camp at one of numerous other sites as low as Chhukung (4730m/15519ft).

CLIMB ESSENTIALS

SUMMIT Imja Tse, 6189m (20306ft).
PRINCIPAL CAMPS Base camp: Pareshaya Gab, 5078m (16661ft). High camp: above Pareshaya Gab, ±5700m (18702ft).
GRADE Alpine grade PD+.

Southeast Flank and South Ridge

About an hour and a half above Pareshaya Gab are the man-made tent ledges of the high camp (±5700m/18700ft), reached by climbing the steep grassy slopes and rocky outcrops with occasional cairns to mark the path. From the right (east) of the high camp cross a broad gully and gain another ridge, by easy scrambling, which in turn leads to a snowy glacier. Climb the glacier, turning crevasses, to reach a snow/ice 150m (492ft) couloir, at 50° – the usual route in autumn. In spring, however, climb the face to the left of the couloir, zigzagging up mixed ground; this is noticeably harder than the autumn line. The summit ridge used to be quite straightforward, though there are now various ice gendarmes and crevasses which are passed on the south side. The summit has awe-inspiring views up Lhotse towering overhead.

Descend by the same route

Imja Tse seen from above high camp, with the main summit just off-picture to the right.

ascent of Chhukung Ri (5559m/18239ft, approximately 3hrs up from the village), from the summit of which there is an unrivalled panorama of the vast basin of the Imja Khola.

From Chhukung it is possible to make the trip up to Imja Tse base camp and back in one long day, though I recommend planning to camp there if you have the equipment and clothing. It's a wild and spectacular spot, as long as you don't mind competing for tent space with large groups of climbers.

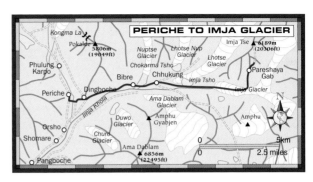

Walk-out to Periche

Whether or not you choose to climb Imja Tse (6189m/20306ft), there are a couple of options on the return. The simplest route, as suggested here, is just to retrace your steps as far as Periche or Dingboche. However, if you are intending to head on to Gorak Shep (see trek 18) and are already acclimatised, you might wish to consider a crossing of the 5535m (18160ft) Kongma La via Pokalde base camp. The base camp for Pokalde is at 5200m (17061ft), northwest of Chhukung, and the crossing to Lobuche in the Khumbu valley can be made easily in two days from Chhukung.

PEAK: POKALDE

Forming part of the Khumbu Himal, Pokalde is dwarfed by the bulk of Lhotse. Nevertheless it is an interesting mountain. It was first ascended in 1953 by Noyce, Bourdillon, Ward and sherpas, via the north ridge, as part of the preparations for the British Everest expedition that year. Pokalde is nicer to climb in a snowy season, and therefore usually better in the autumn than spring. The mountain has a crenellated rocky ridge, rising from the south at the Kongma La (5535m/18160ft), a rarely crossed pass leading to Chhukung.

Base Camp

Establish base camp at around 5300m (17389ft) by a group of (often frozen) lakes southeast of the Kongma La, reached from either Lobuche or Bibre (see trek 20).

East Face Route

From the base camp at Kongma La Lakes, climb broken rocks on the northeast flank of the mountain to gain the south ridge a short way below the summit (crux); approximately 50m (164ft) of rock climbing/scrambling up the narrow crest leads to a tiny summit. It's a good viewpoint.

Descend by the same route

The rocky route leading up to the summit of Pokalde.

CLIMB ESSENTIALS

SUMMIT Pokalde, 5806m (19049ft).
PRINCIPAL CAMPS Base camp: Kongma La Lakes, ±5300m (17389ft).
GRADE Alpine grade PD.

HIMALAYAN GLACIERS AND CLIMATE CHANGE

[By CAMERON WAKE]

Almost as much as the mountains themselves, glaciers serve as a focal point for the scenic beauty and power of the Himalaya. The movement of these large bodies of snow and ice under the force of gravity has carved up the Himalaya and created an alpine wonderland of wide valleys, glacial lakes, sheer rock faces and thick accumulations of glacial debris. The melting of these same glaciers produces the lifeblood of fresh water for great south Asian rivers such as the Ganges and the Indus, upon which hundreds of millions of people depend.

Glaciers also serve as a barometer of our ever-changing climate. In their cycles of advance and retreat, they respond to changes in temperature and precipitation. The fluctuations of past and present glaciers serve as a valuable recorder of change within the climate system.

In the Himalaya, glaciers reached their largest extent during the end of the last ice age (more than 20,000 years ago). The evidence of these larger ice masses can be seen in the U-shaped valleys which characterize much of the high Himalaya and in the large moraines (mounds of glacially deposited rock and debris), some up to several hundred metres in height, that can be found adjacent and down-valley of existing glaciers.

Glacial Retreat

Direct observation of the positions of the snouts of a select few of the thousands of Himalayan glaciers indicates that they have been in a general state of decline over at least the past 150 years. Recent observations furthermore suggest that the rate of retreat has been increasing in the past decade. This is most likely due to the observed temperature increases of 1-2C° in the Himalaya over the past twenty years, although decreases in summer-time precipitation also appear to play a key role for some glaciers.

Researchers extract a section of ice core at 5800m (19030ft) on the Nangpai Gosum Glacier, with Everest, Lhotse and Nuptse behind.

One notable result of the recent widespread glacial retreat in the Himalaya has been the creation of dozens of precarious glacier or moraine-dammed lakes. The glacier ice and moraine dams are relatively unstable and occasionally these lakes burst, unleashing cataclysmic floods. The largest recent outburst flood in Nepal occurred on 4 August 1985 from Dig Tsho in the Langmoche valley above Thame in the Khumbu Himal. This sent a wall of water and debris up to 15m (50ft) high down the Bhote Khosi valley, resulting in the destruction of bridges, homes, agricultural land, trails, and the nearly completed Namche small hydro-electric project (since reconstructed), as well as 5 deaths. This disaster would have been far greater if the outburst had occurred during the busy trekking season in the Khumbu. The current build up of glacial lakes – for example on the Imja Glacier in the Khumbu Himal and Tsho Rolpa on the Trakarding Glacier in the Rolwaling Himal – suggests that similar floods will occur again in the not too distant future.

If the glacial retreat continues over the long-term (several decades), as would be expected in a greenhouse-gas warmed climate, the amount of meltwater will decrease and the flow of rivers in southern Asia become less reliable and eventually diminish, leading to potential widespread water shortages.

Frozen History

Another valuable source of climate change information preserved in glaciers comes from the snow that falls in their accumulation zones. As the horizontal layers of snow build up over extended periods of time, the physical and chemical characteristics of the snow itself hold important clues which we can use to decipher changes in precipitation, temperature, atmospheric circulation, and human activities (for example – agricultural activity, biomass and fossil fuel burning).

Inside the science trench at the drilling site.

Whilst the longest and most detailed ice core records of climate change have been recovered from ice sheets on Antarctica and Greenland, records developed from Himalayan glaciers provide a means of extending the climate record back in time in the region where the Asian monsoon affects almost one half of the world's human population. In addition, the Tibetan Plateau exerts a strong influence on the global climate system, making the study of climate change in this region globally significant.

We access these secrets by drilling ice cores in the accumulation zones of Himalayan glaciers. The deeper we drill, the farther back in time we go. Ice cores enable us to reconstruct changes in climate in the Himalaya over time-scales ranging from centuries to millennia, extending the 150-year instrumental record way back in time. While Himalayan ice core studies are still in their infancy, our initial research has clearly shown that valuable records are indeed preserved in Himalayan ice. For example, ice core records developed from the Far East Rongbuk Glacier on the north side of Everest in Tibet detail variability in the intensity of the summer monsoon and the westerly jet stream over decades and centuries. We have also discovered that springtime precipitation in the Himalaya is strongly polluted by air masses that are transported into the Himalaya from India during the pre-monsoon and monsoon seasons.

As humans continue to alter the radiation balance of the earth through the burning of fossil fuels and other human activities, understanding past climate variability as a means to predicting future change becomes ever more important, and represents one of the great challenges for modern science. Glaciers around the world, including those in the Himalaya, provide a unique medium for helping unlock the secrets of our complex climate system.

TREK 21: MERA AND AMPHU LAPCHA

After the Sherpani Col route from Makalu base camp to the Khumbu (trek 24), this strenuous and committing traverse of the Inukhu and Hongu valleys is the most serious undertaking described in the present volume. The trekking is mostly on reasonable trails, but the isolation of the regions visited and the fact that, if combined with an ascent of Mera Peak, seven consecutive nights are spent at heights in excess of 5000m (16405ft) make this a most demanding outing.

TREK ESSENTIALS

LENGTH (4 weeks ex Kathmandu, including trek 17 to Lukla). Walking from Lukla; 7 days to Khare (Mera Peak base camp), 3 days to Panch Pokhari, 1 day resting/fixing ropes on Amphu Lapcha, 2 days to Chhukung.
ACCESS *To start* Trek 17 to Lukla. *On finish* Walk from Chhukung to Periche (see trek 20), then as for trek 18.
HIGHEST POINT Highest trekking point: Amphu Lapcha, 5780m (18964ft). Highest camp: Mera La, 5415m (17767ft).
TREK STYLE Tents, kitchen and mountaineering equipment all essential.
RESTRICTIONS No permit required for trek, NMA permit for Mera Peak; NRs1000 Sagarmatha National Park fee.
FURTHER OPTIONS Begin trek by flying Kathmandu–Lukla or walking from Tumlingtar to Lukla (trek 22), then walking from Lukla to Namche (see trek 17). Or leave trek at Hinku valley, and walk to Chhukung via Mingbo La or join difficult trek 24.

A party (and its porters and trek crew) travelling this way will have to be thoroughly equipped to deal with mountaineering situations in the remotest of locations, though given good weather even the ascent of Mera Peak by the normal route presents no real technical difficulties. It is when conditions turn foul that the true seriousness of a trip like this becomes apparent. In such an event both your navigation and survival skills will be tested, and help is a long way off if you're caught in the midst of an epic storm at Panch Pokhari. Go prepared!

It is far preferable to begin this trek by walking in from a road-head such as Jiri (trek 17). However, if you do set off unacclimatized from the airport at Lukla, spend two nights at the yak-grazing area known as Chhatanga before crossing the Chhatara Teng La.

Lukla to Khare
An early start should be made before crossing this first pass, as it's a long day, even in good conditions. If there is snow on the ascent it may be necessary to use ropes and cut steps for your porters. Do not underestimate the crossing – people have died here. Given fine weather and no snow, the trail from Chhatanga over the pass should be straightforward, and zigzags relentlessly up the steep hillside to a classic col known as Chhatara Og. The actual pass lies forty minutes further on after a short descent over rock and scree around a buttress, and a final 100m (328ft) climb to the many cairns and prayer flags marking the crest. The descent to Tule Kharka is short and steep, and the site is easily located by a massive and very prominent boulder which provides an excellent bivouac. There are platforms for tents, and a stream five to ten minutes below.

You are now high above the upper Inukhu Khola, and the trail is a joy to walk as it follows a roller coaster route across a series of ridges before descending steeply through dense woodland of rhododendron and conifer to the river itself at what used to be a grassy clearing known as Tashing

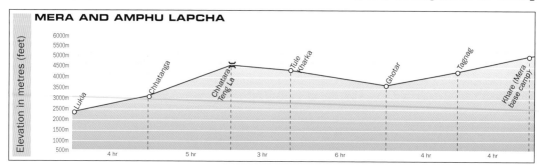

Dingma. This place was all but obliterated by a glacial outburst flood in 1998, and a new trail now climbs through the trees above the huge scar left by the deluge, eventually meeting the old one where it survived the flood. From the last of the ridges crossed before Tashing Dingma there is a particularly fine view of the awesome south face of Mera peak. Take good stock of it if you are planning an ascent of the peak via the normal northern route, and let it bear on any decisions you may have to make later about the wisdom of going up in bad weather if your navigation skills are not excellent!

The stupendous south face of Mera Peak from above Tashing Dingma.

Even if your party is moving well after the Chhatara Teng La, resist the temptation to storm off up this valley – it's a magnificent walk and deserves to be savoured. The changing perspectives on Kusum Kangru's twin summits will have you repeatedly reaching for your camera, and at Tagnag there is more than enough stunning scenery on display to merit a couple of day excursions. Your acclimatisation will benefit enormously too. Possibilities include Sabai Tsho, a moraine-dammed lake beyond the Sabai Glacier, and a walk up onto the eastern flanks of Kusum Kangru.

Khare, or Mera base camp, is also worth a couple of nights' stay for acclimatisation purposes, as you will not now drop below 5000m (16405ft) until you reach the other side of the Amphu Lapcha in almost a week. Whether you're bound for Mera Peak or plan to head straight over the Mera La, rest here a day and hike up the moraine above camp to 5500m (18046ft) for clear views of both the Mera La and the 'trekkers" route up the mountain.

Khare to Panch Pokhari

Those climbing Mera Peak will then move up to camp on the Mera La, but even if you aren't the next few days will be tough enough, commencing with an eight-hour crossing of the pass into the Hongu basin. This is a wild day out by any standards, and the mountain vistas are impressive. After climbing through steep screes, crossing boulder fields and snaking its way up to a rock platform above the western side of the Mera Glacier, the route then ascends 35° ice for a short section, gaining a plateau above. Crampons will almost certainly be required here, and steps should be cut for your porters if they don't have crampons.

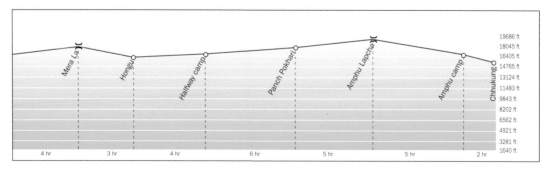

HIGH-ALTITUDE ROUTE

Contributing to the seriousness of this trek is the fact that once over the Chhatara Teng La (often mispronounced as the Zatrwa La) you are in a high-altitude wilderness from which the only escape in the event of someone getting serious altitude problems involves crossing one of two high and far from easy passes. Acclimatisation should be taken very carefully. Many commercial operators run this trip from Lukla, crossing the 4600m Chhatara Teng La on only their second or third day out. Most get away with it, but if you have time it's definitely worth walking in either from Jiri or Tumlingtar before going higher. Few people that set off from Lukla actually enjoy the crossing of that first pass, and if the quality of your entire mountain experience is paramount to you, a walk in will pay huge dividends.

However, unless you are crossing after recent snowfall or you are the first group over in a particular season, you should have few problems routefinding. Steps may already have been cut, and there will probably be a trench worn through the snow weaving its way through the crevasses

MERA AND AMPHU LAPCHA

towards the pass. If you are here in bad weather or fresh snow conditions you would be foolish not to rope up. The descent is immediately steep, plunging down between enormous waves of ice and the flanks of a small outlier peak north of the col, to a spectacular campsite at the foot of an icefall tumbling from Mera Peak itself.

As a prelude to the Amphu Lapcha, the Hongu basin almost steals the show, with a constantly changing and stunning array of leviathan Himalayan peaks. For two days this valley unfolds, revealing Chamlang, Lhotse, Everest, Ama Dablam and Makalu. The base camp for the final crossing is at Panch Pokhari, an open and windy lakeside camp on sparse grass.

Panch Pokhari to Chhukung

Three possible routes exist out of the head of the Hinku valley. The Mingbo La (5817m/19086ft) exits north to the Imja Khola and Chhukung, passing close to Ama Dablam; northeast of this, the Amphu Lapcha crosses to the same valley; whilst further east still, the difficult West Col/Sherpani Col route heads into the Arun watershed beneath the flanks of Makalu (see trek 24). As a crossing into the Khumbu the Mingbo La has fallen out of favour recently due to the receding snow-cover on the northern side, and the Amphu Lapcha has been the safest way to go. Glacier and snow conditions vary from season to season, however, often by startling amounts, and current information should always be sought before setting of. Your sirdar will know!

There are two routes across the Amphu Lapcha from Panch Pokhari. One climbs directly to the lowest point on the skyline before turning up to the left. This is certainly the easiest ascent, being no more than a scramble up a zigzag path on rock and scree. The descent on the Chhukung side, though, involves a lower or abseil of almost 100m (328ft) and then steep (45°) ground for at least 400m (1312ft) to the glacier, the crossing of which presents further problems.

To locate the other route, look left from the lowest notch beyond a birthday-cake topping of ice at the highest visible point, to the very regular steps of an icefall. The route heads to this icefall and climbs it from the middle to its right hand side (two or three 'steps' below its highest point). This will require 100m (328ft) or so of fixed rope and is much the longer and higher of the two ascents. Crucially however, the descent requires only a 50m (164ft) lower over rocks to a reasonable path which heads down around the glacier, thus eliminating a crossing. This way is strongly recommended, although it would require 200–400m (660–1310ft) of fixed rope if under snow.

The precipitous crest of the Amphu Lapcha has to be one of the most dizzying and dramatic crossings in the Himalaya. As you emerge onto its airy promontory, the ground sweeps away down from your feet into the Imja Khola valley, immediately across which the gargantuan south face of Lhotse positively dwarfs the apparently diminutive Imja Tse. Start your day at 2am, for though the distance from Panch Pokhari to Amphu camp in the ablation valley of the Imja Glacier is not great, lowering everybody and their loads safely is time-consuming and you should be pleased with yourselves if you are all in camp by 2pm. From here it's a couple of hours walk to Chhukung, where the route joins up with the trail to Periche (see trek 20).

AMPHU LAPCHA

There is a tendency for members of expeditions climbing Mera Peak to think that after a successful ascent of the mountain their difficulties are over. Far from it! The climb is undertaken by expedition members carrying light personal rucksacks, wearing state-of-the-art mountaineering clothing, plastic double boots and gaiters, accompanied by guides and sherpas. The Amphu Lapcha is also crossed by cooks, kitchen boys and fully laden porters. It is a serious responsibility for everyone involved in organising and participating in trips like this to get these people over safely. Taking inadequately clothed, poorly equipped staff across such a pass is a practise that one encounters all too often even today, and it occasionally has dreadful consequences. If you are organising things yourself, make a point of checking the porters' equipment with your sirdar. Do this at the trail-head rather than in Kathmandu, as things have a habit of disappearing in transit, and only issue the kit when it's needed. Give twenty porters a full set of mountain clothing in Lukla and five of them won't have jackets at Khare.

High camp above the Mera La, with Everest and Nuptse on the skyline beyond.

PEAK: MERA

The first ascent of Mera was made in 1953 by Jimmy Roberts and Sen Tensing, who appear to have climbed the central summit. The next recorded ascent was not until 1975 when French climbers Jolly, Baus and Honills climbed the north summit. Mera is among the highest of Nepal's official 'trekking peaks'. It is also one of the most popular. Access is relatively straightforward, and the climbing uncomplicated. This, combined with its height, gives many neophytes a chance to try their luck at over 6000m (19690ft) for the first time. Combine that with the views on a good day and it is easy to understand the peak's popularity.

The easiest route on Mera starts at the Mera La (5415m/17767ft) and follows the broad northeast ridge towards the central summit, and involves no more difficulty than a simple glacier expedition, with the added pleasure of climbing above 6000m (19686ft). Beware, however, of poor visibility, in which the lack of features on the climb can present serious navigation problems.

Base Camp

It is possible to establish base camp at ±5300 (17390ft) on the east side of the Mera La (see trek 21) on a gravel flat below the ice. This is useful for those intending to cross over to the Hinku valley afterwards. Otherwise establish a base 20 minutes below Khare.

North Flank

From the Mera La, wide snow slopes lead south and southwest to a rocky outcrop that marks the divide between the Mera and Naulekh Glaciers. Establish high camp near the rognon on the Mera Glacier, at ±5800m (19030ft) – some three hours from Mera La. There are magnificent views from here encompassing the eight-thousand metre giants Everest, Kangchendzonga, Lhotse, Makalu and Cho Oyu, (the 1st, 3rd, 4th, 5th and 6th highest summits in the world) as well as the spectacular spires of Ama Dablam, Nuptse and Kang Tega.

From high camp the central summit (6461m/21199ft) stands at the head of a wide glacial bay, with the north summit to its right. The route climbs the bay and broad ridge above high camp (beware of hidden crevasses) to join the ridge at the central summit from the east. There is then a short steep slope to the central summit. For the north summit bypass the central summit on the north side and follow easy snow slopes to top.

Descent is by route of ascent.

CLIMB ESSENTIALS

SUMMIT Mera Peak, 6476m (21248ft).
PRINCIPAL CAMPS Base camp: east side of Mera La, at ±5300 (17390ft), or below Khare. High camp: by Mera Glacier, ±5800m (19030ft).
GRADE Alpine grade F.

The snowy form of Mera Peak seen from the Mera La, with the north summit to the right.

EVEREST REGION DIRECTORY

REGIONAL FLIGHTS
Most people today access the Everest region by flying to the high-altitude airstrip of Lukla. Services are numerous and the frequency of flights depends upon seasonal demand. Normally in high season, there will be at least 10-15 flights available daily. These are heavily over-subscribed, so book early.

Kathmandu–Lukla: Royal Nepal Airlines, Yeti Airlines, Gorkha Airlines, Lumbini Airlines, Sita Air

The author takes a welcome dip in a stream near Simigaon in the Rolwaling valley (trek 16).

Although not cheap, it is possible to privately charter a flight. Fixed-wing aircraft are available for charter through Nepal Airlines and other private airlines; 9-seat or 5-seat helicopters are also available in the event of emergencies.

REGIONAL ROAD TRANSPORT
It's better to walk in! The nearest road-head to the Khumbu region is Jiri, whilst other trekking routes may be accessed from nearby Barabise. Both are served by regular buses.

Kathmandu–Jiri: Local bus departs from Old Bus Park, Ratna Park.
Kathmandu–Barabise: Local bus from Old Bus Park, Ratna Park.
Alternatively it is possible to hire a minibus or hire car as far as Jiri.

ACCOMMODATION
Kathmandu provides the first main base for any trek into the Everest region. The city has literally hundreds of hotels of all standards, a couple of good bets are detailed below, and the main list is in the the Langtang Region directory on page 115.

Dwarika's Hotel PO Box 459 Battisputali, Kathmandu tel (01)4470770, 4479488, fax (01) 4471379 www.dwarikas.com Expensive. A little out-of-the-way, but quite simply an exquisite tribute to Newari architecture. The building features many ancient features salvaged and collected by Dwarika Das Shrestha.
Summit Hotel Kupondol Height, Lalitpur (Patan) tel (01) 5521810, 5524694, fax (01) 5523737 www.summit-nepal.com Very pleasant, recommended if you can't stand the crush of Thamel.

TREKKING COSTS
Nearly all of the areas covered in this chapter are officially an open zone, requiring no trekking permit (fee for entry into Sagarmatha National Park). Tea-house trekking is the norm on the popular routes here. However, the route from Barabise to Namche Bazaar is the exception and is only possible in conjunction with an NMA climbing permit and a fully equipped trek-crew.

LOCAL ACTIVITIES
See Annapurna Regional Directory on page 99
Resorts
For a few days outside of Kathmandu City, consider **Dhulikel Mountain Resort** PO Box 3203 Lazimpat Kathmandu tel (01) 4420774, www.catmando.com/dhulikel-mt-resort 35km from Kathmandu on the valley rim.
Borderlands Resort PO Box 13558 Thamel Kathmandu tel (01) 4700894 www.borderlandsresorts.com 3hrs from Kathmandu by road.

8

EASTERN NEPAL

From Makalu and the Arun valley to the
tea estates of Ilam and the border with
Sikkim, the lush, densely forested hills of
eastern Nepal are mysterious, complex
and thoroughly alluring.

Deep, seemingly impenetrable valleys
carve their way into the highlands from the
south; primaeval, mist-swathed and alive
with the chorus of birds and insects. In
spring enormous rhododendron trees burst
into flower, colouring entire mountainsides
with their vibrant exotic hues. Here you
won't find lodges advertising hot showers,
but isolated pastoral villages populated by
Limbu, Rai, and Lhomi.

In the far north, impoverished communities of Bhotias eke out a marginal existence grazing their animals on pastures
that lie under deep snow for long months
every winter. This is wild country.

Approaching Pang Pema above the Kangchendzonga Glacier (trek 25), with the
north face of Kangchendzonga just coming into view.

BIRATNAGAR

Access to these eastern areas from Kathmandu is usually-gained via the sprawling industrial city of Biratnagar. Nepal's first large-scale industrial enterprise, Biratnagar Jute Mills, dates back to 1936. At an altitude of less than 100m (328ft) Biratnagar is hotter and more sticky than Kathmandu, and has an Indian feel to it. Pedal rickshaws and horse-drawn *tongas* compete for right of way with pedestrians, languid buffalo and overloaded vintage trucks. If you are flying to Taplejung you will certainly overnight here, as these flights depart very early in the morning.

On the borders of eastern Nepal lie two of the world's most formidable peaks, Makalu and Kangchendzonga. Makalu (8463m/27767ft) is the fifth highest – and many would say most beautiful – of all the eight-thousand metre peaks. Hardly less spectacular, Kanchendzonga (8586m/28171ft) ranks as Nepal's second highest peak and was first climbed in 1955 by Joe Brown and George Band.

Two major river systems, the Arun and the Tamur, drain these eastern ranges, upon which the monsoon unleashes its deluge with unparalled vigour every summer. Like the Karnali in the west, the Arun predates the Himalaya, and rises north of Everest in Tibet (where it is called the Phung Chu). Passing between Everest and Makalu at an altitude of only 1000m (3280ft) the valley floor is a veritable sauna even in November, and during the monsoon the leeches are voracious. The Tamur and its major tributaries – the Yangma, Ghunsa and Simbua Kholas – drain the entire western side of the Kangchendzonga Himal before combining with the Arun and the Sun Khosi east of Dharan in the Mahabharat hills to form the Sapta Khosi. Thus, in effect one mighty stream drains this stretch of the Nepal Himalaya from Langtang to Kangchendzonga.

Due to its proximity to Darjeeling and the fact that British Gurkha regiments recruited extensively amongst Rai and Limbu in the vicinity, the eastern Terai is well developed, with extensive air and road links. Biratnagar is the currently second city of Nepal after Kathmandu. However, the people of the northern hills have not shared in this economic progress, and still rely on tenuous economic links across difficult passes on the border with Tibet for their livelihood.

Those with a penchant for tasting local speciality food and drink on their travels will find two unforgettable commodities on offer in eastern Nepal – *gundruk* and *thungba*. The first is a preparation of sour radish greens, pickled and fermented underground, dried in the sun and then cooked in stews. An acquired taste! The second is a pleasant and deceptively potent alcoholic beverage, made by pouring boiling water over fermented millet-mash. This marvellous regional speciality is traditionally served in tall circular wooden flasks with ornate brass bands around them and a close fitting lid with a hole in the centre. Through the hole a thin bamboo straw, called a *pising*, serves both to filter out lumps of millet and to rapidly intoxicate the imbiber. In devout households a tiny dab of yak-butter may be applied to the side of the lid as a blessing.

Bargaining for carpets in Phole village, south of Ghunsa on the trail to Kangchendzonga (trek 25).

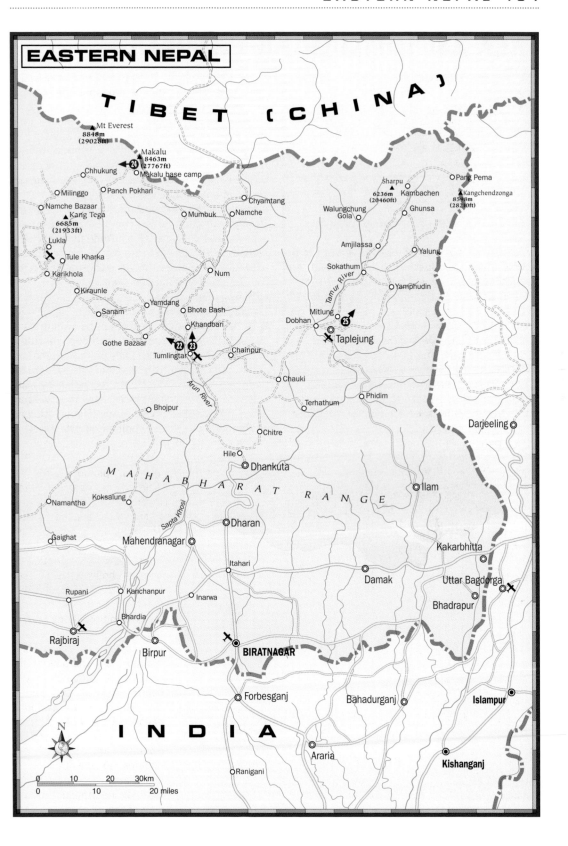

EASTERN NEPAL

TIBET (CHINA)

▲ Mt Everest
8848m
(29028ft)

Makalu
8463m
(27767ft)
◀ 24
○ Chhukung
Makalu base camp

○ Milinggo
○ Panch Pokhari
○ Chyamtang

Sharpu
6236m
(20460ft)
Kambachen
○ Pang Pema

○ Namche Bazaar
▲ Kang Tega
6685m
(21933ft)
○ Mumbuk
○ Namche

Walungchung
Gola
○ Ghunsa
Kangchendzonga
8598m
(28210ft) ▲

○ Lukla
✖
○ Tule Kharka
○ Num

Amjilassa
○ Yalung

○ Karikhola

Sokathum
Tamur River

○ Kiraunle

○ Yamdang
○ Bhote Bash
Mitlung
○ Yamphudin

○ Sanam
○ Khandbari
Dobhan
✖ 25

Gothe Bazaar
22 23
Tumlingtar ✖
○ Chainpur
✖ Taplejung

Arun River
○ Chauki

○ Bhojpur
○ Terhathum
○ Phidim

○ Chitre

○ Hile
◉ Dhankuta
○ Darjeeling ◉

MAHABHARAT RANGE
◉ Ilam

○ Namantha
○ Koksalung

Sapta Khosi

○ Gaighat
◉ Dharan

Mahendranagar ◉
○ Itahari
○ Kakarbhitta

○ Rupani
○ Kanchanpur
○ Inarwa
◉ Damak
Uttar Bagdorga ✖

○ Bhardia
Bhadrapur ◉

✖
Rajbiraj
◉ Birpur
✖ **BIRATNAGAR**

○ Forbesganj
○ Bahadurganj
Islampur ◉

INDIA

N

○ Araria
Kishanganj ◉

0   10   20   30km
0   10   20 miles

○ Ranigani

TREK 22: TUMLINGTAR TO LUKLA

Beginning in eastern Nepal, this is the least trekked of all the approaches to the Khumbu, following an ancient trade route used by the Limbu and Rai people to transport grain to Namche Bazaar and – formerly – on into Tibet across the Nangpa La. For those wishing to experience the entire gamut of trekking conditions found in Nepal, here is the perfect walk, commencing in the sweltering, verdant Arun valley at a height of less than 300m (984ft) and finishing in the Khumbu, with its towering array of Himalayan peaks.

TREK ESSENTIALS

LENGTH (2 weeks ex Kathmandu.) Walking from Tumlingtar: 7 days to Lukla.
ACCESS *To start* Flight Kathmandu–Tumlingtar. *On finish* Join trek 17 at Lukla.
HIGHEST POINT Highest trekking point: Salpa Banjang, ±3800m (12468ft). Highest camp: Salpa Kharka, ±3600m (11812ft).
TREK STYLE Tents and kitchen required.
RESTRICTIONS Open zone: No permit required; NRs1000 park/conservation fee.
FURTHER OPTIONS Begin by taking night coach Kathmandu–Itahari, local bus or hired Landrover Itahari–Hile, then walk from Hile to Tumlingtar. Or leave trek at Kiraunle, walk to upper Inukhu Khola via Panch Pokhari and join trek 23.

This is a marvellous way to walk into the Khumbu. You will be unlikely, even today, to pass more than a couple of other foreigners during the entire week. The route is often far from obvious, and teahouse accommodation cannot be relied upon. Be self-sufficient, and take porters and a local guide. A knowledge of spoken Nepali will be an asset as you constantly ask for directions.

Tumlingtar to Lukla
Particularly on the first two days, the path threads its way through complex terraced hillsides. Climbing above the Arun valley on the second day and skirting around the ridges into the Irkua Khola, there are superb views north to distant Makalu. The snowy summit seems to hang in the sky at an unfeasible height, above lush forests, banana groves and rice paddies. Be prepared to sweat!

Trekking through the terraced paddy-fields of the Arun valley at the beginning of the walk-in to the Khumbu.

The area into which you are headed is sparsely populated by Rai and Sherpa people, and after leaving the heat of the Arun behind you will find yourself in a wonderland of isolated villages and pristine woodland. Climbing from Phedi to the highest point between Tumlingtar and Lukla, the Salpa Banjang, the forest at last begins to thin out as rhododendron and conifer replace the deciduous trees of the lower slopes. At the crest of the pass is a large *chorten*, marking the watershed between the Arun and Dudh Khosi river systems. Camp high here, at the clearing known as Salpa Kharka (the only water on the ridge), for there are magnificent morning views north up the Hongu Khola to Mera Peak and Chamlang from the start of the descent.

Be sure to enquire locally about the timing of fairs held twice a year at Salpa Pokhari. Like those held in Humla in the far west, these are colourful affairs presided over by shamans and attended by Buddhist and Hindu alike – you will not witness a more memorable event in Nepal.

Sanam, passed after a couple of hours on the steep trail from Salpa Banjang down to the floor of the Hongu valley, is the first Sherpa village you come across. As is so often the case in Nepal you have clear views of the following day's walk, tantalisingly close on the other side of the valley, but with a river far below to cross first. In this case the suspension bridge across the Hongu between Guidel and Bung is at 1380m (4528ft), a knee-crunching 2420m (7940ft) down from the pass.

Near Kiraunle above Bung on the west of the Hongu Khola there is an important trail junction. To the northeast a steep and particularly thin path heads off up onto the Chalem Danda to Panch Pokhari ('Five Lakes' – not the same one as the base camp for the Amphu Lapcha!) before dropping into the upper Inukhu Khola and joining the route to the Mera La from Lukla (see trek 23). To the northwest a larger path – the route suggested here – leads over the Sipki La, crosses the Inukhu Khola, climbs again to the Satu La and finally joins the main Everest highway at Karikhola (see trek 17).

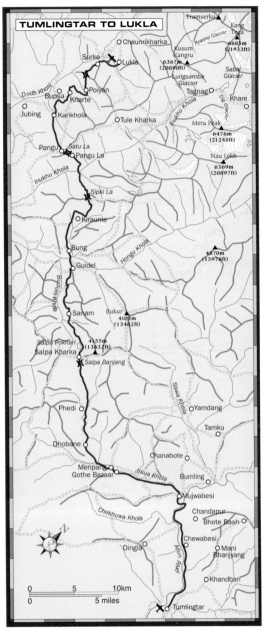

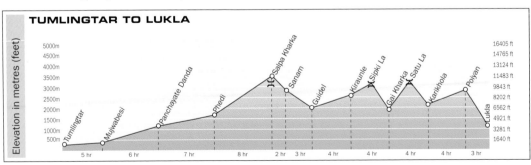

TREK 23: TUMLINGTAR TO MAKALU

Every bit as rewarding as the popular Khumbu valley to the west, the Barun valley approach to Makalu base camp is one of Nepal's many unsung treasures. The ten-day walk-in from the airstrip at Tumlingtar in the Arun valley is as strenuous as any, and the 3500m (11484ft) climb to the Shipton Pass from the suspension bridge over the Arun river between Num and Sedua will have the fittest trekker's heart pounding. The views from the pass and from above base camp in the southwest spur of Makalu itself are unsurpassed anywhere in the Himalaya.

TREK ESSENTIALS

LENGTH (3–4 weeks ex Kathmandu.) Walking from Tumlingtar: 10 days in, 3 days at Makalu base camp, 7-8 days out.
ACCESS Flight Kathmandu–Tumlingtar.
HIGHEST POINT Makalu base camp, 4800m (15749ft).
TREK STYLE Tents and kitchen required
RESTRICTIONS Open Zone: No permit requirted; NRs2000 Makalu conservation area fee; NRs1000 Makalu-Barun park fee.
FURTHER OPTIONS Begin by taking night coach Kathmandu–Itahari, local bus or hired Landrover Itahari-Hile, then walk for three days from Hile to Tumlingtar. Or extend trek by continuing from Makalu base camp to Chhukung (trek 24).

Furnace-like heat in the Arun valley, steep trails, the possibility of snowfall on the Shipton Pass at any time and the quality and variety of the mountain scenery make this a serious but immensely rewarding outing. Pace yourself carefully on the way in, especially on the Shipton Pass, as gaining so much height over two or three days is pushing it as far as altitude acclimatisation goes, and allow time at or above base camp for excursions.

If you don't wish to fly to Tumlingtar, it is possible to begin by walking to Tumlingtar from Hile on the Dharan–Basantapur road. Note that Tibetan Bhotias from Walungchung Gola (in the upper Tamur watershed near Kangchendzonga) have settled in Hile and make excellent high-altitude porters.

Tumlingtar to Tashigaon

Arriving at Tumlingtar by air from Kathmandu it makes sense to walk up to Khandbari the same day and stay there. Khandbari is the regional capital, a good place to provision up and a tad cooler at night, being on the crest of a ridge. Saturday is market day. It is a charming place, with a flagstoned main street, whitewashed houses with gardens and manicured lawns. The Arati Hotel in the main square is the only lodge in town.

From Khandbari it's a pleasant roller coaster ridge walk for two days to Chichira and Num, through magical jungle with tantalising early morning views of Makalu before the clouds roll up from below. The cloud forest on this section of trail is particularly stunning, with giant trees swathed in lichens and mosses and lush, dense undergrowth

Arriving at a high camp on the Shipton Pass late in the afternoon.

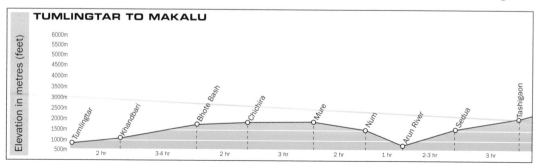

TUMLINGTAR TO MAKALU

of ferns and flowering shrubs. The bird song and insect buzz are deafening.

Sedua looks deceptively close across the valley from Num, but be ready for a strenuous few days from here on, as the trail plunges to cross the Arun via a suspension bridge before beginning the long pull up to the Shipton Pass. Here you come to learn the truth behind the Nepali saying, *raato maato, chipalo baato* ('red mud, slippery path') as the path snakes its way precipitously down to the river through the jungle. Huge fallen trees, enormous roots, rotting leaves and mud polished almost to a shine by the countless bare feet that pass this way all combine to make this a place to keep your eyes down and watch your step. It was here that British mountaineer Alan Hinkes slipped and fell from the trail into a bamboo thicket with almost tragic consequences.

Trekking out from Nehe Kharka in the upper Barun Khola valley, with Makalu beyond.

Tashigaon to Makalu Base Camp

Tashigaon (2050m/6726ft) is the last permanent settlement passed on this route, and unless you had the opportunity to hire Walungchung wallahs at Hile, you would do well to change your lowland porters for the Bhotias living hereabouts. Basic foodstuffs may be available – copious amounts of *chang* and *raksi* certainly are. Above this primitive village, consisting of twenty or so bamboo huts (many on stilts to keep the leeches at bay during the monsoon), the trail to the Shipton Pass ascends steeply into dense jungle, with only a few small *karkhas* providing camping spots. Immediately after the monsoon you may find yourself hacking back the dense vegetation to clear a tent space.

Fresh water sources become increasingly scarce as you ascend, and after mid October there may be none at the highest *karkha* on the Tashigaon side of the pass – a place called Kauma – so check with local people before setting off up. If the Kauma spring is dry you will have to camp lower, at Unshisa. Unless you're already fully fit and acclimatised, crossing the pass from here in a single day is definitely not recommended. The Shipton Pass actually consists of three cols: the Kauma La at 3900m (12796ft), the Keke La at 4127m (13541ft) and the Tutu La at 4075m (13370ft). Ideally you should camp at Kauma if there is water, as it then makes a sensible day over from there. There are, however, lakes between the three crests, so water is always available should a camp on the top be necessary. One should be made anyway on your return journey, on account of the stunning panorama revealed from the Kauma La – east to Kangchendzonga and

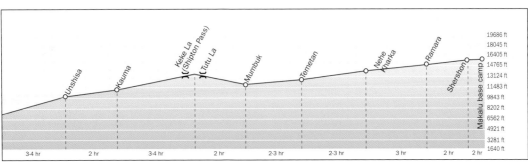

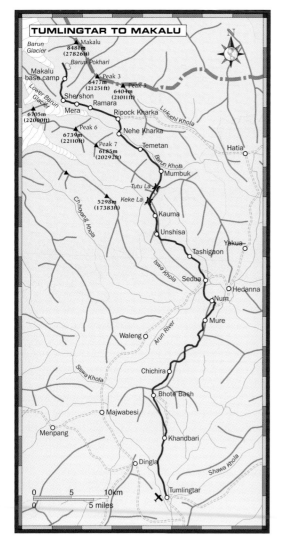

TUMLINGTAR TO MAKALU

Barun Glacier
Makalu 8481m (27826ft)
Barun Pokhari
Makalu base camp
Peak 3 6477m (21251ft)
Peak 5 6404m (21011ft)
Lower Barun Glacier
Shershon
Ramara
6705m (22000ft)
Mera
Ripock Kharka
Lukchi Khola
Peak 6 6739m (22110ft)
Nehe Kharka
Peak 7 6185m (20292ft)
Temetan
Hatia
Barun Khola
Mumbuk
Tutu La
Chhayang Khola
5298m (17383ft)
Keke La
Kauma
Unshisa
Yakua
Tashigaon
Iswa Khola
Sedua
Hedanna
Num
Mure
Waleng
Arun River
Siswa Khola
Chichira
Bhote Bash
Majwabesi
Menpang
Khandbari
Dingla
Shawa Khola
Tumlingtar

0   5   10km
0   5 miles

northwest to Chamlang (7317m/24007ft), Peak 6, Peak 7 and Makalu (8481m/27826ft).

The dramatic views and high trails of the Shipton Pass herald the beginning of a landscape in complete contrast to that encountered so far on the walk from Tumlingtar. Descending steeply into the precipitous Barun Khola, the trail now enters a pristine Alpine forest of conifer, rhododendron and bamboo, with waterfalls cascading from above, eagles and vultures soaring overhead and snow-capped peaks lining the horizon above intermediate hills scarred by monsoon landslides and massive cliffs. The Barun valley feels like another world.

To reach Makalu base camp takes a rugged three-day hike up this valley, which, due to only being accessible via the Shipton Pass (the lower reaches form an impenetrable gorge before

debouching into the Arun north of Num), retains an air of tranquillity few places can match. The first camp over the Shipton Pass – a place called Mumbuk – is in forest and short of level tent-spaces, but the next, Nehe Kharka, is stupendous.

From Mumbuk the trail is uncharacteristically rough for Nepal, plunging down into the valley along stream-beds, slippery gullies and over boulder fields. The valley walls are steep and loose, and a wary eye should be kept on the slopes above for rock-fall as the trail skirts along at river level to Nehe. Here, in a beautiful meadow beneath pines and cliffs, by the rushing waters of the Barun, you enter the heart of Makalu's inner sanctuary.

The final approach to Makalu base camp via Ramara, Mera and Shershon is stupendous. In terms of walking time it takes only six or seven hours, but at this elevation you should take at least two days unless you're previously acclimatised. A rest day would be prudent in most cases.

The valley ascends steeply from Nehe, and in the autumn the colours in the forest are breathtaking. Above all this arboreal splendour a host of peaks reveal themselves one after the other as you steadily gain height – Pyramid Peak, Peak 4, Chamlang, Peak 6, Peak 3 and Peak 5. Makalu itself remains hidden until just before Shershon, where the photographically inclined would do well to overnight. Set in a wide, windy ablation zone, this spot offers magnificent panoramas, and at sunset and sunrise the scene is quite sublime.

An hour or so beyond Shershon the trail emerges onto the grassy plain of the Hillary base camp, which is right at the snout of the Upper Barun Glacier. The southwest face of Makalu from here is as sobering a spectacle as you could wish for, as it sweeps up from the glacier in a dramatic series of pink rock buttresses to the summit.

Walk-out to Tumlingtar
The return to Tumlingtar takes about a week.

AROUND MAKALU

The opportunities for high-altitude exploration above Makalu base camp are almost endless. Excursions to the Upper Barun Glacier and advanced base camp, or via Shershon to the Lower Barun Glacier and the base camps of Chamlang and Baruntse are rewarding. If you are short of time, ascend the southwest spur of Makalu itself on the easy ground above Barun Pokari for the view up the Upper Barun Glacier to Lhotse and the Kangshung face/northeast ridge of Everest.

TREK 24: THREE COLS

Mountain traverses don't come any more spectacular or difficult than this high-altitude route from the Barun Glacier to the Khumbu. Such a venture goes way beyond the bounds of what is normally described as trekking, as it involves spending eight days and nights above 5000m (16405ft) and crossing three high mountain passes, two of which exceed 6100m (20014ft). This is a classic mountaineering outing and should only be undertaken by those with the experience and equipment to deal with such environments.

TREK ESSENTIALS

LENGTH (3-4 weeks ex Kathmandu, including trek 23 to base camp). Walking from Makalu base camp: 7-8 days to Chhukung.
ACCESS *To start* Trek 23 to Makalu base camp. *On finish* Join trek 21 at Chhukung.
HIGHEST POINT Highest trekking point: West Col, 6135m (20129ft). Highest camp: glacier camp 5500m (18046ft).
TREK STYLE Tents and kitchen required.
RESTRICTIONS Open zone: No permit required; NRs2000 Makalu conservation area fee;
NRs1000 Everest park fee.
FURTHER OPTIONS Leave trek at Panch Pokhari and walk to Chhukung via Mingbo La.

Taking porters over this route is impossible, and though the services of trained high-altitude sherpas may save you some load carrying, all members of your party must be fit and proficient at moving over glaciers and snowfields carrying heavy packs. Those fulfilling these criteria will find it a dream route, with challenging terrain and close-up views of some of the most celebrated mountain faces.

Begin by walking to Makalu base camp (trek 23). Spend at least two days here acclimatising before setting off west, preferably ascending to as near 6000m (19686ft) as possible a couple of times.

Makalu Base Camp to Chhukung

From Makalu base camp a thin trail climbs into the ablation zone west of the Barun Glacier before

Descending west from Sherpani Col, with Lhotse ahead.

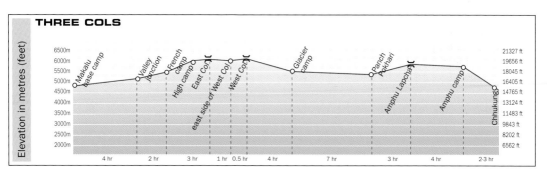

THREE COLS

Elevation in metres (feet)

6500m	Makalu base camp	21327 ft
6000m	Valley Junction	19656 ft
5500m	French camp	18045 ft
5000m	High camp	16405 ft
4500m	East Col / east side of West Col	14765 ft
4000m	West Col	13124 ft
3500m	Glacier camp	11483 ft
3000m	Panch Pokhari	9843 ft
2500m	Amphu Lapcha	8202 ft
2000m	Amphu camp / Chhukung	6562 ft

4 hr   2 hr   3 hr   1 hr 0.5 hr   4 hr   7 hr   3 hr   4 hr   2-3 hr

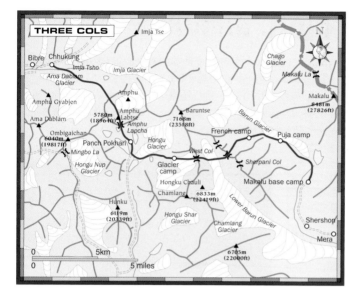

Sherpani Col, and the descent into the Barun basin from the pass is more straightforward. Parties wishing to cross both the first col and West Col in a single day may opt to camp even higher on this middle route, immediately below the final steep ground on the glacier at ±5900m (19360ft).

As the next stage is the crux of this route, spend a couple of nights camped high and reconnoitre your route before setting off. Expect short steep sections of ice-covered rock and be prepared to fix ropes. Aim to be on the move by 3am at the latest for the crossing. Above the bergschrund the climb is steep, rocky and exposed in places, and from the col the entire party should rope up for the crossing of the glacier to West Col. This stunning cirque is framed by Baruntse to the north, Makalu to the east, Chamlang to the south and Ama Dablam ahead to the west.

The descent from West Col (6135m/20129ft) onto the Hongu Glacier is precipitous and may require an abseil and the lowering of loads, before the day finishes with an easy walk across snow slopes to a moraine camp at 5640m (18505ft). Allow 7–8 hours for this descent, and do not set off to cross West Col from the Barun unless you have sufficient daylight.

Two alternatives then present themselves, and again conditions influence the choice of route. Most parties camp at Panch Pokhari before continuing west across the Mingbo La (5817m/19086ft) or turning north to the Amphu Lapcha (5780m/ 18964ft). The latter is more popular, descending to Chhukung in the Imja Drangka valley (see trek 21). Its seriousness should not be underestimated, though. Even with the two higher passes behind you the Hongu is no place to be caught by bad weather. It would be prudent to spend two nights at Panch Pokhari first, both to inspect the final pass and to savour the surroundings.

emerging onto the glacier itself, where the underfoot conditions are loose and rough enough to make progress hard work. Say your prayers as you spend the night at a spot known as Puja camp below the awesome west pillar of Makalu, before climbing the rocky slopes to the west above the Barun and entering one of the hanging valleys below Sherpani Col. You have a choice of three routes across the col – Sherpani Col itself and two others of almost exactly the same height at the head of the next hanging valley. The middle way, the 'East Col' (6100m/20014ft), has been favoured recently – there is a dry but cramped camp at 5500m (18046ft) at the snout of the glacier leading to the pass, the final steep climb is only 200m (660ft) compared with 300m (985ft) to

The view of Makalu from Sherpani Col, with the west pillar clearly visible.

TREK 25: TAPLEJUNG TO KANGCHENDZONGA

For those prepared to devote the time and energy required to complete this route, the trek to the Nepal side of Kangchendzonga (the name is Sikkimese and means 'The Five Treasuries of the Great Snows') is undoubtedly one of the most rewarding walks in the entire Himalaya. Straddling the border with Sikkim in the remote northeastern corner of the country, the massif is the third highest peak on earth and – with K2 in Pakistan – one of the most formidable of the world's 14 eight-thousand metre summits. Steep and narrow trails, magnificent forests, utterly breathtaking mountain vistas, few settlements and a real sense of wilderness characterise this corner of Nepal.

This approach route cuts across the 'grain' of the mountains, crossing a series of ridges of increasing height before following the valley of the Simbua Khola into the awesome amphitheatre formed by the south wall of Kangchendzonga. First opened to trekking parties in 1988, the very inaccessibility of the Kangchendzonga Himal deters all but the most avid mountain enthusiasts. Parties must be self-sufficient in every respect. Provisions are all but unobtainable beyond Taplejung, and the services of a competent trekking outfitter are both a legal requirement and a matter of common sense.

First arriving at the Suketar airstrip above Taplejung involves one of the most hair-raising landings imaginable. On the final approach Kangchendzonga sways alarmingly back and forth through the windscreen of the Twin Otter, as the pilot fights the air-currents to keep the plane level. One second you are cruising high above the Tamur valley, the next you touch down on a postage-stamp landing-strip with mountainside falling away from it on three sides. Lukla may be famous, but it's way behind Suketar in the adrenaline stakes.

Taplejung to Ramze

Flights into Suketar operate early in the morning, so you'll probably want to set off the same day. The path heads northwards along the top of the ridge for a couple of kilometres before dropping east into the valley of the Phawa Khola. At a colourful collection of Shiva shrines in the forest just before the main trail drops away east, a smaller trail heads due north up to Pathi Bara (3794m/12448ft). A small Shiva temple stands on top of this forested hill, to which Hindu pilgrims come from all over Nepal – if you have time, join them and spend an extra night sleeping out up there. Memories of the sunrise views of Kangchendzonga, Makalu and Lhotse will live with you forever.

The first camping place on the main route – reached after about three hours – is the primitive settlement of Lali Kharka, where you can pitch your tents on some disused terraces. From here the

> ## TREK ESSENTIALS
>
> **LENGTH** (4–5 weeks ex Kathmandu.) Walking from Taplejung: 8 days to Ramze, 1 day rest, 5 days to Pang Pema, 2 days rest, 7 days out.
> **ACCESS** Flight Kathmandu-Biratnagar, flight Biratnagar-Taplejung (Suketar).
> **HIGHEST POINT** Highest camp: Pang Pema (Kangchendzonga north face base camp), 5200m (17060ft).
> **TREK STYLE** Tents and kitchen required
> **RESTRICTIONS** Permits US$10 per week for 4 weeks, then US$20/week. NRs 2000 Kangchendzonga area fee
> **FURTHER OPTIONS** Begin by taking night coach Kathmandu-Itahari, local bus Itahari-Hile (or hired Landrover as far as Basantapur), then walk from Hile to Taplejung.

next night's camp is visible on the clearly defined notch in the ridge to the east across the Phawa Khola, at a place called Sinchewa Banjang. The going is immediately strenuous, as the trail descends steeply to cross the river via a small suspension bridge before commencing the sweltering climb up the other side. The villages hereabouts are scattered settlements of beautiful thatched farmhouses, with colourful flower gardens shaded by poinsettia trees, pumpkins ripening in the sun and corn hung to dry under the eaves. Khunjuri, about an hour up from the bridge, makes a good lunch spot as there are several enormous pipal trees affording delicious shade.

There are stunning views to the entire Kangchendzonga massif from the camp at Sinchewa Banjang. Make the most of them, for you will not see the main peaks again until you round the corner of the Yalung glacier above base camp at Ramze, though Jannu makes sporadic appearances along the way.

From Sinchewa Banjang the trail contours gradually around into the huge valley of the Kabeli Khola for two days to reach Yamphudin (1650m/5414ft), the most remote settlement on

Oktang and Kangch south face.

climbs a brutally steep ridge to a single farm-house commanding fine views over the country traversed so far. It continues upwards in dense forest before crossing the Duphe Banjang and descending into the upper Omje Khola valley, where you will probably want to spend the night camped by the river. The final obstacle between you and the Simbua Khola valley is immediately above you now, and it's a steep, waterless climb to the crest of the Deorali Danda ridge at Lamite Banjang (3230m/10598ft), best tackled early in the morning to avoid the heat. Given clear skies, Jannu is visible from this ridge.

The descent into the wild coniferous woodlands of the Simbua Khola commences with an airy traverse of some steep screes – a place to watch your feet! Abruptly the entire environment changes as the trail plunges down from the col. At the head of the valley lies the Yalung Glacier, and at sunset the temperature plummets as the cool air from above sinks to the valley floor.

this route, with plenty of steep ups and downs as it crosses tributary streams. The terracing of the rice paddies around here is quite incredible, and care should be taken to stay on the correct path as it weaves its way through a vast tapestry of tiny emerald-green fields.

Camping sites are hard to find between Sinchewa and Yamphudin, as every last piece of horizontal ground is planted with rice. The schoolyard at Mamankhe village may be your only option, and it will not be a peaceful night. The next day, as the trail descends across steep open hillsides to approach Yamphudin, it finally meets the river, and an hour before the village crosses the Omje Khola debouching from its fearsomely steep and densely forested valley to join the main stream. This is a wonderful place for a combined lunch-stop and Jacuzzi session – the last opportunity for ablution that does not entail potential hypothermia for at least two weeks.

The second half of the walk-in really is a contrast to the first. Above Yamphudin the tiny trail

The last few days to Ramze, camping at Dorondin and Tseram amongst towering, lichen-swathed pine trees and by rushing glacial streams, are simply idyllic. More rugged now, the path follows the boulder-strewn riverbed, ascending steeply towards the snout of the glacier. The flora becomes increasingly alpine and sparse and the valley opens up gradually to reveal a stunning vista of snow-capped Himalayan peaks. Koktang (6147m/20168ft), Ratong (6678m/21910ft) and Kabru (7353m/24125ft) form a scintillating horizon ahead as you enter the ablation zone above Tseram and stroll along through golden grasslands into Ramze. There is a single stone hut at Ramze which is invariably locked, and though it may be tempting to continue further on this easy trail, the

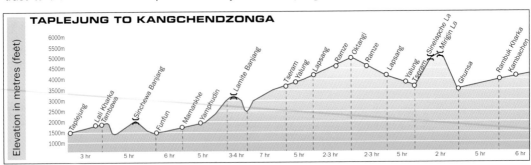

TAPLEJUNG TO KANGCHENDZONGA

last water is here and you should pitch camp. Spend a day resting to acclimatise for the days ahead, and to allow time to gape at the scenery.

Ramze to Pang Pema

There are two options for the next stage of this trek, which takes you across the southern flanks of Boktoh Peak to the Ghunsa Khola and the north side of the massif. A higher route, via the 5250m (17225ft) Lapsang La, is strenuous, takes two long days, and yields only partial views of Kangchendzonga and Jannu. The lower, more southerly route recommended here, via the 4500m (14765ft) Sinelapche La and the 4400m (14436ft) Mirgin La, follows a better trail, takes two or three easy days, and affords outstanding views of both the south face of Kangchendzonga on the way up, and the southwest face of Jannu on the way down. Camp at the small lake above Tseram on the first night, and at the spring-fed meadows of Selele beyond

the Mirgin La on the second. You will then be in Ghunsa village for lunch on the third day.

Ghunsa is a whacky spot. Nestling amongst the pines beneath the near-vertical walls of the Ghunsa Khola valley, this haphazard collection of wooden shacks does not get the sun until late in the morning, losing it again soon after lunch. The population consists of poor Tibetan Bhotias who scratch a precarious living by growing barley and potatoes, grazing yaks and goats on the pastures above, and weaving coarse Tibetan carpets on looms in their houses. These colourful rugs, emblazoned with creatures from Tibetan mythology, are highly durable and make great souvenirs.

The climax of this trek, in both altitude and scenic splendour, is undoubtedly the three-day hike up to the Kangchendzonga glacier and Pang Pema from Ghunsa. It's a steep climb, but having come over the passes from Ramze you'll be fit and acclimatised and enjoy every minute of it. In autumn the larch trees in the forests above the village turn a thousand shades of orange and yellow.

Beyond Ghunsa the trail passes numerous Buddhist *mani* walls and *chortens* as it follows the river to Rambuk Kharka, climbing gently all along. From here the gradient increases, until the summer grazing village of Kambachen (4130m/13551ft) is reached. The views suddenly become overwhelming, as the peaks on the Khumbakarna or Jannu Glacier come into view just before camp. The phenomenal north face of Jannu rears up above the head of this serpent of corrugated ice like a hooded

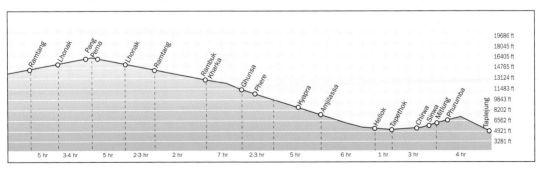

Jannu at sunset from above Kambachen.

apparition, its vertiginous cliffs cold and sinister in perpetual blue shadow. Away to the north leads the Dakhunapo Khola, beneath the jagged bastions of the Sharpu Himal (6236m/20460ft) and Nupchu (6690m/21950ft). An extra day's hike up this valley is worthwhile, as is a trip back across the river and onto the moraine of the Jannu Glacier.

Above Kambachen you enter an area of pure Himalayan magic. Leaving the tiny settlement past a cluster of fluttering prayer flags, the path crosses an open mountainside and finally enters the old ablation zone of the Kangchendzonga Glacier at Ramtang. From here the intimidating north face of Khambachen (7903m/25930ft) briefly appears up a side valley to the south, and there are scattered roofless stone huts that provide good shelter for cooking lunch. Yaks graze on the sparse golden grass, the sound of their bells rising on the cold wind.

Camp is at Lhonak, the coldest night on the entire trip as the wind rips across this huge open space and chills you to the bone. From here a trail heads north over the Chabuk La (5682m/18643ft) into Tibet which is still used today by the Tibetans you will meet at this desolate, airy place. Arriving mid afternoon, do not be tempted to pitch your camp on the fine, level plain – choose a spot up on the moraine or tucked under the cliffs. The reason should be apparent from the quantities of yak dung everywhere. At dusk the herds return, thousands of snorting, bell-donging animals; bull yaks do not step daintily over guy-lines!

The sheer scale and grandeur of the mountain world you now find yourself in defies superlatives, and the final easy hike to Pang Pema is a walk to savour all the way. Ahead, Nepal Peak, The Twins and Tent Peak entice you onward, but to the south across the glacier it is the lesser Wedge Peak (6750m/22147ft) that really draws the eye, with its exquisite fluted summit. Until just before Pang Pema that is, when suddenly the incredible north face of Kangchendzonga itself looms into view. Pang Pema is a place to just sit and relish the mountain prospects. Those seeking an even more dramatic vista can head off up the slopes immediately behind Pang Pema to Drohmo Ri, from the cairned summit of which – at 6200m (20342ft) – you can see the entire Kangchendzonga Himal, Jongsang Peak and the mountains forming the border with Tibet to the north, and even Makalu on the horizon to the west.

Walk-out to Taplejung
The retreat to Taplejung via Ghunsa and the Tamur valley takes a week.

AROUND RAMZE

There are plenty of diversions around Ramze. Climb the grassy slopes above camp for views of the peaks surrounding the Ratong La and the route to the Lapsang La. Look out for *bharal* on the hillsides. Go for a stroll up-valley from Ramze to the lonely Shiva shrine at Oktang (4630m/15191ft), where the ablation zone terminates and the way to advanced base camp for Kangchendzonga descends the enormous moraine onto the glacier itself. About forty minutes walk up from camp, as the glacier curves away to the left, a stupendous amphitheatre is revealed. First the ice-clad buttresses and ramparts of Talung (7349m/24112ft) appear across the glacier, and then the entire south face of the Kangchendzonga massif. Hidden from view for so long during the walk-in, this mountain vision will stop you in your tracks. Cut off the trail and continue along the top of the moraine to Oktang. Take your down jacket and plenty of film and wait for the sun to set. The light show as the alpenglow recedes is sensational.

EASTERN NEPAL DIRECTORY

REGIONAL FLIGHTS

Biratnagar has an airport served by numerous flights daily from the capital. Two STOL airstrips serve the hill-districts of eastern Nepal – Tumlingtar and Taplejung (Suketar). Tumlingtar is in the Arun valley, may be reached from Kathmandu or Biratnagar, and is used as a starting point for treks to the Khumbu, Makalu or Kangchendzonga, whilst higher-altitude Taplejung is further north and east, is only served by flights from Biratnagar, and is only usually used for trips to Kangchendzonga.

Playing on a *roti-ping* (ferris wheel) during Dasain.

seats. Note that passengers to Itahari can also travel on services to Dharan.
Itahari–Basantapur: Local bus

Note that it is possible to charter a Landrover for the drive north through Ilam and Phidim to Taplejung (though only in dry season), or from Itahari to Biratnagar.

BIRATNAGAR ACCOMMODATION

There are a number of hotels in the centre of Biratnagar. The wonderfully quirky Himalaya Hotel has unfortunately closed down.

Kathmandu–Tumlingtar: Nepal Airlines, Gorkha Airlines, Sita Air
Kathmandu–Biratnagar: Nepal Airlines, Necon Air, Buddha Air, Yeti Airways, Sita Air
Biratnagar–Taplejung: Nepal Airlines, Sita Air
Biratnagar–Tumlingtar: Nepal Airlines, Sita Air

REGIONAL ROAD TRANSPORT

Luxury 'night coaches' run from Kathmandu to Biratnagar. If you are planning to walk into the hills from the road-head at Hile/Basantapur or Ilam/Phidim, you should get off the bus at Itahari, north of Biratnagar and take a local bus or hire a vehicle from there. The road to Basantapur is more commonly used, but the Ilam–Phidim road reaches Taplejung in the dry season (winter), and if you are trying to make up time after a cancelled flight from Biratnagar it should prove the quicker route.

Kathmandu–Itahari/Biratnagar: Night buses depart between 16:00 and 18:00 from the New Bus Park at Gongabu, near Balaju. Book 2-3 days in advance in order to get good

Hotel Swagatam Tin Toliya, PO Box 227 Biratnagar, tel (021) (021) 524450, fax (021) 522299 swagatum@bcn.ccsl.com.np A moderate standard hotel – relatively clean, serving Nepali cuisine.
Hotel Namaskar, PO Box 224 Traffic Chowk, Biratnagar, tel (021) (021) 521199, 523399 fax (021) 523499. Comparable to the Swagatam, with a good Indian restaurant.
Hotel Eastern Star PO Box 258, Biratnagar tel (021) 521588, 530626 fax (021) 524408 Given a 2* rating by the Nepal Tourism Board

TREKKING COSTS

Permits are required to trek almost anywhere in this region, and though they are not as prohibitive as those for Mustang and Inner Dolpo, you must still make your arrangements through an accredited agent. Tea-house trekking is not an option here. Kangchendzonga is second only to Humla in remoteness from Kathmandu, and communications in the far north-east are poor, necessitating careful logistical planning.

THE HIMALAYAN ENVIRONMENT

Some 200 million years ago, the Indian subcontinent was attached to southern Africa and Antarctica. After the continents started to rift apart, India sailed northwards across the Indian Ocean and collided with Asia approximately 50 million years ago. The subsequent indentation of India into Asia, by as much as 2000km (1250 miles), created the Himalayan mountain range, the youngest, highest and most geologically active of all the world's mountain ranges.

GEOLOGY OF THE NEPAL HIMALAYA
Nepal lies in the central part of the Himalayan chain and exposes an almost complete section across the leading margin of India. The actual site of collision lies north of Nepal, roughly along the Indus and Bhramaputra valleys. The northern continental margin of the Indian tectonic plate is composed of sedimentary rocks, which are found from the collision zone in southern Tibet southwards to the crest of the Greater Himalaya.

Some of the highest peaks, such as Annapurna and Dhaulagiri, are formed of these sedimentary rocks and show spectacular large-scale folding and faulting, beautifully exposed for example along the Kali Gandaki and Modi Khola valleys. This process of folding and thrusting has led to the unusually large crustal thickness (about 70km/44 miles) under the Himalaya and Tibet, double the normal crustal thickness of continents.

Many of the highest peaks of the Himalaya, however, like Manaslu, Shishapangma, Lhotse, Jannu, Makalu and Kangchendzonga, are composed of a unique type of granite, rich in the minerals tourmaline, garnet and micas which formed at deep crustal levels in excess of 20km (13 miles) beneath the surface. These deep-level metamorphic and igneous rocks were uplifted to their present heights by compressional thrusting as the Indian plate continued to drive north, underthrusting the Himalaya.

The youngest and presently most active thrust fault lies along the southern margin of the Himalaya, where most of the active earthquakes occur today. One interesting aspect of the Himalaya is that the higher you go north of the active mountain front, the deeper the rocks were formed, so that in effect the entire southern boundary of the High Himalaya is inverted or upside-down, with deeper hotter rocks emplaced southwards over shallower, cooler rocks. Many of Nepal's hot springs are located along the traces of these relatively young faults.

The Himalaya are still actively rising at rates measurable in mm per year, and this will continue as long as India keeps moving northwards, driven ultimately by the oceanic crustal spreading occurring along the mid Indian Ocean ridge.

The view across the Ngozumpa Glacier from Gokyo Ri (trek 19) in the heart of the Nepal Himalaya.

Climatic Effects
The Himalaya and the Tibetan plateau also govern the climate of the northern hemisphere. Hot air rises over the uplifted Tibetan plateau during the summer, sucking in warm, moist air, which then flows west along the Equator. This creates the northward driven monsoon winds, which bring life-giving rain to the plains of India and the southern slopes of the Himalaya.

The crest of the Greater Himalaya acts as a 7–8000m (22970–26248ft) barrier and the monsoon system ends somewhat abruptly along the highest peaks. The rain shadow thus created on the northern side has turned the Tibetan plateau into a barren high-altitude desert.

MINIMAL IMPACT TREKKING

Much has been made in recent years of the adverse cultural and ecological effects wrought by the boom in mountain tourism in Nepal. Nevertheless, it is my firm belief that trekking is not inherently damaging, and that its development should bring many benefits to remote Himalayan communities. It is usually the attitudes and behaviour of individual trekkers and mountaineers that cause the problems. As Pietro Segantini of the UIAA says, 'we need political connections, professional behaviour and generous help, instead of missionary eagerness and idle talk'.

There are many ways in which trekkers can, with a modest amount of consideration and a few simple steps, minimize or eliminate the negative ecological and environmental impact of their visit to Nepal. Begin by adopting a mindful and responsible attitude and be prepared to do all you can in a positive way to counteract the damage done by those less caring.

FIREWOOD USE

Undoubtedly the most critical environmental problem facing Nepal is nationwide deforestation. This has been exacerbated by a burgeoning highland population, which is currently rising by 2.3 per cent annually. Of Nepal's 5 million in 1950, only 500,000 lived in the Kathmandu valley; of today's population of 21 million, some 3 million live in the valley. The pressure on marginal districts is thus intense. The frighteningly rapid destruction of Nepal's forest reserves has three immediate causes – conversion to arable land, overgrazing and firewood extraction. Firewood currently accounts for 75 per cent of all forms of energy consumed in Nepal.

In 1988 mountain tourism was responsible for the burning of approximately 5.4 million kg (5315 tons) of firewood – only about 0.12 per cent of the total, but a significant amount nonetheless. The problem is worst in the Annapurna, Langtang and Everest regions, where trekkers are concentrated in small areas. In the Khumbu, for example, 85 per cent of fuel-wood is burned by trekkers, while at Ghorepani on the Annapurna circuit (a village with a population of 250 that annually accommodates over 10,000 trekkers) the average household burns 22kg (49lb) of wood a day whereas the average trekkers' lodge burns over 200kg (440lb). Some lodges have installed solar water heaters, but such technology is far from universal, is expensive, and is not really the answer. You do not need that hot shower!

Before you leave Kathmandu, think about how you will bathe or wash clothes, and prepare yourself accordingly. If you are using a kitchen crew, check that they have enough kerosene and stoves and will not be relying on firewood. On trek, remember to monitor whether your porters are burning wood. If you are

Young boy carrying firewood in Humla.

using teahouses, avoid having hot showers unless they are provided by solar energy. By coordinating your food requests with others staying in the same place you can further help to conserve firewood.

OTHER CONSIDERATIONS

Before setting off on a trek or expedition, study the Himalayan Code of Conduct (details available through Kathmandu Environmental Education Project – see page 29), and assess which points are likely to be relevant to your trip. What sort of clothes are you taking? If taking new equipment, can you remove packaging and labels? What can you do to minimize the number of battery cells you will need?

No matter which style of trekking you opt for, accept that the buck stops with you. You bear total responsibility for your own conduct and that of your party as a whole, whatever its size or purpose. Unilateralism is the key concept. If you see a piece of trekkers' litter and do not pick it up, you are as guilty as the person who dropped it. The tour leader who apologized in advance for the terrible state of a campsite that he had left that morning and to which my party were headed that night in the Kangchendzonga region, explaining that the litter was not his group's, was taken aback when I berated him for his lack of care!

As soon as you get off your internal flight, remove all the airline tags and identifications from your luggage. A feature of the first few days of any trail into

Kitchen crews should be equipped with kerosene stoves.

the hills from an airstrip is invariably the brightly coloured tags that litter the way. Think also about the type of food you are going to eat – is it all freeze-dried imported stuff in foil packets, or rice, *dal* and fresh vegetables in hessian sacks?

On trek, ask yourself the following questions constantly. Is the kitchen sorting waste and dealing with it appropriately? Is paper waste too wet to burn in the morning? (Keep it dry!) Are your campsites spotlessly clean on departure? Are latrines being dug deep enough, covered properly afterwards and sited away from water sources? Is there litter on the trail? (Pick it up!) If you have to make a toilet stop during the day and must use toilet paper, have you a cigarette lighter to burn it? (Take care not to ignite dry vegetation.) Resist the temptation to have a bottle of beer or cold drink – at the back of most lodges is an enormous heap of cans, bottles, cartons and plastic bags.

For women, coping with your period whilst out on trek should be given prior consideration. Disposing of sanitary napkins and tampons correctly is important. Throwing a used tampon into the nearest shrub or dropping it behind a stone wall may sound gross, but it's amazing how many foreign visitors do this. Used personal hygiene products such as wet-wipes, tampons or cotton-buds and the plastic or foil packets they come in are not biodegradable and make the worst possible type of litter. The only ecologically acceptable practice is to wrap them in layers of plastic and take them back to a city for disposal. Prepare yourself for this.

Cultural Awareness

During the course of a trek you are likely to find yourself visiting the houses and temples of different cultural groups. Being familiar with a few basic points of etiquette will save you and your hosts much unnecessary embarrassment.

The exact denomination of temples is not always immediately apparent, so bear in mind that Hindus do not permit non-believers into the inner sanctums of their temples, and that leather goods are strictly taboo. When in the houses of Hindus, remember that you will be considered the equivalent of the lowest caste, and that your hosts will be very concerned about the ritual pollution of food. They will not touch any food or utensil that has been used by you. When drinking from a vessel that will be used by others, avoid touching it to your lips. Always eat with your right hand – Hindus use their left for cleaning themselves after defecating.

Buddhists are less particular, though the hearth is sacred in Sherpa homes, and you should not throw rubbish into the fire. They also believe that burning rubbish in high places offends the mountain gods and brings bad luck, so sensitivity is required when cleaning campsites. Take the time to explain, when clearing quantities of other peoples garbage, that leaving a beautiful place spotlessly clean is surely more likely to impress the gods.

Photography is a major preoccupation with many trekkers, too many of whom feel that they have not seen a thing until they have photographed it. Local people are often treated inconsiderately in pursuit of a photograph, a kind of behaviour which is inexcusable. Despite the temptation to make believe that you are on assignment for *National Geographic*, remember that these are villages, not human zoos, and that ruthlessly stalking someone for a picture is rude. A sad trait of villagers on many of the popular trails in Nepal is the way they run for cover the moment a camera is produced. This is not because they have some notion about losing their souls the moment they are photographed, but because countless trekkers pass by every year and show no interest in them other than as lens-fodder. Show some respect!

Tempting as it may be, the urge to hand out sweets, cigarettes, balloons or money to children on the trail should be strongly resisted. It may elicit smiles and instil a feeling of generosity, but it makes beggars out of children and is really nothing but a cultural arrogance. Ultimately it is demeaning, as anyone who has entered a village to a chorus of 'one pen, one pen, give me miThai, one rupee one rupee!' will understand.

MOUNTAIN PHOTOGRAPHY

In conjunction with a meticulously kept journal, a collection of photographs is the best way of recording your impressions of Nepal – for capturing those precious moments of scenic splendour and remembering the many people encountered along the way. Few travel these days without a camera, but attitudes to photography vary from the casual to the complete obsessive. As you will be carrying your camera equipment for many weeks or months during a season trekking in Nepal, careful consideration should be given to both the type of camera chosen and the film stock used.

THE DIGITAL DEBATE

Film or digital? Camera sales worldwide would indicate that most people have made up their minds in favour of the latter, but for prolonged mountain use the issue is far from settled. Camera and lens design has traditionally been aimed at two ideals – reliability and the best possible image quality. Portability comes a close third. Surely, when traveling in the Himalaya one cannot compromise any of these.

I still shoot film exclusively in the mountains. Here's why. A 35mm image, shot with Fuji Velvia and a prime lens, delivers a resolution equivalent to 25 megapixels. With medium format cameras you can up that to 100 megapixels. The latest 16+ megapixel digital SLR bodies cost £4500 today! Even if you use an intermediate DSLR – say 10 megapixels – and shoot at the highest quality setting, you will only get 60 images in Camera Raw format per gigabyte of memory-card space. During a three month stint in the mountains I frequently shoot 50+ rolls of slide film – that's over 1500 images. Do the maths – that's a lot of memory cards!

Digital cameras are also *very* power-hungry, and cease to function the minute their batteries loose a few percent of their charge. That's fine if you're based in a hotel and can re-charge daily, but in the mountains? You want to be shooting at dawn and sunset. It's cold! Cold sucks the life out of batteries. If you are totally convinced you want to shoot digitally, choose a camera that takes AA cells or similar, and use lithiums. Take lots! Many modern digital cameras use only their own unique rechargables. Also, choose one with a view-finder and use it! Those handy little screens on the back suck the juice out of batteries too! Finally, a word about digital "speed". It is measured using the same ASA units as conventional film,

and reviews agree that few digital cameras – especially compacts – deliver quality at settings above 200 or 400ASA. Fast film suffers from "grain", fast digital settings from "noise", which is worse. If all you require at the end of your trip is a set of small prints to pass round amongst your family and friends, then a carefully chosen compact digital camera *might* be the answer. Even these can deliver upwards of 10 megapixels today, and if you take the above points into consideration you'll probably get by.

SLIDE PHOTOGRAPHY

If, however, you think you may want to give the odd presentation (we used to call them slide shows!), enlarge some of your images for framing, or even consider publishing the odd shot, you should probably opt for colour transparency or "slide" film. As this type of film is developed by a fixed process, any subtle exposure variations made with the camera are faithfully reproduced in the final transparency, giving the photographer a fine degree of control over which parts of a scene he wants to capture.

By 'bracketing', ie. making one exposure at the value indicated by your camera's meter, and then another either side of it by up to one f-stop, you can be sure of capturing the effect you want. For example, if the meter indicates an exposure of 1/250 sec @ f8, also shoot 1/250 @ f5.6 and 1/250 @ f11. Many modern cameras have the facility to do this automatically.

A couple of other factors should be considered for slide photography. The exposure meters of most SLR cameras are calibrated for print film, and slide emulsions tend to be more sensitive. As a rule of thumb I always underexpose slide film by ⅓ or ⅔ of a stop – that is, I shoot 50ASA film at 64 or 80ASA. This is

The contours of Ratong (trek 25) are brought to life by a magical light at sunset.

only a very minor adjustment, but it does allow the film to produce maximum colour saturation. Every camera's meter is slightly different, so if you are taking your photography seriously, shoot a roll of your chosen film at home and bracket each exposure by up to two whole stops and observe the results. This will also give you a good idea of how the film handles over- and under-exposure.

Choice of Film and Lenses

The choice of film is always a matter provoking debate. The faster the film (the more sensitive to light), the less capable it is of reproducing either colour saturation or contrast. Slower films are richer, sharper and have greater latitude. They also require more light to create an image, and in low-light conditions this can be problematic as your shutter-speeds decrease, introducing the possibility of camera-shake blurring the picture. The longer the focal length of the lens, the more pronounced this effect becomes, and for sharp hand-held exposures your shutter speed should be a value higher than the focal length of your lens in mm. Don't shoot slower than 1/125 sec with a 135mm lens. High in the Himalaya the light is often intense, and this problem only really occurs at dawn and dusk, but enthusiasts will want to be capturing just these times of day and thus the choice of lens is crucial.

I'm assuming that you want perfectly exposed, pin-sharp slides with rich colour saturation. Fuji's Velvia is an obvious choice, but it's only rated at 50ASA and 100ASA, and by the time you've put a polarising filter on your camera you've effectively reduced this to 18 / 25ASA. Most zoom lenses have maximum apertures in the f3.5–f5.6 range, and in low light, shooting slow film, you would be struggling with shutter-speeds of 1/4sec or slower, which is way too slow for hand-held exposures. To allow yourself flexibility in these light levels, you should really use a faster lens (i.e. one capable of transmitting more light) and a tripod. Professional photographers always choose this option and use lenses with maximum apertures of f2, f1.8 or even f1.4. It is possible to buy fast zoom lenses, but they are prohibitively expensive and still not sharp enough. Almost 99 per cent of pictures taken with a zoom tend to be at one or other end of its range, where a zoom lens is at its least efficient. If you really want quality images, leave your zoom at home. I would always argue for carrying two or three fast prime lenses. Use a 17 or 24mm f2.8, a 50mm f1.4 and a 80mm f1.4 rather than a 28–80mm f5.6 zoom. You may have to think about your photography a little more, but your results will be vastly improved.

BATTERIES AND CAMERA CARE

Another key point to consider when choosing a camera for the Himalaya is the type of battery required. Modern auto-focus, power-wind cameras of all types rely totally on battery power to function. There is actu-

The sharpest lens in your bag is a tripod!

ally a strong argument for using vintage mechanical cameras. Alkaline cells perform very poorly in low temperatures, though a camera that runs on lithium cells performs better and will be happily snapping away before dawn at 5000m (16405ft) when the thermometer is showing -25°C. All batteries drain more quickly at low temperatures, so keep them warm in your tent over night. Lithium 'AA' cells are now available, though expensive.

Dust, water and physical violence are the enemies of both photographic film and the delicate mechanisms inside every camera. Use a modern padded camera case, preferably one with a dust-gusset. Carry a blower-brush and lens tissues and use them meticulously. Clean the back of the camera every time you open it to change a film – the slightest specks of dust on the pressure-plate inside will give you skies bisected by perfect tram-lines. Heat and humidity both ruin any kind of film, so carry yours in a proper waterproof bag – especially the exposed rolls.

TECHNIQUE

However many books you read, seminars you attend or friends you discuss it with, you'll only ever define your own photographic style and find out what pleases you by travelling with your camera, pointing it at the world and contemplating the results. Mountain landscape photography requires a certain element of technical accomplishment, but most of it is the result of the vision of the photographer.

One essential point to remember is that the definitive mountain photograph does not depend soley on form and composition, but on light. Mountain light. In the rarefied air of the high Himalaya nature puts on a daily light show that often defies language to describe it. Most of the time it defies the photographer to capture it as well, but there are two 'magic hours', around sunrise and sunset, when colour and contrast and shadow bring the contours alive.

HEALTH AND SAFETY

A complex and as yet not fully understood set of physical and biochemical changes occurs as the human body is exposed to the decreased levels of oxygen available in the air breathed at high altitude. The general term used to describe these changes is **acclimatisation**.

ACUTE MOUNTAIN SICKNESS

The symptoms of Acute Mountain Sickness (**AMS**), brought on when a person ascends too fast for adequate acclimatisation to take place, are simply due to the collection of fluid between the cells of the body, or edema. This primarily occurs in two potentially dangerous areas – the lungs (high-altitude pulmonary edema or **HAPE**) and the brain (high-altitude cerebral edema or **HACE**). Initial symptoms may be mild, and are not a reason to panic or disrupt an itinerary. Shortness of breath and a dry, hacking cough are early signs of HAPE, whilst headaches (especially on waking in the morning), loss of appetite and nausea are indicative of HACE.

Other, less serious, signs of inadequate acclimatisation are peripheral edema (swollen fingers, toes or face) and **Chaine-Stokes respiration** at night (a sleeping person stops breathing for half a minute or so, and then takes several deep breaths before slowly tailing off again). The latter is more alarming for any person sharing the tent – it is not dangerous, and the urge to shake the victim awake should be resisted. These conditions may develop together.

Religious adherence to three simple rules will prevent any drama or crisis due to mountain sickness:

- Learn and recognise the symptoms of AMS and do not be afraid to communicate them to your companions.
- Do not continue to ascend while suffering any of the symptoms.
- Do not remain at the same altitude if your symptoms are worsening, even if it means descending at night.

Various medical preparations are available to treat AMS, though none should properly be used prophylactically (as a preventative). Parties travelling to high (ie over 5000m/16405ft) and remote areas where descent or evacuation may be difficult or impossible should perhaps contemplate carrying a hyperbaric chamber such as a Gammov Bag. These are expensive, heavy to carry and need to be used discriminatingly, but in serious cases they can undoubtedly save lives. Their main benefit is that a debilitated victim, placed in one for several hours, may then be capable of walking down rather than being stretchered. For a traumatised party in extremis, this can be crucial. However, Gammov bags should not be used to prolong time spent at altitude by those not acclimatising naturally.

BASIC MOUNTAIN FIRST AID

'First Aid' refers to the initial management of an injured person before they are taken to a doctor or hospital. In many of the remote Himalayan areas of Nepal, a doctor or hospital could be over a week's walk away. Knowing the basics of first aid, and managing an injury correctly in the first instance can often mean the difference between life and death, and prevent the later development of life threatening complications.

In the event of an accident in which immediate action is taken to save a life, the priorities are **ABC**:

A – AIRWAY B – BREATHING C – CIRCULATION

AIRWAY
Establish an open airway.

Listen for breathing sounds and if there are none, lift the chin and jaw upwards, and tilt the head back.

If there is an obvious foreign body blocking the airway, such as vomit or food, remove it.

With any victim who has fallen from a height or received a head injury, be aware that they may have broken their neck, and if at all possible do not attempt to move the patient. Keep the neck straight. In any situation where the airway is obstructed, however, the airway MUST take first priority.

BREATHING
Breathing patient
If, after clearing the airway, the victim is breathing, turn them on their side into the **recovery position**. The lower leg should be straight and the the upper one bent at the knee to act as stabiliser. Ensure that the airway remains open by continuing to extend the head, and tilt the jaw.

Non-breathing patient
Start mouth-to-mouth resuscitation: pinch the nose and blow into the victim's mouth. Form a tight seal with your own lips and watch their chest rise as you exhale. Perform two effective breaths before checking the pulse.

CIRCULATION
If the victim continues not to breath after two rescue breaths then check the pulse in their neck. If there is no pulse, start Cardio Pulmonary Resuscitation (**CPR**).

CPR is performed by placing the heel of your hand, with your other hand on top, on the middle of the victims chest, 2 fingers distance above the bottom of the sternum (chest bone). Press down to a depth of 4cm (1½in), at a rate of 100 per minute. After every 15 compressions give 2 rescue breaths, and continue at a rate of 15:2.

Continue until the victim shows signs of life, until you are exhausted or until skilled assistance arrives.

Bleeding

If there is an obvious site of major bleeding, attempt to stop the flow of blood by applying firm pressure over the site directly for at least 10 minutes, without releasing pressure. Maintain pressure during evacuation as much as possible by applying a firm bandage and dressing. Do not remove during evacuation.

If the bleeding is from a limb, then a tourniquet can be applied above the site of bleeding, taking great care not to over-tighten and stop the flow of blood to the limb entirely.

Remember that not all bleeding sites are visible and the patient may be bleeding heavily inside their chest, abdomen or limb. Always remember ABC (see above).

Hypothermia

Do not forget that an injured person in extreme conditions will become hypothermic very quickly.

Remove wet clothes if possible, shelter from wind and rain and cover with emergency blankets, sleeping bag etc. Lie with the victim if all else fails.

A person is not considered dead until WARMED AND DEAD. With a hypothermic person always continue resuscitation attempts (if possible) until the person is warmed.

Drowning

The priorities for a person who has been pulled from water are the same as for any unconscious patient – ABC (see above). Remember that they will also be hypothermic.

Choking

If the patient is conscious, bend them over forwards and carry out firm back blows. Encourage them to cough. If the back blows fail, then attempt abdominal thrusts ('Heimlich manoeuvre') by standing behind the patient and placing both arms around the upper part of the abdomen. Clenching one fist and holding this with your other hand, pull sharply backwards and inwards. This will hopefully produce a sudden expulsion, causing the foreign body to be ejected from the airway.

If the patient is unconscious, then ABC (see above) are first priorities. An abdominal thrust can be tried by straddling the victim and pushing down into the upper abdomen with your two clenched hands.

Fractured Limbs

Any suspected fractured bone should be splinted as comfortably as possible using whatever means are available. Examples are tree bark, pieces cut from closed-cell mattresses ('Karrimats'), Thermarests, pieces of wood, walking sticks etc.

If the bone is sticking out of the skin then cover with a dressing and evacuate. If evacuation is delayed then consider starting antibiotics such as penicillin to prevent infection.

Straightening a badly deformed limb will help relieve pain and stop internal bleeding.

Dislocations

If a joint is obviously dislocated then it may be worth attempting to reduce it (put it back in place), as this will help with relief of pain. Give adequate pain relief, splint the limb involved afterwards as comfortably as possible and evacuate.

If a limb below a dislocation is white, pulseless and painful then this may mean that a major blood vessel to the limb is compressed. The limb is at risk of gangrene and the joint must be put back in place immediately if possible.

Lacerations and Cuts

The basic rule of thumb is that any cut older than 6 hours should not be sutured (stitched). If a wound is dirty and old, clean it thoroughly with antiseptic (povidone iodine is best) and cover with a clean dressing.

Freshly cleaned recent cuts can be sutured or closed if less than 6 hours old. Consider using paper or 'butterfly' sutures.

If there are signs of infection such as pain, redness and pus, then start antibiotics, such as penicillin, amoxycillin.

Dehydration

If you suspect that a person is dehydrated then if possible give Oral Rehydration Salts (ORS). This should be given in small sips every 10 minutes to prevent vomiting.

If there is no ORS available, it can be made by warming 1 litre of water and dissolving 8 teaspoons of sugar + 1 teaspoon of salt.

If the patient is unable to take oral fluids then intravenous fluids should be started. Evacuation will be necessary.

Confirming Death

A person is only deemed dead when there are no signs of life:

- No breathing
- No pulse
- Pupils are fixed (do not move when a light is shined) and dilated
- Hypothermia has been excluded

Bibliography

Trekking
Swift, Hugh: *Trekking in Nepal, West Tibet and Bhutan* (1989), Hodder & Stoughton, UK. This book, by the late Hugh Swift, is still by far the most engaging, stimulating and inspirational of the mass of literature published to date on trekking in the Himalaya.

Climbing and Exploration
Bremer-Kamp, Cherie: *Living on the Edge* (1987), David & Charles, UK. Harrowing account of a winter attempt on Kangchendzonga.

Evans, Charles: *Kanchenjunga – The Untrodden Peak* (1956), Hodder & Stoughton, UK. The first ascent of Kangchendzonga, by George Band, Joe Brown, Tony Streather et al.

Fellowes, P.F.M. et al: *First over Everest* (1933), The Bodley Head, London. Incredible, frightfully British account of an expedition to fly over the Himalaya in biplanes, with some absolutely stunning aerial and 3D photography of Everest, Makalu and Kangchendzonga.

Herzog, Maurice: *Annapurna* (1952), Jonathan Cape, London. Epic account of the first eight-thousand metre peak to be climbed. Snow-blindness, frostbite, heroic retreat – gripping stuff.

Hillary, Sir Edmund: *View from the Summit* (1999), Doubleday, London. Autobiography of the most famous climber in the world, with typically modest and thoroughly engaging account of his explorations in Nepal with Shipton and his subsequent first ascent of Everest.

Hunt, John: *Our Everest Adventure* (1954), Brockhampton Press, UK. Pictorial account of the first ascent of Everest.

Hunt, John: *The Ascent of Everest* (1953), Hodder & Stoughton, UK. The first ascent of the highest peak on earth.

Shipton, Eric: *That Untravelled World* (1969), Hodder & Stoughton, UK. Marvellous, understated autobiography.

Shipton, Eric: *The Mount Everest Reconnaissance Expedition* (1951), Hodder & Stoughton, UK. Pictorial account of the first attempt at finding a route up Everest from the Nepal side.

Steele, Peter: *Eric Shipton; Everest and Beyond* (1998), Constable, UK. Biography of Britain's most celebrated mountain explorer – the man who discovered the route into the Western Cwm of Everest. Immensely readable account of a colourful life, with fascinating detail on the race for Everest in the 1950s.

Tilman, H.W.: *Nepal Himalaya* (1952), Cambridge University Press, UK. Also in omnibus edition *The Seven Mountain Travel Books* (1983), Diadem. Accounts of the first explorations of Langtang, Ganesh, Annapurna and the approach to Everest. Marvellous! First editions now fetch well in excess of £200, but are essential to connoisseurs on account of the photographs missing from the omnibus.

Altitude and Medicine
Houston, Charles MD: *Going Higher* (1998), Swan Hill, UK. Comprehensive, perhaps too scientific, but the definitive text on the effects of altitude.

Wilkerson, James MD (ed.): *Medicine for Mountaineering* (4th edn 1992), The Mountaineers, Seattle. If you do carry a book on wilderness medicine it should be this one – practical, authoritative, comprehensive and easy to understand.

Mountain Photography
Rowell, Galen: *Mountain Light: In Search of the Dynamic Landscape* (1995), Sierra Club Books. Superlative essay on the subject of mountain photography.

Birds and Flowers
Ali, Salim: *Field Guide to the Birds of the Eastern Himalaya* (1977), Oxford University Press, Delhi. Pocket guide with colour illustrations. Covers eastern Nepal, Sikkim and Bhutan, but useful throughout Nepal.

Ali, Salim and Ripley, S.D.: *Pictorial Guide to the Birds of the Indian Subcontinent* (1995), Bombay Natural History Society/Oxford University Press, Delhi 1995. Larger book, illustrated by John Henry Dick.

Fleming, Fleming & Bangdel: *Birds of Nepal* (3rd edn), Nature Himalayas. The definitive pocket guide. Superbly illustrated. By Nepal's most celebrated ornithologists.

Polunin, Oleg and Stainton, Adam: *Concise Flowers of the Himalaya* (1987) Oxford University Press, Delhi. Extensively illustrated with colour photographs. Pocket version of their definitive *Flowers of the Himalaya* (OUP 1984).

Anthropology and Culture
Fisher, James: *Trans Himalayan Traders* (1987), Motilal Banarsidass, Delhi. Economy, society & Culture in north-western Nepal.

von Furer-Haimendorf, Christoph: *Himalayan Traders* (1975), John Murray, UK. Scholarly but immensely readable account of trading patterns across the Himalaya between Nepali and Tibetan traders. Covers Humla, Mugu, the Arun valley and the Dhaulagiri area (Dolpo).

Snellgrove, D.L.: *Himalayan Pilgrimage* (1981), Shambhala. Travelogue with rich cultural insight and comment on the Tibetan religion, covering the Dolpo area.

Snelling, John: *The Sacred Mountain* (1990), East-West. Lavishly illustrated and authoritative guide to the exploration and cultural significance of Tibet's Mount Kailas.

Glossary

Various Hindi and Tibetan terms, as well as Nepali ones, may be encountered on trek.

achaar = spicy pickle
angrezi = foreigner, from mispronunciation of English
banjang = hilltop clearing
bharal = Tibetan blue sheep
bhatti = primitive lodge
chang = home-brewed alcoholic drink, like beer
chautaara = stone-built resting platform
chiang-lu = mountain goat
chorten = Tibetan word for stupa
chuba = Tibetan wrap-around robe
dahi = yoghurt or curds
dalbat = staple food of lentils cooked as watery soup with boiled rice
danda = mountain ridge
dhami = village shaman
dokpa = human effigy
doqo = porter's basket
gompah = Buddhist monastery
goth = temporary monsoon shelter
gundruk = preparation of sour radish greens
karkha = jungle clearing or grazing ground
khola = river
kora = pilgrim route around sacred mountain or temple

la = pass
lagna = mountain ridge
lama = Buddhist monk
lekh = mountain ridge
lukal = 10kg load carried by sheep and goats
maati baato = upper path
mela = trade fair
panchayat = system of government
pashmina = cashmere wool
pising = thin bamboo straw for drinking *thungba*
puja = religious ceremony
raksi = distilled alcoholic drink
ri = small peak
rimpoche = particularly revered high-ranking lama or 'precious one'
roti-ping = ferris wheel
sulpa = clay and copper smoking pipe or chillum
suruwal = baggy cotton trousers
takaari = vegetables
tal = lake
tamak = pungent mix of tobacco and molasses
tan = tiny shrine
thangka = Tibetan sacred painting, usually on canvas
thungba = alcoholic drink
tse = lake
yersa = occasional summer grazing pasture

Index

AUTHOR'S ACKNOWLEDGEMENTS

I owe a debt of enormous gratitude and appreciation to many generous friends and colleagues, without whom the scope of this book would have been seriously limited. Space limitations preclude a complete list here, but certain people deserve special thanks. To all my trekking companions, respect is due, especially Gill Solnick, Rex Munro, Glenn Rowley, Harry Gill and Karen Long, Lisa Melhuish, Pete Royall, Karl Farkas, Pam Andrews, Bart Jordans, Colin Wells and Karen Stanley, Elly Whitford, Rob Riddell and Natalie Hawkrigg. Good Nepali staff make a trip into the hills all the more enjoyable, and I have been blessed with the company of the very best. Here I must thank Kumar Tamang, Karma Lama, Dorje Sherpa, Lakpa Sherpa, Lakpa Tamang, Ang Kaji, Chet Gurung, Ratan Tamang, Rinjin Sherpa, Pema Lama of Jumla, Wungri, Mungri and Chiring Lama of Mugu, Bovita Lama and Jonpol of Humla, Wong Chhu, Gombu Sherpa and Pemba Chiri. Namaste!!

My parents instilled a deep love of the hills in my young psyche during family camping holidays in the Alps, and have long tolerated my peripatetic and wandering lifestyle. My mother proof-read the text of this volume on more than one occasion. My partner, Natalie Hawkrigg, has put up with my late nights at the computer and encouraged me throughout. Glenn Rowley, Tim Greening and Kit Wilkinson at KE Adventure Travel have long pandered to my whims, employed and supported me. In Nepal, I owe the success of most of my exploratory trips to the organizational skills of everyone at Himalaya Expeditions, especially Bikrum Pandey and Satish Neupane, who also patiently and painstakingly replied to my frequent emails during the writing of this book. I must also thank Suman Pandey of Explore Himalaya and Ang Zambu of Highland Sherpa for similar help. Pablo Segovia provided an essential thread of continuity and communication during the crazy comings and goings of seasons in Nepal. Sincere thanks also go to Nawang and Tenzing Bista and their families at the Mustang Holiday Inn in Kathmandu for their kindness and hospitality.

Finally, many people have given unstintingly of their time and enthusiasm to this project. Victor Saunders, Mike Searle, Cameron Wake and Natalie Hawkrigg wrote sections of text. Pam Andrews, Stuart Miller, Mick Bromley, Kit Wilkinson, Richard Eaton, Ronnie Faux, Steve Berry and Pete Royall gave me access to their photographic material and provided valuable feedback and criticism of the text. Tim Jollands, Pete Duncan and Bill Smuts at New Holland had the confidence to trust me with the writing of this book. To all of you, and everyone I have failed to mention here, my eternal gratitude.

I would like to dedicate this book to the people of Nepal, and to the memory of Mark Miller, who died in the PIA Airbus that crashed approaching Kathmandu on 28 September 1992.

CONTRIBUTORS

Additional text contributors: Dr Natalie Hawkrigg (Health and Safety, pages 169–171); Mike Searle (The HImalayan Environment, page 164); Victor Saunders (Climbing in Nepal, pages 36-7; Annapurna, page 69; Mountain No XV, page 129; peaks, pages 74, 77, 110, 114, 123, 124, 132, 138, 139, 146); Cameron Wake (Himalayan Glaciers and Climate Change, pages 140–141).

Additional photographic contributors (copyright © in photographs rests with Steve Razzetti with the exception of the following individual photographers):

Pam Andrews title page, pages 32, 37, 107, 109; Stuart Miller contents page (middle top), pages 36, 122, 125, 128, 133; Kit Wilkinson pages 85, 86, 88, 90, 91, 93, 94, 100, 101 (bottom), 145, 152; Richard Eaton pages 42, 44; Lindsay Abbotts pages 70, 77; John Lyall pages 74, 114; Kath Murphy page 110; Mike Searle pages 112, 129, 137; Mick Chapman pages 123, 138, 139, 146; Pierre Schmidt page 124; Bruce Goodlad page 132; Cameron Wake pages 135, 136, 140, 141; Mick Bromley page 143; Pete Royall pages 157, 158

Tibetan prayer flags.